The Search for the Perfect Golf Club

The Search for the Perfect Golf Club

Tom Wishon

with Tom Grundner

Copyright © 2005 Thomas Grundner

All rights reserved. No part of this book may be reproduced in any manner without the express written consent of the publisher, except in the case of brief excerpts in critical reviews or articles.

All inquiries should be addressed to:
Sports Media Group
An imprint of Ann Arbor Media Group LLC
2500 S. State Street
Ann Arbor, MI 48104

Printed and bound at Edwards Brothers, Inc.,
Ann Arbor, Michigan, USA

09   08   07   06   05   10 9 8 7 6 5 4 3 2

Library of Congress Cataloging-in-Publication Data

Wishon, Tom W.
 The search for the perfect golf club / Thomas Wishon with Thomas Grundner.
   p. cm.
 Includes bibliographical references and index.
 ISBN 1-58726-185-5 (alk. paper)
 1. Golf clubs (Sporting goods) I. Grundner, Thomas. II. Title.

GV976.W585 2005
688.7′6352′028′8—dc22

                                    2005000792

ISBN-13: 978-1-58726-185-5
ISBN-10: 1-58726-185-5

This book is dedicated to:

My wife Mary-Ellen, for her complete love and support through all of the good and less than good times in my work and my life.

My father Winston, who introduced me to this great game and thus provided the spark for me to be able to find real passion in my life's work.

My friend Peter Farricker, who refused to let Lou Gehrig's disease prevent him from enjoying his last two years, and in doing so, inspired me to find the courage to finally do what I should have done many years ago.

ACKNOWLEDGMENTS

I wish to thank my mentor, Art Mittendorf, for being there with the guidance and answers when I was not smart enough to figure things out on my own.

I want to thank Tom Grundner for his perseverance in convincing me to do this book, and for being there to make sure my words would make sense.

I also wish to offer special thanks to Duffy Brook for his incredible skills in doing the cover photography, cover design, and all photography and illustration work inside the pages of this book.

And finally, I want to acknowledge and say thanks to some of the truly nice people I have met in my work in the golf equipment industry for being willing to share a little of what they too have learned along the way—Robin Arthur, Graeme Horwood, John Oldenburg, Chinneng Lin, Tim Gist, Charles Su, Thomas Chen, Mondher Lattiri, Elmore Just, Jeff Ellis, and Bob Kuntz.

CONTENTS

AN INTRODUCTION YOU REALLY NEED TO READ

Oh, the Humanity!!!

This book is about golf clubs. More specifically, it's the first book written for the average golfer that explains how and why golf clubs work the way they do.

It is designed to deal with two very real problems that, taken together, I believe are seriously compromising your ability to play the game and very possibly compromising the game itself. I would like to touch on those problems in this introduction so you will have a better idea of what this book is all about.

The first problem has to do with golfers themselves. The sad fact is that the average golfer knows little more about golf clubs than what he or she reads and hears in advertising or sees in Golf Channel infomercials. This lack of golf equipment knowledge results in millions of golfers attempting to play an already difficult game with equipment that not only won't, but CAN'T POSSIBLY meet their needs. This, in turn, contributes to an equipment-generated frustration with the game that I call the "grass ceiling."

If you doubt the existence of the grass ceiling, go to any driving range on a busy day and watch for a while. People of all shapes and sizes, sexes, and ages will be at the tee line flailing away. A few shots will be good, some indifferent; most of them will be bad, and some downright dangerous to surrounding life, limb, and property.

Watch especially when these golfers take out their drivers. If you see two or three golfers out of 10 who can consistently hit the ball straight on a nice trajectory, you're there on a good day. I am not talking about hitting 300-yard drives down the middle. I am talking about the ball flying high and straight, landing downrange at any reasonable distance, within 20 yards on either side of its intended target.

Now, think about what you're seeing.

Name one other product that, in the hands of the average consumer, is so difficult to use that it works properly only two or three times out of 10. In any other industry it would be a scandal, and companies would be going out of business overnight. But not in the golf industry. In the world of golf, we give each other knowing winks and say, in tones of sympathetic camaraderie, "It's a hell of a tough game, isn't it?"

Why? Why is there such a gap between intention and result among most players even after years and years of practicing the game? There are two possibilities.

The first is that our nation has somehow become overrun with the athletically impaired, but that makes no sense. Many golfers, perhaps even most golfers, were in their day reasonably proficient athletes in a variety of other sports. There is no way that someone who could once routinely hit 60 percent of his or her free throws under game conditions or bat .300 in high school baseball could somehow now lack the eye/hand coordination to hit a golf ball solid and straight a reasonable percentage of the time. I have watched professional athletes in football and basketball (and please don't question their coordination) look like fools with golf clubs in their hands.

No, that can't really be the only reason.

The second possibility lies in the equipment the golfers are using. Winston Churchill once said, "Golf is an ineffectual attempt to direct an uncontrollable sphere into an inaccessible hole with instruments ill-adapted to the purpose." He might have been right about inaccessible holes, but he was definitely wrong about the equipment.

The golf club and the ball today are among the most superbly designed instruments and objects ever crafted for use in a game. Every inch of the club has a purpose and a clear rationale for why it is the way it is. It is 100 percent pure, engineered function. So, why then are so many golfers out there slashing away like cavemen with tree limbs in their hands?

One source of the problem, I believe, is that most golfers know next to nothing about how to select golf clubs that are designed to maximize the strengths, and minimize the weaknesses, in their swings. They know little more, really, than what they read in golf equipment advertising and see in Golf Channel infomercials. Now, I will admit these ads rarely lie, but they also almost never tell the whole truth. So, armed with nothing more than these semitruths, the golfing public spends $4.7 BILLION dollars a year on equipment hoping and expecting that with the "right stuff" they will play the game better and enjoy it more.

Yet if you don't understand how club length, the loft angle of the face, and the flex and weight of the shaft all have to be properly matched to the way you swing, the club remains simply that, a club—in the Cro-Magnon sense of the word. You will pick clubs with attention only to the name and the price, and wind up standing there on the tee, looking sheepish, titanium tree limb in hand, saying, "It's a hell of a tough game, isn't it?"

The Archer or the Arrow?

Okay, I know what you're thinking. "That's interesting and all of it might be true but what the heck, a club is a club. It's not the arrow; it's the archer. It's not the equipment that makes a good golfer."

Really?

Most golfers think the clubs played by the tour pros are the same ones they can buy in their local pro shop or retail golf store. In reality, the clubs the pros play are to the clubs you buy off the rack as Jeff Gordon's NASCAR race car is to the Chevrolet Monte Carlo in your driveway. All the pros know full well what I will tell you in this book—that they can't possibly play their best with standard-made off-the-rack clubs.

You think that custom fit golf clubs are only for good golfers? That myth could not be farther from the truth. Look at it this way: The pros are skilled enough to be able to play well with almost any golf club. You, on the other hand, are not, which means YOU need properly fitted golf clubs even more than THEY do. You need them to minimize the swing errors the pros don't have and to maximize your swing strengths.

Now, let's be clear—I am NOT saying you can "buy" skill as a golfer. I am not saying that by spending enough money you can somehow go from being a double-digit handicapper to qualifying for next year's U.S. Open.

Learning and "grooving" the proper swing fundamentals are the keys to game improvement for any golfer. Look at the people you know who are excellent players. Look at the professionals. Almost none of them are completely self-taught. They have each spent many hours with professional instructors to learn the proper technique, followed by many more hours of practice to make the changes permanent. Buying new clubs is NOT a substitute for making that kind of commitment. Never has been. Never will be.

I AM saying, however, that equipment that doesn't fit—that is the wrong length, or loft, or weight, or balance—can keep you from being all that you could be as a golfer (at any level), and it might even keep you from becoming a golfer at all.

You see, golf is inherently a difficult and often frustrating game, but that's part of its charm, part of the fun. As with any game, however, if things are rigged so you can't possibly win, suddenly it becomes a whole lot less charming and not fun at all.

That brings us to the second problem.

I'll put it to you in a nutshell: According to a study by the National Golf Foundation (NGF), each year something like three million people LEAVE the game of golf. When surveyed as to why they left, a variety of reasons are given, but underlying them all, dropouts say, is the frustration of the game being "too difficult." This fact was perhaps best summarized by Ron Drapeau, former chairman of Callaway Golf: "It is so difficult that about two-thirds of those who try the game quit because they don't think they will ever be able to play [it] respectably."

Frustration with the game? Sure, the game can be frustrating to even the best players in the world, but how much of what we're talking about is caused by "equipment-induced frustration?" How many of those golfers simply hit a "grass ceiling" where they found themselves trapped in a nightmare of publicly embarrassing poor performance? Thinking they are playing with equipment that is properly designed and fitted (after all, they paid enough for the stuff), they can then only ascribe their failings to themselves—to their own ineptitude—and give up on the game.

How many know that perhaps a good part of their frustration was due to a driver they bought that is essentially unhittable in the hands of an average golfer? How many know that their 3- and 4-irons are made unhittable, at the factory, BY DESIGN? How many know that all these things are well known, but nobody ever bothered to tell them (until now)? I don't know that this story has any true villains, but many people have certainly had a hand in creating the problem. I am talking here about people, corporations, and organizations that should know better because it is their own economic interests that are at stake.

Look at it this way.

As mentioned above, each year some three million people leave the game of golf. Now, again according to the NGF, the average golfer spends over $900 a year on the game—that's for equipment and fees, clubs, balls, bags, gloves, shoes, the whole ball of wax. If three million people are leaving, that means almost $3 billion dollars in potential revenue is walking out the door with them. $3 BILLION!! ($2,782,440,000 to be exact.)

Now it's true those numbers are offset somewhat by golfers that enter or return to the game, but they are still staggering. No industry can sustain that kind of loss, over time, and expect to remain healthy. Something must be done and must be done NOW.

Mostly, however, I have spent my 33 years in golf researching the performance of golf clubs in the hands of real golfers. I have probably designed more models of golf clubs than any person in the 500-year history of the game, and I have 44 "firsts" in original clubhead design technology. I have created custom designed clubs that have been used to win tournaments on the PGA Tour and in Ryder Cup competition. I've written five books about clubmaking and fitting and over 400 golf equipment magazine articles; I've been a member of *Golf Digest* magazine's Technical Advisory Panel since 1994; and I am currently the Technical Advisor for the PGA of America's Web site, www.pga.com.

I am uniquely prepared to write and teach you about this stuff, if you are prepared to read and learn.

How to Use This Book

Think of this book as being an "owner's manual" of sorts—the manual you DIDN'T get with your last, or any other set of clubs. In it we will dissect the golf club like a first-year medical student. Breathe easy, we will not take it to the point of your becoming a surgeon, but we will learn that the hip bone is connected to the thigh bone, and WHY it is connected the way it is.

We will look at clubheads, shafts, and grips and show you how they can all fit together to bring out the best in each skill level of golfer. We will look at special populations of golfers: seniors, children, women, and the disabled, and how their equipment needs are different. You will learn things that you can do to, and for, your equipment to make yourself a better golfer. Finally, you will be asked to take the proverbial bull by the horns and learn YOUR specific equipment needs that are dictated and ordained by how you swing the golf club.

In doing all this, you will also learn some of the foibles of the golf industry itself.

I will admit there will be places where I will be quite hard on the industry and the organizations that surround it. This is mainly because there are times when I believe they have not served you, the golfing public, very well. Do not mistake these criticisms as disrespect, however, because they are not intended that way. The industry is filled with people who love this game as much as you or I, and are trying to do their best. But sometimes things don't work out as they should and when that happens I will blow the whistle.

Golf is about having fun. Simply put, this book is about understanding its tools and removing some of the barriers that keep it from being MORE fun for more people.

"GAME IMPROVEMENT" GOLF CLUBS

The pros, especially the senior pros, are forever telling us how recent improvements in golf equipment have "transformed their games" and allow them to continue to play at a high level. That is probably true—for them; but does it have anything to do with YOU?

Consider:

The average male golfer shoots a 97. The average female, 114. It's an even 100 for all golfers. Only 6 percent of the men and 1 percent of the women say they break 80 regularly. Only 0.1 percent of all golfers shoot par.

Now, pick up your favorite golf magazine or flip on the Golf Channel and think about the people at whom those advertisements are aimed? Is it YOU and YOUR game? Is your problem how to get 15 more yards on your drive, or how to keep it from going 15 fewer yards into the woods?

The point is: 90 percent of the "improvements" in golf clubs in recent years are completely unusable by 90 percent of the golfers. Yet you pay for those unusable advances every time you buy a club.

CHAPTER 1—GETTING A HEAD

The Quest

As with the game of golf itself, you could spend the rest of your life studying the technical vagaries of golf clubs and still not know everything there is to know. The problem is that most golfers need to know a lot more about the performance of golf clubs than they do.

I am not expecting you to become a physicist, a metallurgist, or a trained clubmaker. But there are some things related to your golf clubs that affect your game every time you practice or play, and that stuff you should know.

For example, if I were to design a fully customized set of golf clubs for you, there are 21 things I can tailor to your swing which, on their own or in combination with each other, could change the way you hit the ball without your ever having to change your swing. Each of those 21 golf club design points interacts with the other 20 in a spiderweb of cause and effect that would bring a supercomputer to its knees.

Fortunately, you don't have to know what these 21 different things are that determine the performance of a golf club. Most of them have such a subtle effect on the flight of the golf ball that they are not worth worrying about, except to the occasional marketing executive who wants you to buy his company's clubs. What I hope to accomplish in this book is to show you the things about golf clubs that really matter and that will truly make a difference in how you play.

We are all too aware that today we live in an era of high tech. Every time you turn around there is an ad or commercial reminding us that technology will make everything better—including golf clubs. There is no question that advances in the application of physics and material science have made today's golf clubs far better than those made even 10 years ago. But what makes the task of choosing a new set of golf clubs so confusing is that some golf companies routinely use these high-tech claims simply as a means of loosening your hold on your credit card—whether or not those claims will result in noticeable differences in the flight of the ball.

Here's the first fact I want you to keep in mind as you read this book . . .

> We who design and engineer golf clubs can now design differences between golf clubs that golfers cannot perceive. They are all very real, but some of them will have more of a visible impact on your game than others.

My goal will be to show you which golf equipment features will increase the probability of your playing to the best of your ability and which, in all likelihood, will not.

Getting a Head

When you walk into a golf store and wander over to the club racks, the first thing most golfers look at are the clubheads attached to the end of the shafts. (I sometimes think the main reason shaft companies have produced so many attention-getting color schemes in recent years is finally to get you to look at THEIR products, because it's a well-known fact that golfers browsing through racks of clubs are chiefly attracted by the clubheads!) So, let's start with the head and begin with some terminology.

Every clubhead has three parts: the hosel (pronounced: HAW-zul), the face, and the body (see figs. 1.1 and 1.2). The hosel is the neck of the clubhead and is designed to secure the shaft. (Yes, I know, several Callaway brand clubheads do not have a hosel, but let's stay away from the exceptions for right now.) The face is the surface where impact takes place and the energy from the swing and clubhead mass is transferred to the ball. Everything else is termed the body of the clubhead.

The end of the clubhead and area of the face furthest from the shaft is called the toe; the area on the other end where the shaft is attached is termed the heel; and the bottom of the head is the sole. I should point out that this terminology is centuries old and there is no truth to the rumor that the clubhead is named after the parts of the foot because of the way some golfers are prone to getting their ball back into play!

You might also have noticed that most golf clubs have a little plastic piece wrapped around the shaft at the top of the hosel. This is called a ferrule (pronounced FAIR-ul). We like to joke that the ferrule has no purpose except to irritate clubmakers and club-repair technicians! Actu-

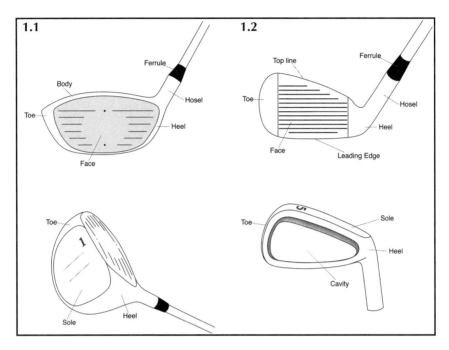

Figures 1.1 and 1.2. While clubhead designers have a wide vocabulary when referring to specific clubhead parts, the above terms are the minimum that the average golfer should know.

ally, the ferrule's purpose is twofold. The first is a cosmetic one; it affords your eyes a smooth, tapering visual transition from the shaft to the clubhead. Second, it offers a small amount of extra support for graphite shafts when the head crashes into the ball and as much as 4,000 pounds of impact force is applied.

Early in your golfing life you learned there are four types of clubheads: woods, irons, wedges, and putters. While each of the four looks quite different, each shares two design features in common—loft and lie.

Loft is an angle, so it is expressed in degrees. It indicates how far the face of the clubhead is tilted back from an imaginary vertical line that runs through the hosel. So if you are in the market for a driver, the first thing you will want to know is if the loft angle is 9 degrees, 10.5 degrees, 13 degrees, or whatever. (I'll explain later why loft doesn't always work on distance the way you think it does.)

Lie is also an angle, so it too is expressed in degrees. Lie represents how far the hosel is tilted back from an imaginary horizontal line running along the sole of the club, and, in the irons, is very important in determining accuracy (see figs. 1.3 and 1.4).

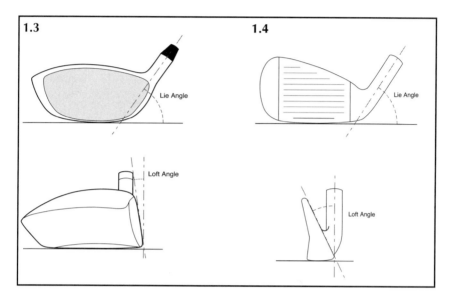

Figures 1.3 and 1.4. The loft angle is the angle between the face plane and a vertical plane running perpendicular to the sole of the clubhead. The lie angle is the angle between the axis of the hosel and the ground line.

It is the rare golfer who knows the loft angles of his clubs (except maybe his driver), and even rarer the one who knows the lie angles, yet both are extremely important to your game.

A Lofty Quest

The loft angle controls the speed, launch angle, and amount of backspin imparted to the ball. This is important because how far you hit the ball and the angle of its flight are all about those three things. The faster you swing the club and the lower the loft angle of the clubhead, the higher the ball's speed, the lower the launch angle, and the lower the backspin will be when it leaves the clubface (i.e., distance). The faster you swing the club and the higher the loft angle of the clubhead, the higher you will hit the ball (i.e., trajectory). This is because a higher swing speed means a higher ball speed, a greater loft means a higher launch angle, and a higher ball speed plus loft means more backspin. Put 'em together and it means a higher trajectory.

Each clubhead is designed with a different loft angle, which is the primary reason you can hit each club a different distance. Each of the different loft angles generates a different ball speed, launch angle, and amount of backspin on the ball, which is precisely why each club hits the ball a different distance. Even if you had a set of clubs all made to the same length, as long as the lofts between each club were different, you would still hit each club a significantly different distance. That is why the loft angle for each club is so important to playing consistent golf.

The exact distance each club will hit the ball will vary from golfer to golfer depending on the speed of their swing, the loft of the clubhead, and the launch angle their swing plus the loft creates on the ball. Tiger Woods hits his 5-iron MUCH longer and higher than I do. Actually, to be honest, he hits his 5-iron farther and higher than I hit my 5-wood (but he can't design golf clubs as I can, so I feel I have at least a shred of respect left!). And my 5-iron might go longer or shorter, and higher or lower than yours. The main reason is that of differences in how fast we all swing each club due to our size, strength, athletic ability, and swing mechanics. Regardless of how far we each hit the ball, it is critical for each golfer to spend time at a driving range so when you are standing on a golf course, 100, 150, or however many yards from your target, you know exactly which club will carry the ball that distance.

First, you should know the loft angle of each club in your bag. If the shop from which you bought your clubs can't provide that information, the Web site of the company that made your clubs might archive it. Depending on your swing speed, the shot hit with each clubhead is designed to travel about 10 to 15 yards farther than the previous one. The slower your swing speed, the closer together will be the distances of your clubs. The faster, the farther apart their distances will be. However, this consistent difference in distance between clubs will result only IF the loft angles are spaced evenly, and IF the lofts on each club are true to what each company intends them to be.

Here's the problem.

There are a zillion golf clubs manufactured each year. What do you think the odds are that all of them are coming from the factory with the correct loft angles and loft spacing built in? Even the best clubhead production foundries on the planet produce heads for their customers with a +/- 1 degree tolerance for the loft angles. That means if the intended loft spacing between two clubs in your set is 4 degrees, if one is a "plus" and the clubhead next in line is a "minus" within the accepted production error tolerance, you could have two clubs that are only 2 degrees apart, or another two clubs which are spaced at 6 degrees from each other.

Have you ever found yourself with NO club that seems to give you 100 yards reliably, or two adjacent clubs in your set that hit the ball very close to the same distance? It's probably because the loft angles are screwed up with one or two clubs being too steep (termed too "strong") or too shallow (termed too "weak") to give you the right distance increment between each club. This is not the case only with "cheap clubs," but with EVERY model of club made.

Whenever you buy a set of clubs, you should have the loft angles checked by a qualified clubmaker.[1] Do not assume that a new set of golf clubs will have heads that are true to their stated lofts (or lie angles). In addition to common +/- tolerances for the lofts and lies in the production of the heads, if you hit many balls, if you have a high swing speed, and you have a tendency to tear out serious divots, the loft angles on the clubs which you've been playing for a few years might have been knocked out of whack. Either way, get them checked. If the irons are out of whack with each other they can usually be corrected by an experienced clubmaker. If the woods are out of whack . . . well, sorry about that, but there isn't much you can do, other than take them back to the shop that made the sale and ask for a more accurate replacement.

To achieve consistency in shot distance, the lofts between your fairway woods and irons should have no less than 3 degrees, and no more than 5 degrees, of separation from club to club. Any less than 3 degrees and you will have two clubs that hit the ball too close to each other. Any more than 5 degrees and you will have a spread that will cause you to have to hammer one club or ease up on another to get the right distance. Although the difference in the length of each club has something to do with this distance difference, the loft separation accounts for 80 percent and the length spacing for the other 20 percent of the distance difference between any two clubs in your bag.

The loft difference between your driver and 3-wood depends on what driver loft is best for you to achieve your maximum distance and

---

[1]To find a competent clubmaker in your area, look for listings in your yellow pages under "Custom Clubs," "Clubmakers," or "Golf Equipment Repair." In addition, you can find a clubmaker in your area by accessing the Web site of the Professional Clubmakers Society at www.proclubmakers.org or the Clubmaker Locator at www.twgolftech.com. In all cases, be sure to inquire if the clubmaker has the necessary equipment in their shop with which to accurately measure the loft angles of your clubs.

how easily you can get a low lofted fairway wood into the air ("off the deck"), given your swing speed. (We'll explain more about the particulars of that later.)

The Dreaded Vanishing Loft Disease

You must also beware of the "Dreaded Vanishing Loft Disease," something that's been inflicted upon us by all the club manufacturers.

Gradually, over the past 30 years or so, to be able to advertise that their clubs "hit longer," manufacturers have been tinkering with, among other things, the loft of the golf clubs, making them ever lower ("stronger"). Thus, when you try, for example, a 5-iron from the NEW IMPROVED AND LONGER big-name golf club set, you might find yourself exclaiming: "Huzzah [or words to that effect], this 5-iron hits as far as my 10-year-old 4-iron used to go." Well, yeah, but the reason is that your shiny new 5-iron IS, at least according to its NEW AND IMPROVED loft, a 4-iron (see table 1.1).

You see, back when I was a kid the average 5-iron had a loft of 32 degrees (see table 1.1). By the late '90s that 5-iron loft was as low as 25 degrees on many club models. Today the average loft of a 5-iron has "settled" in the area of 26–27 degrees. Will the "new and improved" modern equipment hit farther than the gear built 30 years ago? You bet, "stronger" lofts ensure that. But what they are not telling you is that the new brand-name 5-iron is approximately the same loft as the club they stamped with a #3 or #4 in the '60s and '70s. Of course it's going to go farther!

This Vanishing Loft Disease has had its effect on other clubs as well. In fact, it has forced the golf industry to invent a new club out of thin air. Have you noticed all the companies now offering "gap" or "approach" wedges (aka 52 degree wedges) lately? Ever wonder why, suddenly, this club is now needed?

In the 1960s the difference in loft between the pitching wedge and the sand wedge was typically four or five degrees, which will give you the 10- to 15-yard difference you want between full shots with these clubs. By the mid-'90s, because of "vanishing loft disease," the loft relationship between the PW/SW had grown to as much as 10 degrees, in the process creating a HUGE gap in distance between these two scoring clubs.

The loft of the sand wedge could not be changed. It had to stay at 55–56 degrees because you need that kind of loft to get the ball up quickly

Table 1.1—The Dreaded Vanishing Loft Disease

Club	1960s–70s (degrees)	1980s (degrees)	Early 1990s (degrees)	1997+ (degrees)
Evolution of Men's Wood & Iron Lofts—Industry Average				
1-iron	17	17	16	16–17
2-iron	20	20	19	18–20
3-iron	24	23	22	20–21
4-iron	28	26	25	23–24
5-iron	32	30	28	26–27
6-iron	36	34	32	30–31
7-iron	40	38	36	34–35
8-iron	44	42	40	38–40
9-iron	48	46	44	42–44
PW	52	50	48	46–48
SW	56	56	56	55–56
Driver	11	11	10	9–10.5
3-wood	16	15	15	13–14
5-wood	22	21	19	17–18
7-wood	28	27	23	20–21

Note: A quick look at the information above shows how drastically golf club companies have reduced their loft angles over the past few decades. This was done primarily so they could say their clubs hit the ball farther and thereby sell more clubs.

and out of bunkers. So a "new" club had to be invented to fill the "gap" between the two clubs. Thus, the "gap wedge" was invented. And what an appropriate name that is!

When the first big-name golf company started to shrink their lofts to lure golfers into buying their clubs because they hit the ball farther, every other golf company had no choice but to follow. After all, when have you not been impressed by hitting a club with the same number farther than the one you currently have? If you are a golf company that chooses not to follow the trend, what are you going to say to your potential customers? "Well, the other companies are just fooling you—keep hitting ours although you won't hit the ball as far." Yeah, right, that'll keep sales going.

I'll never forget several years ago how I got hit right between the eyes with the effect of the golf industry's steady decrease in clubhead lofts. During a business trip to Pinehurst, the eastern Mecca of golf in the United States, I had a couple of hours to kill so I was wandering around outside the Pinehurst Resort's golf shop. They had a whole fleet of carts parked side by side, each with golf bags all loaded and ready to take off in a shotgun start.

Being a club designer and professed club nut, what do you think I'll stop to look at while walking by 60 or so loaded golf carts? After perusing about three-fourths of the players' varied selections of "weapons of grass destruction," it hit me like a 2 x 4 between the eyes how SHINY the #3- and #4-irons in every bag were compared to the other irons in the set!

So now you know why: (a) only God can hit a 1-iron, (b) club companies no longer even offer a 2-iron, (c) you and your buddies can't come close to hitting a 3-iron (and probably the 4-iron, too), and (d) you have to fork over the cash for another wedge!

What the brand-name golf companies have done to lofts, however, is nothing compared to what they've done with the lengths of the clubs, all in the name of "hitting it farther" and ultimately selling more clubs. What this means is that set-makeup (i.e., the clubs you select to fill your bag) has become a VERY important part of golf club fitting.

Length, Loft, and Accuracy

The loft, lie, and lengths of your clubs all interact with one another and your swing speed to give you the direction, distance, and trajectory of your ball flight. In terms of accuracy, the most important of these three is club length, followed by lie and loft. Let's look particularly at length.

Length and accuracy is a no-brainer. Think about it. If I put a clubhead at the end of a 10-inch shaft and ask you hit a golf ball straight down the fairway it would be a pretty easy task. OK, so you'd only get to put one hand on the club; you'd be on your knees to address the ball; and the ball wouldn't go very far. But it would be easy to make solid contact and to hit the ball straight. Now, let's say I switch you from a 10-inch to a 10-foot club and ask you to do the same thing. What do you think is going to happen?

Right. The 10-foot-long club would be almost completely uncontrollable.

I remember when long drive competitions had just started, and golfers were in awe of the humongous long drivers these gorillas used. All of a sudden there was so much interest among regular golfers in superlong drivers that many shaft companies began to manufacture specially designed superlong shafts to meet the demand.

One day I built a 60-inch-long driver with a graphite shaft finished in a bright fire engine red. My wife Mary-Ellen happened to work with LPGA Tour player Tammie Green's brother at the time. We were headed out for a picnic at the Green family farm outside the quaint little town of Somerset, Ohio that weekend. I knew Tod would just love to get his hands on that club, what with all the talk at the time in golf about superlong drivers, so I shoehorned all 60 inches of it into the car.

The 9-hole golf course where all the Greens learned to play bordered the family's farmland so as soon as I pulled this 60-inch driver out of the car, Tod and Tammie got this gleam in their eyes and said, "Let's go over to the club." In a flash the three of us hopped on the family John Deere, headed out across the fields, and made it over to the Perry County "Country Club." Some vehicle to head into a golf course parking lot with, eh?

As soon as we rolled in, Tod hopped off the tractor, took the 60-inch driver and strolled into the "clubhouse." Conspicuously waggling the driver in front of him, Tod hollered out, "Tammie 'n' me got us a new driver here and we're a'wonderin' if any of you boys want to give it a whack." Sure enough, the "boys" all jumped up and insisted on heading outside the front door to the first tee to try it out. Once there Tod posed a little proposition—you know, a group of guys hanging out drinkin' beers in the shop can't possibly do anything golf-related without "putting something on it"!

Tod said, "OK, you guys give me a buck for each swing you take with this driver and I'll give you two bucks if you hit it over the ditch out there in the fairway." I took a look and figured the ditch that crossed the first fairway was out there about 210 yards, and probably a hazard most of these guys feared with their "mini-drivers."

With visions of massive drives from this 60-inch driver, tongues were hanging out and hands were reaching into back pockets before Tod could finish uttering the challenge. Of course, Tod's "shill" was sister Tammie. After several of the "boys" paid the buck and topped, heeled, or dropkicked the driver, Tammie would step in and say, "Tod, you sure there ain't nothing wrong with that driver that's causin' the boys to hit it so short"? At which point Tod promptly handed the club to his tour player sister Tammie, who blew the ball WELL over the ditch on the fly.

Well that just stirred things up even more with the boys of Perry County C.C. To make a long story short, Tod and Tammie walked away with over $100 that day! And the guys all left with a lesson about long drivers, on-center hits, and accuracy. The most-heard phrase that day? "Gimme that damn thing again, I know I can fly the ditch." So Tod, Tammie, and I all headed to the Somerset butcher shop and had grilled steak at the picnic instead of burgers and dogs!

What all this means is this. Somewhere between 10 inches and 10 feet is the correct length for a golf club to hit the ball solid with distance and accuracy. But I'll guarantee the right length for you is far closer to 10 inches than 10 feet! Do NOT assume that the "standard" length found on the clubs in the golf shop, especially the woods, will be right for you. Ninety-eight percent of the men's drivers these days are built to a "standard" length of 45 or 45.5 inches, and I am here to tell you that a 45-inch driver will not fit 90 percent of all golfers and will never allow them to achieve their best combination of distance AND accuracy.

Let me put it another way. Tiger Woods has swung a 43.5-inch driver most of his career on tour. If he could hit the ball straight with a 45-inch club—he would. He can't, so he doesn't. And he knows if he did use a longer driver, he'd have even more trouble keeping it in play. The average driver length for all the other pros on the PGA Tour today is 44.5 inches. Now if Tiger and the rest of his pals know they can't control a 45-inch-long stick, what are the chances that you can?

Golfers come in all combinations of height and arm lengths, which are just two of the important elements that have to be considered in determining the best club lengths for golfers. If you do nothing else, get measured for the correct length when you buy golf clubs—EVEN IF YOU ARE A BEGINNER. All professional clubmakers and even some retail golf stores will do this for you, usually for free. You can even do it yourself by taking a very simple measurement called a "wrist-to-floor dimension."

While standing comfortably erect with your shoulders perfectly level and arms hanging relaxed at your sides, measure the distance in inches, plus any fraction, from the major wrist crease at the base of your dominant hand to the floor. Reference that measurement to the club lengths in table 1.2.

If you are considering buying your clubs at a pro shop or off-course retail golf store, your length requirements will likely be different from what they carry. Thus, you will definitely want to inquire if the shop can specially order the right length clubs for you from the manufacturer. Some

Table 1.2—Driver and 5-Iron Length Recommendations Based on Wrist-to-Floor Measurement of the Golfer (in inches)

Wrist-to-Floor	Driver Length	5-Iron Length
27 to 29	42	36.5
29+ to 32	42.5	37
32+ to 34	43	37.5
34+ to 36	43.5	38
36+ to 37	44	38.25
37+ to 38	44.25	38.5
38+ to 39	44.5	38.75
39+ to 40	44.75	39
40+ to 41	45	39.25
41+ to 42	45.5	39.5
over 42	46 and up	39.75 and up

Note: An accurate measurement of your wrist-to-floor distance is the best starting point for club length. Your final length, however, may be different based on your swing plane, swing path, swing tempo, and general athletic ability.

of the large brand-name golf companies do provide this service through their custom departments, but they will likely be limited in how much they can deviate from their normal "standard length" and still keep the clubs in a proper swingweight balance. In addition, such custom orders can take from 2 weeks to 2 months because building to custom order is not exactly how most of the big companies have set up their assembly lines.

If the golf store or pro shop offers to "cut down" or alter the length from a standard set they have in stock, BE SURE to inquire about their experience and skills in this area. Specifically it will be critical to the performance of the clubs that the heads are reweighted to restore the proper swingweight for their adjusted length.

At the end of the day, though, your best bet would be to place your needs in the hands of a competent clubmaker in your area to perform the proper length adjustments or, even better, to have him/her custom build a new set precisely to your length needs. (And yes, I do mean "him/her." There are some VERY competent female custom clubmakers out there!)

In the hands of an experienced professional clubmaker, the difference in accuracy and on-center hit frequency after being properly fitted for length, compared to standard off-the-rack clubs, will be immediate and profound!

Backspin, Loft, and Distance

One of the biggest trends in golf has been to buy a driver with a lower loft. The theory is that the lower the loft, the more distance you will get. It sounds logical. The problem is that with the driver, and for the 3-wood as well, it isn't true. Most golfers do not realize they have at least 10–12 more yards available to them off the tee if they will just give up that 8, 9, 10, or even 11 degree driver and start using a driver with MORE LOFT. Yes, that's right. Most golfers need a higher loft on their driver to maximize their distance potential and enable them to hit the ball farther.

I know that sounds counterintuitive, so let me explain.

The main players in this little mystery are backspin, loft, swing speed, and a little-known factor in your golf swing called the "angle of attack" into the ball. The angle of attack is an expression used to describe whether you hit the ball on a downward blow, whether the head is traveling level to the ground into impact, or whether you hit the ball on the upswing (see fig. 1.5).

Now, I told you that more loft means more distance with the driver. I can prove it scientifically but, instead of boring you with formulas and all that scary stuff, let me explain it this way.

Let's say you're washing the car with your kids. Kids being kids, they lose focus and start goofing off, so to get their attention you decide to give them a quick shot with the hose. As you start to raise your "weapon," they catch on and take off running. What angle do you need to aim the hose to shoot that stream of water far enough to nail your fleeing kids?

Well, you better aim that hose at a 45 degree angle with the most water pressure your hose can muster or you've got no prayer of delivering your message! If you angle the hose at a "lower loft," the stream cannot carry as far because gravity will force the water to the ground too soon. And if you point the hose up too much, you won't achieve the best "launch angle" so the force of the stream will be wasted in shooting the water too high, thus falling short of its target. Either way, you'll be standing there with your kids laughing and no help to finish the car!

What you've just discovered is that the correct angle for shooting the stream of water its maximum distance depends on the angle at which you hold the hose (loft) and how fast the water is shooting out of the nozzle (swing speed/ball velocity). Well, pretty much the same thing is true for a tee shot. How far the ball will go depends on the launch angle, which is first determined by the clubhead loft, second by your swing

Downward Angle of Attack

Level Angle of Attack

Upward Angle of Attack

Figure 1.5. The angle of attack describes whether your swing delivers the clubhead to the ball on a downward, level, or upward path. It is a critical element in the selection of the best driver loft to maximize your distance off the tee.

angle of attack, and then by the speed with which the ball is traveling when it leaves the clubhead.

The more downward your angle of attack and the slower your swing speed, the higher the loft must be to maximize your driver distance. Conversely, the more you hit the ball on the upswing (upward angle of attack) and the higher your swing speed, the lower your loft would need to be to maximize distance. This is precisely how all the national long drive competitors can use drivers with 5, 6, 7 degrees and still achieve a high ball flight for their gargantuan carry distances. They train themselves to hit the ball on a severe upswing so they can use a much lower loft to maximize their distance. In other words, *you have to match your clubhead loft to your swing speed and especially to your angle of attack!*

If you still doubt me, look at the numbers in table 1.3. Look at the listing for a 90 mph swing speed based on a +2.5 degree upward angle of attack in the swing, which is about average for most men with a driver. The distance achieved by your "water hose" increases as the launch angle (loft) goes UP, not down. This holds until you get to about 13 degrees of loft, then the distance goes down again. If the angle of attack from your swing is level or downward, you'll need even more loft to achieve your maximum carry distance. (Don't have a clue about your angle of attack? Don't worry. Later on we'll teach you how to determine your swing angle of attack.)

So you still want to buy that 9 degree driver? If so, you'd better have about a 110 mph swing speed and hit the ball a little on the upswing or you will be FAR better off with about 11 degrees. The ball will go farther and will have a little less tendency to fly off-line.

Okay, fine. All that makes sense, but what does swing speed have to do with it? To use the water hose analogy again, the more you turn the faucet and dial down the nozzle, the farther the stream will travel at whatever angle you have on it, right?

Yes, that's true for a stream of water coming out of a nozzle, but it is not true for golf balls. The reason is that, unlike hoses, golf balls have dimples and fly off the face with backspin.

Did you ever wonder WHY golf balls have dimples on them? All golf balls made before the 1870s were as smooth and as round as the ball makers could make them. It wasn't long, however, before golfers found out that balls that were scratched or slightly cut seemed to fly farther and straighter. Smart caddies looking for a good tip started filing a sharp edge on their belt buckles to put several gouges on the cover of their players' balls. Taking their lead from the savvy caddies, the golf ball

Table 1.3—The Effect of Launch Angle on Driver Distance[a]

Swing Speed (mph)	Driver Loft (degrees)	Launch Angle (degrees)	Carry Distance (yards)
60	11	12.1	106
	15	15.2	117
	19	18.1	122
70	11	12.1	145
	15	15.2	154
	19	18.1	156
80	9	10.5	174
	11	12.1	181
	13	13.7	185
90	9	10.5	206
	11	12.1	211
	13	13.7	213
100	8	9.6	231
	9	10.5	234
	10	12.1	236
110	7	8.8	254
	8	9.6	256
	9	10.5	257

Note: To achieve maximum distance, every golfer from pro to beginner must be fitted with the correct driver loft angle to match their swing speed. It is the only way to obtain the best launch angle for maximum distance.

[a]Table information based on a swing angle of attack of +2.5 degrees, which means hitting the ball on the upswing with the driver traveling upward at an angle of 2.5 degrees. The average golfer will have a slight upward angle of attack with the driver. For golfers who do not hit the ball on the upswing, the optimum driver loft for maximum distance will be a little higher loft than what is shown in the table.

makers immediately started making balls with all sorts of crosshatches and patterns on them. Eventually, it was found that the application of a simple dish-shaped depression (what we now call a "dimple") would yield the maximum distance. Even later, we found out why.

When the ball comes off the clubface it does so with a certain amount of backspin. Believe it or not, with a driver it's somewhere between 2,000 and 4,500 rpm. That spin causes the dimples to (for lack of a better word) "bite" into the air. This bite actually creates an aerodynamic lift under the ball (like an aircraft wing) which, in turn, holds the ball up in the air longer, allowing its speed to carry it farther. If you don't have backspin on the ball, instead of getting aerodynamic lift, you'll get a ballistic knuckleball where the only thing that's holding the ball up is the speed at which it was hit.

Not good.

So let's put it together. To get aerodynamic lift on the golf ball you need backspin. To get backspin you can either (a) increase the loft of the driver, take your normal 90 mph swing and get the right launch angle with enough backspin on the ball, or (b) you can opt for a lower loft and smash the 110 mph bejeebers out of it, providing you have a high level of bejeebers in you. *What you can NOT do is hit it with a single-digit loft AND a slow swing speed and expect your longest drive.* Unfortunately, that is what most golfers end up trying to do by choosing a lower driver loft in the mistaken belief that a lower loft means more distance.

Want even more proof I'm not blowin' smoke here? How many of you hit your 3-wood as far, if not farther, than your driver—even though the 3-wood is probably 1 to 2 inches shorter than your driver and has a lot more loft? If you do hit the 3-wood as far as your driver, it's because that higher loft is generating a higher launch angle with more backspin, which holds the ball up in the air longer, so the ball carries farther.

In their cover story, the November 2003 issue of *Golf Digest* magazine reported even the majority of professionals on tour had slightly increased their driver loft to gain more distance. It's a fact. Choosing the right loft for your swing speed and your swing angle of attack WILL maximize your distance potential.

If your driver swing speed is, like those of most golfers, under 100 mph, if you have a level or downward angle of attack into the ball—and you want to maximize distance—you may actually need a driver with a loft of 14–15 degrees or even more. If your swing speed is between 100 and 110 mph with a downward angle of attack, you should be looking at heads with 11 to 12 degrees of loft. And you should use lofts lower than that ONLY if your swing speed exceeds 105 to 110 mph and your angle of attack into the ball is level or slightly upward.

So how do you know exactly what driver loft is best for you? A trip to see an experienced clubmaker in your area who has a fancy piece of analytical technology called a "Launch Monitor" can nail down your optimum driver loft with precision and eliminate the guesswork.

One last item before we leave this topic. Does moving to a 13 or 14 degree driver mean you should get rid of your 14 or 15 degree 3-wood? No, absolutely not, not as long as you have the swing skills to easily hit a 14 or 15 degree 3-wood well up in the air "off the deck" so it will carry its full potential distance. Remember, the first task of a 3-wood is to give you the longest possible SECOND shot where the ball is sitting on the ground, not on a tee. Drivers are not designed to do that. That's why fairway woods have a face height and head size that are so much smaller than drivers. And if you don't have the skill to attain a high ball flight with a 3-wood, then chuck it and make your second longest hitting wood be the lowest loft fairway wood with which you can get the ball well up into the air to carry. If you "rope" the 3-wood at gutter height, you are not doing yourself any favors by keeping that 3-wood in your bag—well, unless your greenkeeper doesn't water your fairways and the grass is a shade of tan.

In recent years 3-woods have also become "infected" with a bad case of the "dreaded vanishing loft disease" which has made them much more difficult to hit for the majority of golfers. The old standard 3-wood loft of 16 degrees has recently shrunk to 14, 13, or, yeouch, even 12 degrees—caused, again, by the geniuses at the big golf club companies

YOUR CHOICE OF DRIVER LOFT

A check of the majority of the big club companies' offerings shows that the highest men's driver loft you'll ever encounter in a trip to the pro shop or off-course looking for a big brand-name driver is 12 degrees. The highest loft on a women's driver made by the big club companies is 13.5 degrees.

The average man swings the driver 86 mph with a slight upward angle of attack into the ball. The average woman swings the driver 68 mph, also with a slight upward angle of attack into the ball.

Launch monitor research shows that all golfers with a swing speed of 80 to 93 mph or less with a slight upward angle of attack, regardless of gender, need at least a 13 degree loft on their driver to maximize their distance. What about a swing speed lower than 80 mph? Simple, more than 13 degrees of driver loft is necessary to achieve the longest possible carry distance.

And what does all this mean? Way, way more than half of all the golfers on the planet can't achieve their maximum potential for distance with any of the big golf companies' driver offerings.

who want to claim more distance and therefore sell more clubs whether you can actually hit them or not. Just as 9, 10, and 11 degree drivers will not maximize the average golfer's distance potential, neither will a 12, 13, or 14 degree 3-wood perform the best for the average golfer's long second shot requirements. Only golfers with a higher swing speed and the ability to swing so that they "stay behind the ball" at impact will have a chance to be well matched to a 12, 13, or 14 degree loft 3-wood. So for the rest of us, if you do not have the natural ability to hit your 3-wood high in the air, quit fooling yourself and hunt down a 3-wood with no less than 15–16 degrees of loft. And if you still hit the ball barely above the height of your first floor gutters, shift to a 5-wood with 17–18 degrees of loft for your next-to-longest wood.

Putter Hop and Wedge Bounce?

I know that putters look as if they have no loft, but they really do. They all have at least two or more degrees of loft.

The reason for this is that a golf ball sitting on the green is nestled down slightly in the grass. It's short grass, to be sure, but the ball does sit down a little in the grass nonetheless. You need a certain loft on the putter to get your ball up out of its nest and rolling smoothly. Without it, the initial movement of the ball would be an unpredictable "hop," which is definitely not a good start for rolling the ball straight and true.

I hate to sound like a broken record about this matter of loft angle, but *having the right loft with the putter is of huge importance for making more putts*. Spend some time on the practice putting green and try to note the position of your hands in relation to the putter head at the moment of putt impact. If your normal putting stroke puts the hands in front of the ball when the putter makes contact with the ball, you would very likely benefit from 5–6 degrees of loft on the putter. If your hands are directly in line with the ball position at impact, a putter loft of 3–4 degrees will be suitable. And, although this is rare, if your hands are behind the ball when you make contact, you will do better with a 1–2 degree putter loft.

If you suspect a different putter loft could help you reach in your partners' pockets more often, here again, take a trip to your local professional clubmaker's shop. The vast majority of putters can be adjusted for a loft change through a minor bend in the hosel, or the shaft if your putter is one of the models without a hosel where the shaft is inserted directly into the head. And, in fact, some clubmakers are starting to offer more detailed putting analysis, often using a video camera, and can very accurately gauge the correct loft, along with the right lie and length for individually fitting the putter to your individual stroke. I'm sure the majority of golfers are aware of the importance of the putter to their score, so why anyone would NOT spend the time to be properly fit to the length, lie, and loft of their putter is beyond me.

Wedges, on the other hand, are . . . well . . . they're simply strange clubs because they come in so many different combinations of design specifications. They look like irons but technically they're not. Unlike irons, wedges are designed to be used primarily with something less than a full swing and in a multitude of different shot-making techniques. They are WEDGES—a class all their own. They are more steeply lofted (weaker) than your other irons; they are heavier and, especially the sand wedge, have a built-in characteristic on the sole known as a "bounce sole angle" (see fig. 1.6).

Compare the sole of your sand wedge to any of your numbered irons. If you rest the wedge on its sole on top of a table as though it is addressing the ball, you'll note that the rear or trailing edge of the sole of your sand wedge is what touches the table first, while the front or leading edge of the wedge sole sticks up off the surface of the table (see fig. 1.6). This is a design feature of the sole angle called "bounce" and it helps keep the head from digging down too deep into the sand and leaving the ball in the bunker. Want an example? Try this.

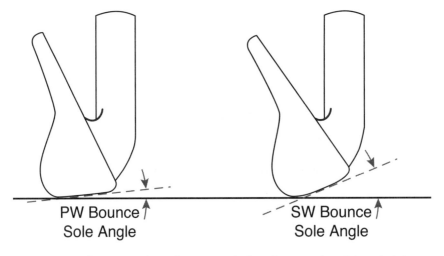

PW Bounce
Sole Angle

SW Bounce
Sole Angle

Figure 1.6. A "bounce" sole angle is created when the rear edge of the sole is lower than the front. Bounce is measured in degrees. The higher the degree, the greater the bounce, which is excellent for golfers who tend to leave the ball in the sand.

Take your pitching wedge into a bunker, and try blasting five or six balls out of the sand. Without the hands and touch of a young Seve Ballasteros it will be an artistic disaster, but you will at least be able to see what happens when you use a wedge with not enough bounce in the design of its sole angle. Most likely you'll leave the ball in the trap as the pitching wedge dives deeper under the ball. The pitching wedge (PW) has far less of a bounce sole angle than does a sand wedge (SW)because it is designed for use off the grass.

When the sole of the SW cuts downward into the sand behind and under the ball, the bounce sole angle meets with resistance from the sand and prevents the club from digging too deep. Think of the bounce sole as the elevator on an airplane, and the sand as the air through which the plane's rear wing flies. When the pilot wants to increase altitude, the angles of the elevators are tilted so their "leading edge" is higher than the "trailing edge." The result is that the rear wings generate more lift, and the plane increases in altitude. Same thing with a sand wedge traveling through sand—or at least it will as long as your swing does not become too steep and force the leading edge down lower than the trailing edge, which will cause the SW to "dive, crash, and burn" in the bunker!

A bounce sole angle's effect is magnified or reduced by the width of the sole. This is the reason that wider sole sand wedges are advised for golfers who have a chronic problem with leaving the ball in the bunker on sand shots. The wider sole will magnify the effect of the bounce to prevent the wedge from digging as deep under the ball, while allowing the ball to be lifted out of the sand more easily. Likewise, it is also the reason that very good sand players opt for more narrow sole wedges—a good sand player can control the depth of the wedge into the sand with the swing and thus needs less sole width to prevent the head from digging too deep. Following are guidelines for selecting the type of wedge for various shot requirements.

Many golfers suffer from a lack of consistency in hitting shots from sand. They either tend to hit the ball first or take too little sand—both resulting in the screaming line drive that ends up way over the green and costs the golfer at least two extra shots on the scorecard. Or they tend to dig too deep under the ball and leave the ball in the bunker.

There is no question that lack of the proper swing technique is the primary cause of both examples of the poor bunker play just described. Leaving the ball in the sand is most often caused by the player swinging the SW down to the shot on much too steep a downswing angle, thus causing the ball to dig too deep in the sand. Blading the ball, or not entering the sand far enough behind the ball, is normally a case of the golfer letting the wrists "break" and flex forward so the clubhead passes the hands too soon before the shot is hit. Such movements cause the clubhead to begin traveling upward too soon, thus either hitting the ball with the leading edge of the SW (an outright bladed shot), or entering the sand very close to the ball so that the length of the swing carries the ball much too far for the intended distance of the shot. While severe problems in the sand should be addressed through instruction with a competent teacher, there are definite wedge design features which can enhance the golfer's ability to allow the wedge to do its job a little more easily, and help overcome some shot-making problems with the wedges.

If you tend to leave the ball in the sand too often . . .

- A SW with a much wider sole can help because the wider the sole, the more the wedge resists digging too deep under the ball.
- A SW with more than 12 degrees of bounce sole angle will also resist digging too deep under the ball.
- A combination of both more bounce sole angle AND a wider sole design will further magnify the ability of the SW to dig too deep under the ball.
- Using a SW of much more loft, such as 60 degrees, will lay the face back more and also present a little less resistance to the wedge traveling all the way through the sand under the ball. In addition, if a very steep downswing is the cause of leaving the ball in the sand, that type of swing will hit a normal 55–56 degree loft SW much lower, which also may be a problem for the golfer in getting the ball up and out of the sand. Thus, more loft on the club used from the sand will help as well.
- A lighter swingweight for the sand club may also help the golfer get the club all the way through the sand under the ball. Normal SW clubs are made to an average swingweight of D6. Using a SW of D0 swingweight might allow the golfer's swing strength to generate more momentum to keep the SW moving through the sand under the ball.
- Check the consistency of the sand in the bunkers where you play. Sand that is very fine and fluffy and deep will tend to present far less resistance to the SW traveling too deep under the ball. Thus SW design factors such as a wider sole, greater bounce sole angle, and/or shorter SW club length can all help to prevent the club from traveling too deep through such light and fluffy sand.

If you tend to take too little sand and hit the sand shot too thin, the equipment remedies for possible help are the opposite of those just mentioned for the problem of the SW traveling too deep under the ball . . .

- A more narrow sole SW can help because the more narrow the sole, the more the wedge can dig deeply under the ball.
- A SW with less than 12 degrees of bounce sole angle will be able to be swung deeper under the ball.
- A combination of both less bounce sole angle AND a more narrow sole design will further magnify the ability of the SW to dig deeper under the ball.
- Check the consistency of the sand in the bunkers where you play. Sand that is very coarse and shallow will tend to present much more resistance to the SW traveling under the ball. Thus if your sand is of this consistency and you are using a wide sole SW or one that has a lot of bounce, this alone could be the cause of the thin shots. Thus SW design factors such as a more narrow sole, less bounce sole angle, and shorter SW club length can all help to allow the wedge to penetrate a little deeper into such coarse and shallow sand.

CHAPTER 2—TRUE LIES AND THE RIGHT STUFF

True Lies?

The lie angle is another very important characteristic of the clubhead that needs to be custom fitted to each golfer to ensure accuracy. If the lie angle is wrong for your size, setup, and swing moves, as the loft of the clubhead increases you will almost certainly hit the ball crooked. As mentioned earlier, the lie angle represents how far the hosel is tilted back from an imaginary horizontal line running along the bottom of the club (see fig. 2.1). Within the golf industry, there is a generally accepted notion of what constitutes a "standard" lie angle for most golfers. Whether this factory norm is right for you and your swing, however, is something all golfers need to discover for themselves because accuracy with the irons is so important to good scoring.

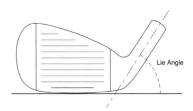

Lie Angle

Figure 2.1. Because golfers are so different in height, arm length, and body position, it is vital that the lie angle of the irons be fitted for each golfer. It is a critical aspect of golf club accuracy.

Here's the deal. When the club meets the ball, the sole of the head must be parallel to the ground. If it is, and if you have delivered the face square to your intended target, the ball will go straight every time. On the other hand, if the toe of the club is sticking up in the air so the point of sole contact with the ground is toward the heel, you will tend to pull your shots. Here, the clubhead would be considered to be TOO UPRIGHT for the player, and would need to have the hosel adjusted flatter, with a lower angle between the hosel and the ground to fit the golfer.

The opposite, in which the club makes contact with the ground on the toe side of the sole, indicates the club is too flat. In this situation, you will push the ball when you make a perfect swing at the ball . . . every day, every time.

There is a myth associated with the lie angle that I can testify from experience exists with ALL levels of players from pro to high handicapper. Many golfers think that if the lie is wrong so that the sole contact with the ground is on the heel, the reason the ball flies left is that the heel is grabbed by the ground, which makes the face rotate closed, and the ball fly to the left (right-handed golfer verbiage here). And vice versa; they think that the pushed shot from an incorrect lie comes from the toe side of the sole digging into the ground, which causes the face to turn open. WRONG. No matter how square you hold the leading edge of the clubhead to your target, as the toe rises up, the face AUTOMATICALLY points to the hook side of the target. And the opposite is true for when you hold the leading edge of the face square to the target but tilt the heel up off the ground—the face now points to the fade side of the hole. Want proof? What happens to your shot direction when you hit the ball from a side hill lie? That's a classic example of how the face is automatically pointed off line and creates a pulled or hooked shot when the ball is above your feet (toe tilting up compared to horizontal) or a pushed/faded shot when the ball is below your feet (heel tilting up compared to horizontal).

Now here's the real kicker with lie—the more the loft, the more pronounced the misdirection will be. As a result, the lie angles are far more critical to be fitted correctly in the higher-lofted short irons, for example, than they are for the woods (see fig. 2.2).

I remember many years ago having a little fun with this relationship between loft, an improperly fitted lie angle, and the misdirection tendency that will result. I was watching a trick-shot show; you know, the people who amaze us with their ability to hit balls with all sorts of weird clubs from all types of convoluted positions. As most trick-shot artists will do, this guy eventually came to the part in his show where he was hitting balls with a regular driver from tees that varied in height from 2 inches to 3 feet off the ground.

After he finished hitting the driver with the ball teed about three feet high, I stood up, young and cocky, and called out, "Let's see you do that with a 9-iron." The guy looked at me with a "What the heck, if it'll make him shut up so I can keep going" sort of look, and promptly pulled a 9-iron from his bag. OK, so visualize this. The ball is waist high, the club is a 9-iron with, say, 45 degrees of loft. You should have seen the look on the guy's face when he almost killed a couple of people standing on the left side of the range!

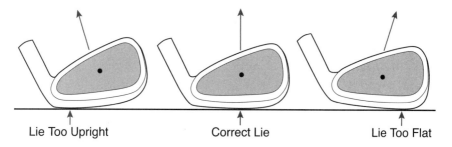

Lie Too Upright   Correct Lie   Lie Too Flat

Figure 2.2. When the lie angle is fitted perfectly to the golfer so the center of the sole touches the ground at impact, the ball will fly straight (center head). However, if the lie is not fitted properly to the golfer so that the toe or heel is up off the ground at impact, the ball will fly off line as shown, regardless of how square you have delivered the face to the ball.

God only knows how many golfers have altered their swings in unimaginable ways, or run screaming to a golf pro for emergency lessons because of balls that insist on going off to the left or right from ill-fitted lie angles, no matter how pure a swing they make. Most golfers automatically assume it's their swing because most golfers have no idea that something called "lie angle" even exists. Most clubs are bought standard, off-the-rack, and most golfers have no idea of the importance of properly fitting lie angles to their size, setup, and swing.

If every golfer were 5 feet 10 inches tall with a 32-inch sleeve length and swung through the ball with the same posture, then fine, the one lie angle design of standard made irons bought off the rack would fit everyone and I would be happy to shut my mouth. But golfers are not all built the same, so if you want to avoid the certainty of making a good swing only to see the ball head off-line, you and every other golfer along with you, regardless of handicap, need to be custom fitted for the correct lie angles on your irons. It's probably fair to say that fewer than 10 percent of all golfers have ever been fitted for lie, and had their clubs adjusted accordingly.

The process of determining the proper lie angle for each club is simple. You could do it yourself, but it's best to have it done by a custom clubmaker. Place a piece of masking tape on the bottom of, say, your 5-iron. Now hit some balls off a rubber mat at a driving range so you feel the sole of the iron make contact with the mat on each shot. After each one, check to see where the scuff mark is on the masking tape put on the sole. If the scuff is right in the middle of the sole, you're fine, the lie is perfect for your size, setup, and swing. If the scuff mark is pretty much consistently out toward the toe, or back toward the heel, you will need to get your lie angles adjusted. This little test you just did is called "Dynamic Lie Fitting" and is the method experienced clubmakers use to note the correct lie for ALL irons in the bag. So if you want to get fitted for lie properly, when you call your local clubmaker, just ask, "Do you perform a Dynamic Lie Fitting for checking lie angles?" If so, you're on your way to eliminating an incorrect lie angle as a possible cause of off-line shots. If not, say thanks, hang up, and call another clubmaker until you find one who does offer this form of lie angle checking for your irons (see fig. 2.3).

Figure 2.3. Iron lie should be fitted "dynamically" as shown. Tape is applied lengthwise on the sole of each iron. The golfer hits shots from a hard surface so the scuff marks indicating where on the sole the iron has hit the ground can be seen on the tape. If the scuff marks are in the center of the sole, the lie of the iron is correct for the golfer. If the scuff marks are on the toe or heel side of the center of the sole, the hosel of the iron must be bent to change the lie angle to fit the golfer.

Adjusting Loft and Lie

Adjusting loft and lie on the irons is a fairly simple procedure and can be done by most experienced clubmakers. The clubmaker will have a machine that looks like a miniature torture device from the Middle Ages with which the loft and lie of your clubs can be checked and altered. Your irons and wedges are clamped into the machine, one at a time, and the current loft or lie angle is read. The clubmaker will then place the hooked end of a specially made bar around the hosel of the club and then, literally, bend the hosel of the clubhead until the angles are correct. (Who says brute force has no place in this game?)

This may sound like a task to make you cringe, but for an experienced clubmaker it's a piece of cake. When the whole lie fitting and adjustment procedure is completed, from then on, whenever you hit a crooked shot, you'll at least know for sure it's YOU and not the club (see fig. 2.4).

In short, the good news is that lie angles are easy to adjust on most irons. Almost any custom clubmaker will do the entire fitting and adjustment for around $5 per club, and the entire procedure from fitting to bending each iron takes less than an hour to do. The bad news is that

Figure 2.4. From the dynamic lie fitting test the clubmaker will know how much to alter the lie angle of each iron to properly fit the lie to the setup and swing of the golfer.

most woods cannot be done because the metals from which wood heads are made are too rigid to bend, and their hollow construction does not allow the rigid metals to stretch that much. The good news about this, however, is that because woods have so little loft, their misdirection tendency from an improper lie angle is minimal at best. So don't worry about the woods, but do take the time to get fit for the proper lie in your irons.

Bulging and Rolling Along

If you look straight down on your driver head from above, you'll notice that the face is curved running from the heel to the toe. This curvature is called the "bulge." If you look at the club from the side, you'll notice the face is also slightly curved from top to bottom. That is called the "roll." Both curvatures are measured and expressed in inches of radius (see fig. 2.5).

Here's the deal on that.

If you had a clubhead with a perfectly flat face and you were to make contact with the ball right on the sweet spot, the ball would go straight. No problem. However, if you hit the ball even a fraction toward the toe or heel side of the face it will go sailing off to either the left or right. With bulge, if you hit it a fraction off center, something called the "gear effect" will take place.

Let's pretend both the clubface and the ball had teeth—like gears. Let's say the ball makes contact with the clubface toward the toe. The clubhead would then rotate back slightly in response to being hit off center. In doing so, the "teeth" of the clubface would begin sliding along the "teeth" of the ball, causing it to generate a counterclockwise (hooking) sidespin (see fig. 2.6).

As a result, the ball will start out to the right and the hooking spin created by the "gear effect" will curve the ball back in toward the fairway. The same thing happens (only in reverse) when the ball hits near the heel.

So, who was the brilliant guy who figured this out? Clubmaking historians are not sure, but it was probably an obscure clubmaker from the late 1800s in Scotland who got tired of seeing wild hooks from the toe of his totally flat-faced woods and just had a hunch!

But before you do a dance on your desktop thinking that your slice has been cured by the magic of the gear effect, you need to know that it is there for off-center hits and has nothing to do with what really may

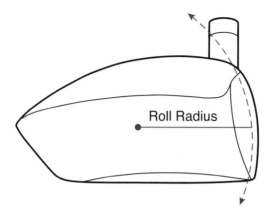

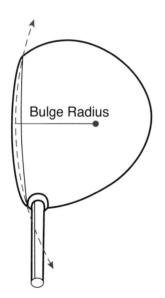

Figure 2.5. The bulge is the horizontal radius on the face of every woodhead. Its purpose is to start the ball a little further off line when the shot is hit off center as a means of balancing the sidespin put on the ball from the "gear effect" of the off-center hit. The roll is the vertical radius designed on the face of almost every woodhead (except most of my wood designs!). Since woodhead loft is always measured at a point that is located halfway up the face, with roll on the face, the loft is considerably less if the ball strikes low on the face and considerably more if it strikes higher.

cause your slice. It is still possible (as you probably well know) for the swing to overcome the gear effect with terrible mechanics and banana-slice or snap-hook that puppy into the trees with no problem.

Roll is another thing entirely. I gotta be honest. As far as I've been able to discover in my design experience and research, it has no useful function and I have no idea why every golf company still puts as much roll radius as they do on their woods. And yes, I know of the so-called

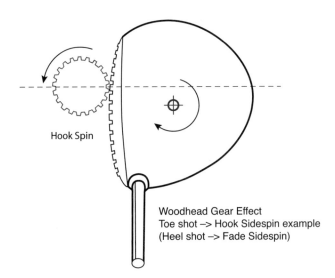

Hook Spin

Woodhead Gear Effect
Toe shot –> Hook Sidespin example
(Heel shot –> Fade Sidespin)

Figure 2.6. When the ball is hit off-center, the woodhead will rotate. The friction between the ball and the clubface then causes the ball to develop a "hook spin" from a toe shot, or "fade spin" from a shot mis-hit off the heel. The purpose of bulge is to start the ball off a bit more to the side so that when the hook or fade spin occurs, the ball will end up back in the fairway.

vertical gear effect that can change backspin from the effect of a high or low shot on the face, which I can assure you is not even close to enough spin change to cause any visible alteration in the flight of the ball.

I started reducing the roll on all my woodhead designs in the mid-1990s, and now I am moving in the design direction of eliminating it almost entirely. I do know the roll radius on everybody else's woodheads was invented after the Scottish clubmaker's friends saw how well his idea for bulge worked. If curving the face from heel to toe was a good thing, what would happen if we also curved it top to bottom? I mean, back in the 1800s who was to argue? Besides, all driverheads back then were one-fourth the size they are today, so a vertical radius on a face that was little more than an inch tall had no real effect on the loft and caused no real shotmaking problems. (See "Rock and Roll" at the end of this chapter.)

There is one good thing about the roll curvature now that drivers have become the size of a grapefruit. If you make contact with the ball high on the face, because of roll, there is more loft at the top of the face than at the center, so a high face hit will cause the ball to take off at a higher angle. For some people, who are too skeptical to believe that more loft on the driver is good for more distance, that's a good thing. The roll on the top of the face has tricked them into a better tee shot, as long as they tee the ball up high enough. But conversely, if you hit the ball low on the face, the roll will deflect it even farther downward, creating a shot that would have easily taken care of Carl Spackler's gopher. Terrific. Just what we need when science has shown that most of us need more loft on the driver to max out our distance potential.

Bulge and roll are found only on woods, and to a lesser radius on some hybrid long ironheads. For several complicated reasons having to do with how close the ironhead's center of gravity is to the surface of the face, irons can't produce the same degree of gear effect from shots hit off the toe or heel. Also, their increased loft generates less hook and slice from off-center shots than woods—well, most of the time. And finally, the people who make the rules of golf pertaining to equipment regulations made it a moot point when they created the rule that says "Irons shall have a flat face." More about them later.

So when you look at the two directions of curvature that reside on the face of most woods, be thankful for bulge and then go hunt for woods with less roll. Your wood shots will be more consistent.

Offset and Face Angle

We'll be talking about clubhead design in more detail a bit later, but offset and face angle are two strategies that are also designed to help people hit the ball straighter.

You see, most people slice because they swing down on an outside/in swing path and leave the clubface open at impact. (You can read all about that and why the ball flies as it does in Chapter 9.) The ball then slides across the face from heel toward toe and picks up that awful tilting of its backspin that causes the banana curve. By putting the hosel a bit more in front of the face (offset), it gives the golfer a split second more time to square up the face before impact—and believe me it can help a slicer (see fig. 2.7). But not as much as face angle, which I guarantee is the #1 best solution for accuracy problems.

If you have ever soled a driver on the ground and wondered why the face was pointing in a direction other than straight, you're looking at a design feature called "face angle." Most woodheads are designed so the face points directly at the target. Those woods have what we call a "square face angle." Some woodheads are designed with the face pointing to the left of the target; hence they have what's called a "hook (or closed) face angle." (For you left-handers, that closed face angle of course points to the right side, your "hook" side of the hole.) Very few woods are offered anymore with a "slice (or open) face angle" (for obvious reasons I am sure you can figure out, given most golfers' misdirection tendencies). The idea is, if you tend to deliver the clubhead to the ball with the face open (a slicer), a woodhead with a hook face angle will automatically deliver the face less open at impact and hopefully eliminate the slice, or at least make it less brutal (see fig. 2.8).

Does it work? Darn right it does, as long as you don't get freaked out by looking at a wood pointing to the hook side of the hole and react by pushing your hands forward at address to get rid of it! But you don't see many hook-faced woods when you look at the big companies' standard clubs on the racks. They all know that most golfers don't like to look at a closed face, so they make most of their woods with a square face angle. They know they can't be with you in the pro shop or retail store to explain what a hook face can do for you. They also know you make most of your buying decisions based on what you see in the store and what you know about golf clubs when you arrive there (which is why we wrote this book). So the big companies keep making square-faced woods, and slicers keep buying square-faced woods, and golf balls keep slicing as they always have.

You say you want to get rid of that slice, and you know you don't have the time or commitment to really retrain your swing as you should?

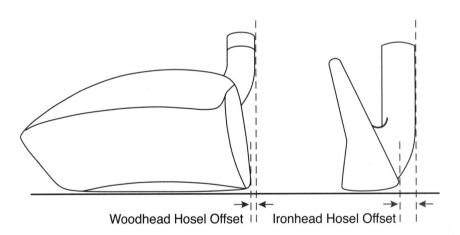

Woodhead Hosel Offset   Ironhead Hosel Offset

Figure 2.7. Offset is the term given to clubhead designs in which the hosel is located ahead of the face. This feature allows the golfer to have slightly more time to rotate the clubface back to square, which reduces the tendency to slice the ball.

Great! *It's simple. Go find a driver that has both an offset hosel AND a hook face angle.* Your ball attrition and handicap should decrease immediately. If it doesn't—get thee to a golf pro for some lessons because we poor clubmakers have done just about all we can to help you.

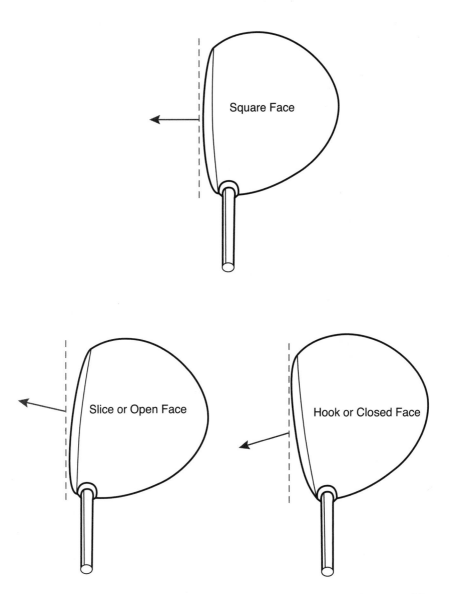

Figure 2.8. Choosing the correct face angle with the driver and woods is one of the best examples of how custom fitting can offer real game improvement to any golfer with accuracy problems.

Remember, if you are a slicer and muster up the courage to buy a driver with a hook face angle, just don't push your hands forward in the address position. Let that face point to the hook side of the fairway like it's supposed to when you set the club down behind the ball!

Seriously, many big golf club companies don't like to make very many of their wood models with a hook face angle, so if you have a problem with a slice, you will probably need to go to your local professional clubmaker's shop. Custom clubmakers are not tied to any one design approach or any one clubhead manufacturer. They can order from many clubhead design suppliers and can custom build virtually whatever you need for accuracy correction.

Home Sweet Spot

What is the "sweet spot?" I hear you cry. Actually, it's a term that is commonly found in golf club ads and misused a lot by almost everyone in the golf industry. You frequently see ads boasting that this club or that has a "larger" or "wider" sweet spot. Technically that can't happen because the actual sweet spot (officially known as the center of gravity) is a point that's about the size of the sharp end of a pin. It can't get "larger." It can't get "smaller." It just . . . is. If you deliver the face of the club square to impact and hit the exact center of the golf ball directly in line with this tiny spot, the ball will fly straight, true, and at the highest speed your swing speed can muster. Any deviation from this perfect contact and the head will start to twist, not only imparting sidespin to the ball but causing a reduction in ball speed from the face. The farther your point of contact is removed from this tiny sweet spot, the more ball speed you lose and the more sidespin you gain. Lose 5 to 7 mph of ball speed, which only takes missing the sweet spot on most drivers by one inch, and you lose about 14 to 20 yards. Ouch! When club companies talk about an "increased sweet spot," what they are really saying is that they've done things in the design to increase the Moment of Inertia (MOI) of the clubhead. (Now, come on, don't panic with these terms. Just follow along.)

Think of figure skaters doing a spin. When their arms are out, their moment of inertia (i.e., their resistance to twisting) is increased, so they spin more slowly. When they draw their arms in close to their body, their moment of inertia is immediately decreased, so they spin faster. Hence, low Moment of Inertia, less resistance to twisting—high MOI (a buzzword acronym to use on your golf buddies to psych them out) means it's more difficult to twist the object (see fig. 2.9).

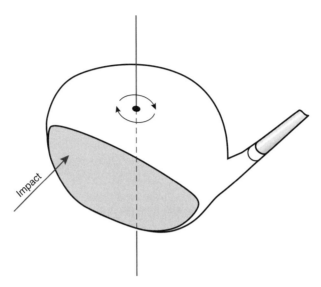

Figure 2.9. The amount the head twists around an axis straight through the center of gravity in response to an off-center hit is determined by the clubhead's Moment of Inertia. The higher the MOI of the head, the less the head twists and the higher the ball speed will be from the off-center hit. Moving more of the head's weight around the perimeter of the head increases the clubhead's MOI.

A BRIEF MOMENT OF INERTIA

The moment of inertia (i.e., MOI—resistance to twisting) of a clubhead is especially important with putters. Basically, the higher the MOI, the better the putter will perform when you look up or move or do whatever you do to hit the ball somewhere other than the sweet spot. So . . . when you are thinking about buying a putter, look at the heel and toe areas. If you see gobs of weight in those areas, compared to the middle, you know you are on the right track. In addition, putters that are much longer from face to back will also provide a better chance of reaching the hole with the putt you hit one-half to one inch off the sweet spot. But you will NEVER EVER putt well with any putter no matter elevated its MOI is unless you are fitted properly for the correct lie, length, loft, grip feel, and overall weight.

Well, the same thing happens with the golf clubhead. The clubhead has some natural resistance to twisting around its center of gravity, which can be increased, for example, by putting extra weight out at the heel and toe and back of the clubhead (i.e., by extending the clubhead's "arms"). The more you can do that, the more resistance to twisting you have, and the "larger" (i.e., more forgiving) is the so-called "sweet spot."

How to Add 28 Yards to Your Drive without Really Trying

Golfers will spend hundreds of dollars on new golf clubs in hopes of hitting the ball an extra five to 10 yards. What they don't understand is that you can get that added distance and more with your current club by simply hitting closer to the sweet spot more often. *Look at the test data.*

Let's assume you normally hit your driver 200 yards on the fly. If you hit it one-half inch off center (either way), you lose roughly 10 yards. Let's assume you hit your 5-iron 165 yards on the fly. Again, if you hit it one-half inch off center (either way), you lose 10 yards. You want more distance with your existing clubs? Go see your professional clubmaker to be properly fitted for length and swingweight balance of the club so you have a much better chance of hitting the ball more often on the sweet spot. It will work—as long as you realize that the sweet spot might not be where you think it is. Later on, we'll show you how to find and mark the actual sweet spot on your clubs so you can squeeze a little more out of your driver.

About Face!

Naturally, the above information concerning distance loss on off-center hits is disturbing to golf club engineers, and vigorous efforts have been made to find a way around it. One of the current leading candidates for a solution is something called "variable face construction" (you've probably seen ads for this), where the center of the clubface is designed to be thicker than the area all around it. To understand this approach, however, let me give you an analogy between the clubface and a trampoline. Imagine you are jumping on a trampoline, and, further, imagine that you are a golf ball and the trampoline mat is the face of your driver. If you (the ball) jump in the exact center of the mat (the clubface) and the direction of your jump is straight up and down (square clubhead path) you will get the maximum rebound effect; you will go straight up (accuracy) and you will go high (distance). This is not exactly what happens when you hit a ball because the golf ball is stationary while the clubface travels to hit it, but it's a reasonable analogy for what happens on a dead-center hit with a "uniform face thickness" clubhead. Now, suppose you jump off to the side of the trampoline center point (off-center hit). You will get less rebound (distance) and you will probably be propelled in a direction other than straight up (accuracy). This is what happens when you hit a ball off-center with a "uniform face" clubhead.

Now, let's suppose further that you stiffen up the center area of the trampoline by sewing in a much thicker mat of some sort—making the center a lot thicker compared to the outside perimeter area all the way around the trampoline. And because you made the center of the trampoline mat thicker so it can't deflect down as much as before, let's loosen all the springs around the trampoline a bit. This time, when you jump away from the center of the trampoline, the difference between the flex in the middle and the flex on the edges is not so great. Indeed, you would get about the same amount of rebound no matter where you jump on the thicker center area. This is somewhat analogous to what is meant by a variable thickness face on the clubhead. The center of the clubface is made slightly thicker to help reduce the distance penalty for off-center hits. In some ways this is not the best example because a golf ball does not "slingshot" off the face like a jumper does on a trampoline, but you get the general idea. Starting a few years ago and continuing today, clubheads are offered with various types of variable thickness faces. You see ads touting cone shapes, oval shapes, concentric rings, and so forth, all of which are intended to still maximize the ball speed from dead-center hits, but minimize the loss of ball speed from off-center hits. This is a tough task for the designer because in making the attempt he has to contend with the first rule of club design—what the golf gods giveth, the golf gods taketh away. Loosely translated: every potential benefit of a design change brings with it a potential loss in some other performance area. Fortunately, as in this case, the good clubhead designers know how to trick the golf gods every once in a while!

Woods and "Woods"

We call them "woods" not because that's where our shots usually end up, but because that's what they were originally made from—wood. After centuries of cutting down any type of tree that had the strength and density to stand toe to toe with a golf ball, clubmakers finally turned to metal. Calling them "woods" is simply a tradition, which, you've probably figured out by now, golf has in abundance. Besides, you've got to admit, when you hear the occasional TV golf announcer say that the player has just hit "a 3-metal," it just doesn't sound right, does it? If you grew up with the game in the "wooden wood" era and you want a good laugh, go dig one up from your attic, hand it to the budding junior golfer in your house, point him or her to the range, and ask for an opinion on the shape, style, performance, and feel! Then, while you're at it, tell them how you used to do calculations in school on a slide rule! It will redefine the word "ancient" for them. Now, don't get me wrong. If you have a "wooden wood," the club will still work. If you hit the ball on the (proverbial) sweet spot, it might not go quite as far as with a well-designed titanium wood, but it'll be darn close. The difference is that the "metal woods" have allowed drivers (in particular) to be designed a lot larger and allowed the ball to lose less energy when smashed. If you miss the sweet spot on a wooden wood by, say, a half-inch, the head will try to twist like a top and you are looking at a more serious second shot into the green. If you miss it by the same half-inch with a well-designed metal wood, it will still twist but not as much (remember our discussion of Moment of Inertia?), and the result will probably just be your basic everyday bad shot.

The Right Stuff

Golf clubheads have been made from nearly everything—trees, steel, plastic, aluminum, graphite, titanium, and ceramics. Once the golf industry quit cutting down trees and moved to consuming inorganic materials, its marketing mavens realized they had free rein to tout almost any nonwooden material as the "next greatest" substance for crafting their equipment. If the material was harder than wood, it had to hit the ball farther, right? Well, at least that became a major subliminal message heralding the onslaught of each new high-tech woodhead material. The vast majority of clubs today are made from various alloys of steel or titanium because clubhead designers have realized these families of metals possess "the right stuff." But even within these families of proven head materials, there are a variety of different steel and titanium alloys; and yes, each one represents yet another opportunity for the marketing mavens to spin their promises of greater performance. Within the maze of different clubhead materials, there are different methods of forming those materials into the finished clubheads. Some clubhead materials lend themselves to one kind of manufacture, others to another. Iron and wedge heads are manufactured chiefly by either investment casting or forging.

Investment casting, also called the "lost wax" process, involves making a mold which is used to create a perfect wax replica of each head to be produced. The wax heads are then coated with a thick, heat resistant, ceramic slurry material. Once the layers of ceramic slurry harden, the wax heads are melted out to leave an empty shell into which molten steel is poured to make each head. Investment casting is used by manufacturers of iron and wedge heads because it can accurately duplicate each head. It is also good for making heads with very deep cavities and with intricate weight distribution shapes, and, above all—it is inexpensive. It is by far the most common form of iron, wedge, and putter head manufacture, and has been since the early 1970s.

The other popular form of iron and wedge head production is forging. Think of forging as using massive machines to beat a solid bar of metal into the appropriate head shape. Because forging hammers the bar of metal into the shape of the head, it cannot be used to make very deep-cavity back irons/wedges, or to make intricate shapes on the head. Casting can do those things because the metal, in liquid form, will flow into all the little nooks and crannies of the designed mold. Forging is a much more expensive process for making clubheads because the production molds are far more expensive to make than investment cast molds, and there are many more labor-intensive steps in the manufacturing process. This is why you see such a big price difference between investment cast and forged irons and wedges.

The vast majority of iron and wedge heads are investment cast from medium-strength grades of stainless steel with relatively high hardness. I know I touched a little on the perceived effect of hardness before, so I better stop and put that one to rest, lest it begins to grow into a gnarly weed. Clubhead material hardness has NOTHING to do with distance in a clubhead. If anything, it has more to do with how much your clubheads will get "dinged" up, banging into each other when the cart hits a speed bump or your kids start hitting rocks off the driveway with your sticks. To complete the picture, the hardness of the metal can have a little to do with the vibration or "feel" you receive back from your clubs upon impact with the ball, but that is normally an area that is the domain of those golfers born, blessed, or cursed with a very fine sense of neurotic, excuse me, I mean neurological feel. No way, no how, does hardness have anything to do with how far the clubhead can hit the ball. So the next time

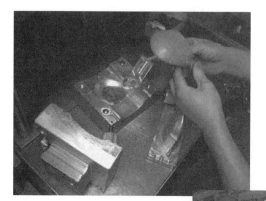

Steps of Investment Casting

1. Every investment cast clubhead begins life as a precisely molded wax replica.

2. Multiple wax heads of the same head number are attached to a wax "tree" and covered by multiple coatings of a ceramic slurry material.

3. After each ceramic coating, the wax trees of each clubhead are carefully dried.

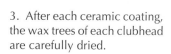

4. After the wax heads are melted out of their ceramic shells, molten metal (in this example stainless steel) is poured into the shell to make the real clubheads.

you see an ad touting more distance because of the hardness of the head's material, ignore it. It's bunk.

Virtually all the "deep" cavity back ironheads are investment cast from either 17-4 or 431 grade stainless steel. The reason I mention the steel alloy identification numbers is because the only difference between them from a clubhead design standpoint is how much work it will be for your clubmaker to alter the loft and lie angles to fit your size and swing. Heads made from 17-4 stainless are more difficult to bend for loft and lie changes than are heads made from 431 because the 17-4 stainless has properties that just make it that way. However, if your clubmaker has a number of years of experience in the trade, he/she will have the skills to be able to accommodate the loft/lie adjustment needs of your investment-cast irons regardless of the stainless steel alloy.[1]

The materials of choice for investment-cast ironheads and wedges are 17-4 and 431 grade stainless steel alloy because they are (1) relatively low in cost, (2) very compatible with the investment casting process for accuracy and quality of manufacture, (3) possessed of enough strength to keep the hosel from bending when you pound the iron into the ground or into a driving range mat, but not so much you can't bend it for loft and lie fitting, and (4) easy to polish to any finish luster desired by the marketing department (yes, in big companies the marketing people make the cosmetic "fashion" decisions for the heads, usually not the designer or the engineers).

Many golfers think that stainless steel won't rust, but that's not exactly true. Quality casting foundries know they have to perform special surface treatment procedures to prevent 431 and 17-4 ironheads from rusting. After all, the name is "stain less," not "stain never." Want proof? When you see those little blue fertilizer granules on the grass on your golf course, moisten a bunch of them in water, scrunch them in the scorelines of your stainless steel irons, leave the clubs for several days, and you might see what we mean by "stain less."

Or the other way you can react to that term is to say, "Stains less than what?" Well, the "what" is in reference to the other popular steel used in iron and wedge head production, good old carbon steel. While

---

[1] If your ironheads are cast from zinc, they cannot be bent for loft or lie alteration. Zinc ironheads are the cheapest ironheads sold in the game and are primarily offered only by the mass merchant retailers or some sporting goods stores. You'll know them by their excessively large diameter hosel, and by how easily they ding and mark up from normal play.

there have been investment-cast carbon steel irons and wedges, carbon steel reigns supreme in the forging process.

Forged carbon steel—ah, the mere mention of the category dredges up another dose of golf tradition within the minds of devoted equipment aficionados. From the introduction of irons in the early 1800s to the middle 1960s to early 1970s, almost ALL ironheads were forged from carbon steel. Carbon steel is different from stainless steel by virtue of how many times the manufacturer had to dip into the Periodic Table of the Elements to make the metal. (You remember the Periodic Table, don't you? That big chart that was on the wall of your chemistry classroom—the one you used to gaze at for relief when the lecture turned from boring to stupefying.)

All steel starts with good old Fe, otherwise translated from the Periodic Chart to mean iron. If you add things like nickel and chromium, and a few others from the chart in tiny amounts, you get stainless steel. If you just chiefly have iron with some carbon mixed in, you have carbon steel. Carbon steel differs from stainless steel in two primary ways. One, it rusts like crazy so you have to cover it with a protective coating, usually by electroplating with nickel and chromium. And two, it is much softer and more malleable than 431 and 17-4 stainless steels, which explains the main reason forged carbon steel irons still possess a moderate level of popularity in the game.

Many golfers have always demanded their clubs "feel solid" when the head strikes the ball. Since 17-4 and 431 stainless steel became the predominant iron and wedge clubhead materials in the 1970s, a loyal band of golf equipment traditionalists has remained dedicated to the belief that "forged is better than cast," because they cling to the belief that forging means a softer-impact feel. The truth is that golf's equivalent of the "tastes great, less filling" debate has it all wrong. Forging and investment casting are but methods of *manufacture* and speak nothing of the "impact feel" or "workability" (ability to intentionally draw or fade a shot) of one clubhead vs. another. Carbon steel and stainless steel are classifications of different steel alloys. You can have hard carbon steel alloys just as you can have soft stainless steels, depending on what other chemical elements and how much of each are present in their composition. And to make it even more confusing, you can investment cast the soft carbon steel alloys or you can forge the harder grades of stainless steel!

In the end, impact feel (and for the forging aficionados, soft impact feel) is the product of several factors, from the shaft to the construction of the ball, with a part coming from the final internal molecular structure of the steel. Don't worry, we won't go into molecular chemistry here, but there are additional processes in both casting and forging that can be used to "pack" the steel more densely in the head and have an effect on impact feel.

The second factor, performance or "workability," also has nothing to do with the material that is used to make the clubhead. Performance and the perceived "workability" (ability to intentionally fade or draw the ball) of the head are all about its DESIGN—how the weight is distributed, where its center of gravity is placed and what the heads' MOI may be. There are some golfers, however, who don't want to be confused by the facts concerning "feel" or ability to "work the ball" with the head. Some of the followers of forged carbon steel already have their minds made up, and people who do what I do—design and manufacturer golf clubheads—are all quite happy to make heads to meet that predilection!

Among woodheads and the hybrid long iron replacement heads, investment casting and forging also reign as the primary methods of production. But for metal wood and hybrid heads, the processes are a little more complicated because these heads are hollow and irons are not—well 98 percent of the irons are not—hollow, but that's a story for an advanced edition of this book.

To make today's typical metal woodhead you have to make anywhere from two to four separate pieces that are welded together to create the final head model. Moreover, the number of ways these pieces can be brought together can be mind-boggling. Welded on sole, welded on face, welded on top, welded on top and sole and hosel and face, press-fit face—it's another reason why clubhead designers also have to be "total gear-heads" and know the ins and outs of all possible design and manufacturing processes. The vast majority of drivers today are made from one or more forms of titanium, while most fairway woods are made from different alloys of stainless steel or ultra-high-strength steel. Why are there so few titanium fairway woods? Two reasons, with number two being the kicker.

First, the smaller size of fairway woods reduces their chance of developing as much spring-face effect as the much bigger drivers. But reason number two, the main reason, is that club companies have found golfers like you will pay $300–$500 for that one big stick, but you won't pay that much times two, three, or four. So they make steel fairways to go with titanium drivers primarily to ease the strain on your wallet. If they thought for one minute that you would shell out the additional money for titanium fairway woods, the market would be awash with them.

So does titanium make a better driver than steel? It can, at least as far as the potential for higher ball speed off the face, which of course is what distance is all about. Certain titanium alloys possess a better combination of strength plus elasticity than do almost all steel alloys. Higher ball speed is all about allowing the face to flex inward as much as possible without caving in or breaking. But some designers have figured out how to design faces from a special group of steel alloys which are given the collective name of "high-strength steels" and can achieve the same high ball speeds from increased face flexing as well.

So why is titanium and not high-strength steel used to make virtually all the drivers today? No, this time it's not because the club companies always want to charge more money for their drivers. It's because BIG is very IN. In addition to being really good for strength and stretchability, titanium also is lighter than steel for the same size piece of the metal. In material terms, that's called density. Because titanium alloys all have a lower density than any steel alloy, designers can use titanium to make bigger driver heads that still weigh the same and not have to worry about the heads caving in when we thrash at the ball.

After reading that, you probably just thought, "But is bigger really better?" Well, technically that's debatable, but it certainly is in vogue these days. I mean, there are some very fine performing high-strength steel drivers that golfers now view as being "too small," despite the fact they are still big enough to pack two of the old wooden drivers of the 1960s inside one of them. Technically, the larger the driver size, the greater the Moment of Inertia (MOI) of the head as measured about its center of gravity. So yes, it's possible to make a larger driver to be more forgiving and get you a couple more yards when you mis-hit the ball. But, here comes that darn law of club design again, "the golf gods giveth and the golf gods taketh away."

There happens to be more than one MOI that governs the performance of a clubhead. First, there is the one I told you about already where the head twists around its center of gravity when you make an off-center hit. The other one is the MOI that determines how much the head can twist or rotate around the shaft during your downswing. And, when you increase the first MOI, you also increase the second, which is not such a good thing for accuracy.

During the swing you have to rotate the clubhead back to square on the downswing, and that rotation centers around the shaft. Hence, the larger the head becomes, the more resistance it has to being rotated back to square during your swing. But we can still trick the golf gods by using a more closed face angle when we make huge driver heads to overcome this. Which is another reason to shy away from a square face driver when you go shopping for that 460 cc size grapefruit on a stick. That is, unless your natural draw happens to turn into a "quacker" from time to time. Where bigger really is better is in what "big" does to the size of the driver face. Bigger driver, bigger face. Bigger face, bigger trampoline. Bigger trampoline, bigger ball speed and more distance. Well, until the United States Golf Association stuck their nose into the issue several years ago.

The Great Spring Effect War

One of the great controversies of recent years has been over the so-called spring-face effect. It really began back in the mid-1990s when an unnamed tour player with a fast tempo made a comment to one of the members of the USGA's Executive Committee, the people who really make the rules. "You guys really need to do something about these new titanium drivers. They hit the ball so far they will ruin the game." So the USGA started to look at driver distances on the PGA Tour and discovered that the average tour pro's driving distance had increased by some 20 yards over the past 15 years. Unfortunately, at the time they began to look into this, nobody pointed out that titanium woods had only been around for the last 2 or 3 of those 15 years. It also did not seem to register that during those same 15 years: (a) the average swing speed of a tour player had increased, (b) the average length of a driver used on tour had increased, (c) the average driver loft had decreased, (d) tour pros were now all being custom fitted for their equipment, and (e) the tour began shaving fairways down to stubble, and starving their tour venues of water, to make the courses "play faster." This last fact alone began to allow the tour players to get 50 yards of roll on a drive when they "piped" it straight down the middle.

It was somehow concluded that the game had a problem, and it must be because the manufacturers were trying to squeeze their new-fangled titanium drivers through loopholes in the rules. Trust me on this, there is nothing that will raise the hackles of the USGA faster than if they think someone is trying to substitute technology for human skill. So in the late 1990s the USGA revived the old rule that said, "The face shall not act like a spring" and devised a limit for the Coefficient of Restitution (COR) to limit the "spring-face effect" of drivers. The USGA decreed that no golf club could have a COR greater than 0.830. In other words, if the

USGA shoots a golf ball at your driver head at 100 mph, it better not rebound off the face and come back at them any faster than 83 mph, or your driver is "nonconforming."

The Royal and Ancient Golf Club of St. Andrews, Scotland (The R&A), which writes the golfing rules for the rest of the world outside the United States and Mexico, did not immediately fall in line with the USGA because they felt the spring effect of the titanium drivers didn't really make that much difference, especially to the average player.[2] I'll tell you why in a minute but, first, another dose of Physics 101.

When the clubhead and the golf ball collide, the ball squashes against the face, and the face flexes inward. This double compression results in a loss of energy, with the ball, by far, losing the most. Anything you can do to cause the ball to compress less (like allowing the face to flex a little more) will result in less energy loss from the ball, and greater ball speed off the face, which of course translates into more carry distance. Since titanium has an outstanding property of strength plus elasticity, titanium woods would flex inward more, thus allowing a higher ball speed coming off the face and more distance than the stainless steel woods of the 1980s and '90s. A test for determining the COR of a driver was devised, and the COR limit of 0.830 was written "into the books." Things then got REALLY interesting.

Along came the giant Callaway Golf Company, who saw the rule as an unfair roadblock to their club design capability. Putting on the gloves, Callaway decided to market a nonconforming driver with a COR higher than the 0.830 limit and let the public decide what they wanted. Battle lines were drawn. Callaway complained about the USGA, the USGA complained about Callaway, pundits complained to each other about the sanctity of the rules, lawsuits were hinted in all directions, and the Royal and Ancient sat around scratching their heads wondering what the Americans could possibly be thinking. The R&A was right.

Upon further review it was found that a nonconforming club in the hands of a very high swing speed player will gain maybe seven to eight

---

[2] The USGA test procedure for determining spring-face conformity has since been changed from a COR test to a test called "Characteristic Time" to measure the spring-face characteristics of the driver. A steel ball on a pendulum swings down to contact the center of the face. The time the steel ball remains on the face before rebounding off is measured with sophisticated sensors. The resulting measurement is termed "Characteristic Time" and is expressed in microseconds. Thus today the limit for driver spring-face conformity is a measurement of 239 microseconds with a tolerance of 18 microseconds for a total allowable measurement of 257 microseconds.

yards. Certainly not the 20 yards for which the USGA originally thought it was responsible. But what was even more interesting was that while the USGA and Callaway were arguing, the R&A let the high-COR Callaway driver be used in all the European PGA Tour tournaments. And you know what happened? Only four of the Euro Tour pros used it in competition for that whole season. Why? Because it was more difficult to keep in the fairway.

You see, more distance also equals more problems with accuracy because the same swing error is magnified over the increased distance the ball flies. In the hands of the average weekend golfer, frankly, it would do little or nothing because the average golfer does not have a high enough swing speed to fully flex the face at impact with the ball. Eventually, the USGA lobbied the R&A to agree to adopt the COR limit for drivers, largely because the USGA wouldn't back down and it looked bad to the golfing world if the two rules-making bodies of the game disagreed.

But what was really odd about all this was that the USGA never actually tested high-COR drivers for distance using either a swing robot or real golfers. During this time my chief engineer had been communicating with one of the USGA's engineers about the development of a more compact and efficient form of spring-face testing. During one of their conversations my chief engineer asked whether the USGA had ever created drivers of differing COR and subjected them to a real hit test, either with a robot or humans. He was told no, they had not. The USGA had devised the rule completely from theoretical calculations because they had apparently concluded in advance that the COR of the driver face was the source of the "distance problem" and simply "knew" these clubs hit the ball "too far." The USGA had initiated a rule on the basis of emotion, rather than on the basis of scientific testing.

Now don't get me wrong here; I have the greatest respect for the USGA. As an organization it has served the game well for over 110 years. The people I have known within the USGA are as dedicated as any you will find anywhere, in any occupation. To a man (or woman) they genuinely love this game. But, no human and no human organization is perfect, which means every human and every organization has room to improve. The USGA is no different.

For example, the USGA has often said it does not want the manufacturers to develop golf equipment that replaces skill with technology and will rule against such developments when and if they are made. What makes that statement so strange is that, at the same time, there are a number of things the USGA allows in the game that really DO replace skill with technology. We can use yardage books created by GPS and laser rangefinder equipment during any tournament to nail distances down to the inch to take the skill out of club selection. We can have an open or closed face angle on the woods to correct for the inability of our swing to deliver the clubhead square at impact; and we can use launch monitors to nail down precisely what driver design specifications will maximize any golfer's distance. We now can move weight around on clubheads to correct for whatever directional or trajectory problems we might be having from one round to the next. And those are just a few examples. Let's not even talk about not being able to tamp down spike marks left from previous careless golfers, or having to trudge back to the tee to hit another ball if we lose or knock the ball over the white stakes. As it was explained to me once by a high-ranking USGA official when I questioned the logic and methodology of their rule making process: "Tom, you know the USGA is not a democracy. We're a benevolent dictatorship." I think he hit the nail right on the head. But, as much as I respect them, they are not perfect. There are things that the benevolent dictatorship needs to examine about itself. I believe the greatness of the game requires that kind of greatness from its ruling body.

So what happened after the COR rule became "law"? Even more rules were legislated limiting what you can take to the golf course—rules that had no scientific reason behind them. Suddenly, the maximum length of a club is now limited to 47 inches, and any clubhead larger than 460 cc in volume is now nonconforming. And again, these rules were made despite the fact no USGA testing was ever done to determine the effect of longer length or larger head size on performance. And to top it off, the lowly long and belly style putters are being reconsidered for critical USGA review, even though only one professional tour event has been won by a player using such a putter in the many years since its introduction. Go figure.

All I am asking is that the USGA at least consult with good old physics before it changes the equipment rules, because the gods of physics will trump the gods of golf every time. To hit the ball farther with a much longer driver, you have to deliver the clubface more precisely to the ball. It takes more skill to do that. If you make a clubhead larger, yes, you could make the face so its COR is very high. But with their COR rule in place, that negates any possible advantage from such a huge size head. Limiting the length of clubs and the size of heads is not technology replacing skill, so why not let the marketplace decide the issue?

ROCK AND ROLL

Many golfers are very particular about the loft in their clubs, especially their driver. It MUST be 9.5 degrees, or 10.5, or whatever. What they don't understand is that, because of roll, the actual amount of loft you have is completely dependent upon where on the clubface you hit the ball.

Vertical roll, as we discussed, is the curvature from top to bottom that you see on a driver's face. In designer's lingo, woodhead loft has always been measured at a point one-half the vertical face height of the woodhead. Thus, there is only one area on the face where the loft is what it says it is, that being if you hit the ball right at the midpoint of the vertical face curve, you will get your 10.5 degrees. If you hit it above that, the loft is more than 10.5 degrees, and below that, less than 10.5. How much more or less your loft is at the top or bottom of the face depends on how curved the vertical roll radius is that was put on the face (see fig. 2.10).

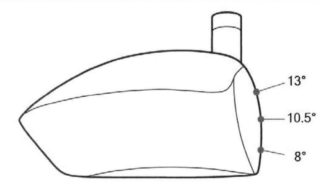

13°

10.5°

8°

Figure 2.10. The vertical curvature on the face of woodheads means the loft will be different at the top or bottom of the face from what it is at the center. The greater the club face height, the more the loft will change.

With virtually all the standard made brand-name drivers being made with 9 to 12 inches of vertical roll radius, that means your 10.5 loft driver could have as much as 13 degrees at the top of the face and as little as 8 degrees at the bottom. Now you know why the "bottom rail" shots you hit when you straighten up on the downswing are called "gopher goosers" and the shots you hit high on the face are said to bring rain! I'll allow you to calculate on your own how many loft fetishists can consistently predict where on the clubface, top to bottom, they will hit the ball. But, if you buy into the TV analysts' comments about the "hot spot" of your driver being above the center of the face, it's really because you bought a driver with too little loft, and hitting it above center gets you closer to the loft you need to have to maximize your potential for distance.

CHAPTER 3—MR. WIZARD VISITS THE CLUB DESIGN STUDIO

What Makes Clubheads Work (and Not Work)

Let's talk about clubhead designs and the real effects of design differences on shotmaking. Because it has always been a major aspect of my job to advise custom clubmakers on the fine points of clubfitting, I have spent most of my 32 years in the golf equipment and design business researching what all the different golf club design specifications really do (or don't do) to change the flight of the ball. After all, if you are looking for game improvement through a change in the design specifications of your clubs, the equipment changes need to result in a different ball flight than what you had before, or else it wasn't worth making the change. I need to add that there are golfers who change clubs for the purpose of a different "look" or a different feel of the shaft or the clubs' impact with the ball. But if you are talking real "game improvement" changes in the clubs, then you are talking about trying to change those fitting aspects in golf clubs which really *will* result in a visible change in the flight of your shots.

For my last book, written to teach clubmakers the principles of accurate clubfitting, I chose the title *The Practical Clubfitting Program*. This was because I had come to the realization that, of the many things you can change in custom fitting any golfer, there are only a few that really matter. What I mean by "really matter" is, which design features are really going to show up to the golfer as a perceptible change in the golf club's performance, visibly seen in the flight of the ball.

Remember, thanks to high technology testing equipment and procedures, we in the design side of the business can measure differences between golf clubs that most humans cannot perceive. When you change some of the club design factors, it has a visible effect on ball flight; others have little or no effect. In other words, one has to be very practical and technically hardheaded when it comes to viewing design differences in clubs. Marketing mavens usually shade to the softer side of things because, all too often, they like to take some of these small measurable differences and magnify them into big differences that can be used in their advertisements. In the end, you, who simply want a set of clubs that works best for your swing, just end up confused.

So welcome to the REAL world of clubhead design. Here, I will list some of the major design features of clubheads, tell you what they are, offer the truth about how they work and their real effect on shot performance. From that I will address the actual ways you may wish to effect a change in how you hit the ball and tell you realistically what can be done with the clubhead to bring about a change in distance, accuracy, or the trajectory of the shot as well.

General Design Features of Clubheads

Center of Gravity: The intersection of all the balance points of the clubhead is called the Center of Gravity (CG). That means, if you balance the head on its face and then on its sole, the intersection of those two imaginary lines going straight through those balance points is the CG. It is located well inside the head's cavity for a wood, and typically somewhere just behind the face of a conventional iron (see fig. 3.1).

I know you've all read this at one time or another in an advertisement: "Low Center of Gravity for ease in getting the ball up." Or, more

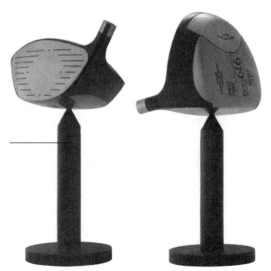

Figure 3.1. The Center of Gravity is located at the intersection of all the possible balance points of a clubhead. Even a simple method of balancing the head on a small pointed object can be used to locate the CG of the head.

recently, "with the Center of Gravity located farther back from the face for higher trajectory." As a result, if you need help getting the ball up higher in the air, you look for clubheads with a low and/or rear-located CG, and if you want to lower your ball flight, you look for heads with a higher and/or more forward-located CG.

Right, that's fine; but how the heck do you know WHERE the CG really is, or more important, whether the CG is in any different position from those in your current clubs? From the ad? You surely can't find it when you browse in a golf shop for clubs because the ONLY way it can be determined is when the head is removed from the shaft. I have yet to see a golf club with the CG position marked clearly on the head, or identified in the club company's literature.

Don't worry, because I can make this easy. First, don't fret too much about a high or low CG. For example, if you take the same numbered head from all the golf industry's iron models, the CG is within about a 3–4 mm range from high to low. That's because virtually all the same numbered irons are made within a few millimeters of the same height. Sure, there are some wide sole irons and a few "oversize" irons as well. Those design features chiefly bring about the 3–4 mm low-to-high range in the vertical position of the CG; but, seriously, the variation in shot height from a 3–4 mm vertical difference of the CG is minimal at best. Very minimal. Like not quite one degree in launch angle higher (or lower) minimal.

How far the CG is back from the shaft will have more of an effect on your ability to hit the ball higher or lower than how high or low the CG may be in the clubhead. Take it to the bank—there is a far greater range in front-to-back CG location than there is in the top-to-bottom CG location. The more offset the hosel is in front of the face, the farther back the CG will be from the shaft and the easier it will be to get the ball up in the air.

What about big drivers vs. small drivers? Yes, there is a big difference in height of the head, BUT . . . think about it for a second. You use a tee with the driver, so that all but eliminates the vertical CG difference in the size of the driver heads. With a tee you can adjust the ball height so the point of impact on the face is about the same whether you use a tall or more shallow face driver (see fig. 3.2).

The rearward location of the CG demonstrates its effect on ball flight far better in a wood than in an iron. Why? For that matter, why does a CG located farther back in the head cause us to hit the ball higher at all? The first reason is that woodheads are much deeper in size than ironheads. That automatically pushes the CG farther back from the shaft. In a

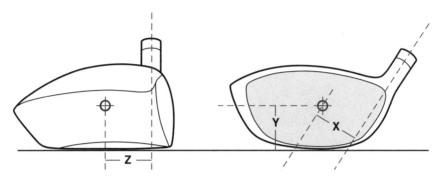

Figure 3.2. The Center of Gravity is a very small point inside the head which can be defined for its position by referencing how far back it is from the face (Z), how high it is up from the sole (Y), and how far it is from the shaft (X).

woodhead the more rearward location of the CG causes the shaft to bend forward more just before impact with the ball, thus functionally increasing the loft. Again, physics dictates a limit to the amount the shaft can bend forward before impact. Since wood shafts are longer and smaller in diameter at the head end than iron shafts, the rear CG of the woodhead will bend them forward much farther than an iron. An iron shaft is shorter and has a bigger diameter tip so it just can't bend as much as a wood shaft, no matter what you do or how hard you swing. If you add the fact that no ironhead has a CG located as far back from the shaft as does a woodhead because of its much smaller breadth, you have a triple whammy for creating a big difference in CG-induced shot height between woods and irons.

The newer hybrid long ironheads hit the ball higher than a conventional ironhead of the same loft simply because the hybrid clubhead is fatter. Being fatter, again, the CG is farther back from the shaft, and the resulting shot trajectory will be a little higher than the normal ironhead of identical loft.

So if you're shopping for an iron that will hit the ball higher, you can pick a wide sole clubhead and that will help a little. Or, you could pick a head with more offset and use a more flexible shaft. This will enhance the forward bending to increase loft at impact. In a wood, pick a head style that has offset or has a greater breadth from face to back (or has a pile of weight stuck into the very back of the head).

For you golfers who want to hit the ball lower, stay away from offset, keep your head shape choices to more narrow-bodied clubheads, or look for heads where more of the mass is piled up toward the face. After that, if you want to change trajectory you're going to have to change your swing.

Perimeter Weighting and Cavity Backs: Here's another ad line you've probably read a thousand times: "Deep-cavity back design for maximum forgiveness." Or how about, "We've deepened the cavity and added more mass around the perimeter for even greater shot forgiveness."

There is no question that when basic ironhead design moved from no hole on the back to a big hole on the back, a quantum leap in off-center hit forgiveness was realized. Prior to the late 1960s all irons were a variation of a style known as a "muscleback." The term was coined to describe any iron in which the thickness of the head from face to back was about the same thickness all the way across the back of the blade from heel to toe (see fig. 3.3).

When Karsten Solheim, founder of the PING brand of golf equipment, began messing around with machining holes on the back of an ironhead, he changed the face (or I should say the back) of iron design forever. Woods soon got a dose of the same concept when hollow metal woods replaced the solid wooden woods.

Previously, you'll recall, I mentioned a little about the Moment of Inertia of clubheads. Increasing the weight around the perimeter of the head by moving more of the head's mass out to the toe, heel, and farther

Figure 3.3. Ironhead design today runs the gamut from muscleback (left) to moderate-cavity back (center) to deep-cavity back (right) as a way to change the Moment of Inertia of the head about its center of gravity.

away from the center means the head has a higher Moment of Inertia around its Center of Gravity, and thus, more resistance to twisting. Thus, a deep-cavity-back ironhead design twists less when the ball is hit off-center, and we get a little more distance from the shot that is hit off-center. So the moral of this story (so far) is, if you can hit 99 percent of your shots on center, you will play just as well with a muscleback style iron as a cavity-back iron.

If you are, however, a mere mortal and you don't hit it on center 99 percent of the time, then get smart and get a cavity back. I mean, over half of the tour pros use cavity-backs, so that should tell you something about MOI, shot forgiveness, and plain common sense among the best ball strikers on the planet.

But here's the kicker about cavity backs and high MOI. Let's say you own a golf company and you've been selling the same cavity-back iron and oversize driver for the past three years. You know it's time to put new models in front of your followers. The "boys in the back room" who do the designing tell you that they can deepen the cavity on your existing iron model and they can also make your current driver model larger still. Samples get made, and the boys report a 10 percent increase in the MOI of the new heads. Your marketing people now have their story—"more forgiveness than ever before"—and the whole picture is ready to be painted in living color and three-part harmony in advertisements across the country. Unfortunately, you have not composed a new symphony; all you've done is slightly change the lyrics of the same old song.

If you want a perfect example of the credo ". . . can measure differences between clubs that golfers cannot perceive" AND obtain a dose of practicality in club design, read on.

Moving from a muscleback to a cavity back of even moderate depth, or increasing a driver's size from 150 cc to 300 cc is akin to filling an 8 ounce glass with 7.5 ounces. In short, you've made a quantum leap in shot forgiveness. You can further deepen the cavity and go still larger in the driver from there, but the real effect in shot distance from an off-center hit will end up being more like just squeezing that last half-ounce into the glass. In other words, not much in the way of real, visible performance enhancement. Once a designer has created a reasonably deep cavity or fairly large head, he has unleashed about as much of the real measurable distance improvement from off-center hits as he will get. Sure, you can work to increase the MOI a little more, but it won't make any difference to the vast majority of golfers. The bottom line is: Don't be lured in by a higher and higher MOI in the head, because once you get to a certain point, any more won't pay off in measurable distance improvement from off-center hits.

Big, Bigger, and Biggest

You know, sometimes it must seem like the golf companies have a big air pump in their factories that they use to make last year's driver even larger, and announce the "new and improved" model is now here. I mean, even the USGA got so concerned about it that they finally said: Enough, we'll let you stay with heads the size of grapefruit, but no way are we going to let you go to watermelons. Now, if you believe that the USGA imposes restrictions on equipment to keep designers from making the game too easy, then you would probably conclude that bigger must be better, right?

Well, theoretically, it's possible to design a bigger driver head, with a commensurately bigger face area that has a greater "spring-face" effect, thus increasing the ball speed off the face and giving you more distance. But when the USGA put the handcuffs on the maximum COR measurement for a driver, that possibility of increasing driver head size to make the face "spring more" was eliminated.

So when we designers make bigger and bigger drivers, we have to make the faces thicker to prevent them from generating a ball speed that would exceed the USGA's rule for spring-face effect. And that, dear reader, cancels out any possible advantage of bigger heads being better.

What about the bigger head having a greater resistance to twisting, and thus offering better performance from off-center hits? Nope. Remember the discussion we just had? Once you get to a certain MOI level, any further increase will never show up in distance improvement for off-center hits. Worse, it brings with it an increase in the effort needed to square the face at impact.

So what's left? How can we make a bigger head be a better head? There IS one way, but it's only for a certain segment of players who need it.

As we pointed out earlier, the bigger the head, usually the farther back from the shaft the Center of Gravity will be. That will bring about an increase in the height of the shot over a smaller head of the same loft, when using the same shaft. So, if you need a higher ball flight to improve your carry distance and you don't want your friends to see you with a loft number of say, 13 or 14 on the sole of the driver, you could go bigger with a little less loft increase than what you really need, and thus possibly get the ball height necessary to maximize your carry distance. The problem is that you're taking a risk that when the manufacturer says the club has a "more rear-located CG," it really HAS a "more rear-located CG." It's much more of a sure thing to optimize your launch angle for your swing speed via the club's loft.

Making the Grade

How often have I seen an ad like this in my career? ". . . with the face made from a brand-new stronger and harder titanium, recently declassified for commercial use by the aircraft industry . . ."

As you've probably figured out, I really like metallurgy. You know, the science of metals where you look at all the individual elements in the metal and the strength and elasticity and hardness and all that stuff? As a result of my experience in metals for clubhead design, I have to tell you, don't believe everything you read in golf advertising. The only improvement that more sophisticated titanium alloys could really bring to head design disappeared with the USGA's rule limiting the COR of driver faces.

What the heck, maybe that secret aircraft titanium does have a higher strength with better elastic properties. If so, perhaps it *could* have been used to make faces that were tailor made for further increasing the COR of the face and raising the ball velocity on your drives. But not now. Not unless the company wants to publicly defy the USGA, like Callaway did with the ERCII, and make a nonconforming club. To make a long story short, a conforming driver with a face that comes right up to the limit of the USGA's COR rule can be made from all sorts of different titanium alloys. But to tout one as being better? I will defer to the marketing mavens for that explanation.

You CAN Get What You Want

I have spent the past several pages giving you the inside story on some of the more popular clubhead features, and I have done so on the basis of having personally tested and observed the results from the more than 200 different sets of wood and ironhead models I have designed in my career. I also understand that you might now be thinking: "Well, what the heck WILL work to help me play better?"

I can summarize the whole thing when it comes to what you've read about clubheads in this book so far. But to do so we will have to revert to being practical again. Think about it this way.

Your game improvement desires can probably be summed up as follows. You either want to hit the ball farther, straighter, higher, or lower, or to change the backspin you put on the ball; or, you want some combination of these added together. Right? The good news is that all these desires for improvement can be assisted through the proper selection of the head, shaft, grip, and how it's all put together. But please note that I said "assisted." You cannot now, nor will you ever, be able to buy your way into being a really good golfer. There will come a time when even the most diplomatic clubmaker will have to tell you: You don't need a new club—you need lessons.

Be that as it may, there are still many things that can and should be done—many things that you need to consider when you are purchasing or modifying your clubs—that will help you "be all you can be" and become a BETTER golfer. Some of those things have to do with head selection, some with shaft selection, some with grip selection, some with how the three parts are put together, and we will cover those things in later chapters.

When it comes to golf clubheads, the subject of this chapter, let's review for a moment some of the things you need to remember.

Face: Let's start with the face. If you're still playing with a tree on the end of the shaft, we can help you. Same thing if you're using a small steel 200 cc size driverhead. On the other hand, if you already have a 2000-era jumbo titanium driver with a COR approaching the limit imposed by the USGA, scratch this item from your list, at least as a source of distance improvement.

As far as the other contribution of the face, its ability to improve the ball speed from your off-center hits via some type of variable face thickness construction, that's still possible. Unfortunately, as yet there is no way to know which variable face is best for you unless you "try before you buy." And if you do your trying by hitting the clubs on a launch monitor, you will be able to know the ball speed from on- and off-center hits, and thus be able to know how well the head covers up for your swing mistakes. Another reason to visit a competent custom clubmaker with a launch monitor in his or her shop.

When it comes to the faces of fairway woods, here is an area of woodhead design that is just starting to really flower. Thanks to the experience of thin face design engineering of the drivers, some of us are now able to hit that USGA COR limit with the 3- and 5-wood now. More will be able to do it by the mid-2000s as well. So do watch for higher COR fairway woodheads because they now are possible to make so the COR is the same as your high-COR, USGA-conforming driver.

Loft: Now, here's one that you have a pretty good chance of parlaying into an additional 10 yards or more off the tee! If your driver swing speed is 90 mph or less and your current driver has the number 8, 9, or 10 engraved somewhere on the head, today is your lucky day because you learned there is no way that club will work the best for you.

Generally, you need more loft on the driver, but there are some complications attached in terms of your swing angle of attack. So get to a launch monitor to find out what loft will end up maximizing your distance and accuracy. This is one of the reasons God invented golf club makers who live, eat, and breathe golf club technology. The potential improvement in distance off the tee from being fitted with the correct driver loft is huge and is definitely out there for most of you if you will just take the time to take advantage of it.

Headweight: Physics tells us that a heavier head, if swung with the *same speed* into the ball, will result in a higher ball speed off the face. This comes from the same logic that asks which one would you rather get hit by—a feather traveling 50 mph or a car traveling the same 50 mph? But the rub in the golf club application of this science is that you need to be sure, if you do go with a heavier headweight, that you will still be able to swing the club with no loss in swing speed, AND that the higher headweight won't mess up the swing balance of the club for your specific swing strength and tempo.

If you think you can just go out and slap several strips of lead tape on your current driver, think again. All that will do is increase the swingweight and the total overall weight of the driver, which will probably slow down your swing speed.[1] But if you are currently using a steel shaft or a heavier graphite shaft (>70 grams), you have a chance. You can be fitted into a much lighter graphite shaft, with the club's headweight being increased to restore the swing balance. This will give you a lower total clubweight with a higher headweight, and you should be able to pick up a few more yards.

---

[1] If you're hitting your driver off-center a LOT of the time, putting 2–3 four-inch-long strips of half-inch-wide lead tape anywhere on the head to increase the swingweight might result in your finding a better overall balance of the club, which in turn could increase your on-center hit percentage and offer you more consistent distance.

Center of Gravity: More specifically, how far is the CG behind the shaft in the driverhead? Granted, this is tied to the loft, because both the loft and the rear location of the CG will alter the trajectory or height of the shot. So you have to watch out, if you increase the loft to improve your carry distance AND move the CG farther back from the shaft, because that might combine to make your trajectory too high. But here's a trick you can play on the golf gods, provided you are working with a well-supplied professional clubmaker.

First, find a clubmaker who has a supply of driverheads that offer successively more rear-located CG positions. Then, once you find the right loft for maximizing your carry distance, select the driver with the most rear-located CG and then reduce the loft and trick the golf gods in the process. How? Because if you can get to your ideal launch angle and trajectory through the rear-located CG, then you can reduce the loft and increase your ball speed off the face a little more. But only a launch monitor can tell for sure, and only a clubmaker with a good selection of driverhead designs can offer you this fine-tuning to eke out more distance.

One Size Fits All?

Then there is the whole element of standard-made clubs vs. the vast differences among golfers in height, arm length, strength, swing tempo, swing plane, swing path, wrist-cock, and so on. You might have heard the comment, "Golfers are like fingerprints—there are no two alike." Well, it's not quite *that* diverse, but let's just say there is no way that any company's standard way of making each club model can possibly allow every golfer to play to the best of his or her ability. This game is hard. To expect all golfers with their physical and swing differences to be able to play their best with standard made clubs is, well, it's impossible. Period.

So what happens is that each year some three million people take up the game of golf and each year some three million quit. Why do they quit? One of the major reasons given is frustration with the game being "too hard." But is it really frustration with the difficulty of the game or frustration with a game made harder than it needs to be by equipment that doesn't fit the golfer and even worse consumer decisions to buy that standard made equipment?

Yet I can't tell you how often I have heard middle handicap players tell me, "I'm not good enough yet for custom fitting." I am sorry, folks, but that's just plain WRONG! Every single golfer, from beginner to professional can and will benefit from being custom fitted. Let me tell you a few things that pertain to ALL golfers, despite handicap.

Club length is a matter of height, arm length, swing plane, swing tempo, and swing consistency. If all golfers were the same in each of these factors of length determination, fine, I would be the first one to advocate one standard length for all golf clubs. But golfers are not, and, as a result, one length does NOT fit all. Length is also a fitting factor that is more critical for success among less skilled golfers than it is among the single-digit players. Really good ball strikers have the athletic ability to play with a reasonable variety of lengths. Less skilled players still trying to develop a sense of swing consistency simply cannot. So, think you're not good enough for custom fitting? That's definitely not true for club length.

Getting the proper driver loft, for example, is a matter of your swing speed and angle of attack. When you go into a big golf store, they probably carry a choice of driver lofts in their men's drivers between 8 and 11 degrees and 12 or 13 degrees for the women. The problem is, men, you need a swing speed of 100 mph or more to take advantage of those clubs and most guys swing the driver 90 mph or less. And ladies, you need at least a swing speed of 80 mph to make the 12 or 13 degree drivers bring out the best in your ability. THESE golfers need drivers with a 12, 13, 14, or 15 degree loft, lofts which are not even offered by most of the large companies that make standard clubs.

Fitting the lie angle of the irons is a must for ensuring accuracy. Lie is determined by your height, arm length, your swing speed and your posture, and your strength and body position when you swing through the ball. Again, this important feature has nothing to do with handicap. It needs to be calculated and fitted, whether you are a rank beginner or a PGA touring pro.

Wood face angle is the number one way for a club to offer relief from your slice. As mentioned, your options in finding a closed face angle among the drivers on the racks are limited. And in this case, the need for a closed face angle on the driver is far more for the middle to higher handicap player than the single-digit golfers who have learned how to square the face when the club reaches the ball.

In the end, it is no "marketing hype" that all golfers could and would benefit greatly from proper custom fitting and enjoy the game a lot more than they do now.

The fitting carts you see parked on the driving range of your golf course on "club days" allow for only a slight change in length and iron lie angle. They fall well short of the full realm of fitting specifications that could and would allow every golfer to play their best. That's why your real playing needs are truly in the best hands when you visit your local professional clubmaker. At the very minimum, go into the purchase process armed with the information we are giving you here.

To Clone or Not to Clone . . .

To clone or not to clone: that is the question. From my comments about custom clubmakers being a tremendous source for real custom fitted golf clubs, you might be thinking, "Oh you mean the guys who build the knockoff clubs?" No, I don't. I am talking about the custom clubmakers who are intensely interested in the science of golf club technology and how it affects the fitting process for ALL golfers. Different from them are many people who "assemble clubs," who are not as interested in the real science of the equipment, and who are more into their hobby of being able to assemble clubs just for themselves to have fun tinkering around with different combinations of heads, shafts and grips.

Every major industry has clones, it's just how you define the term. For example, within a couple of years after Dodge marketed the first minivan in the 1980s, every carmaker in the U.S. was offering their version. Same thing with the SUVs today. In the computer industry, cloning runs wild, with little companies buying the chips and boards and CRTs to copy the larger hardware makers. You might have a clone of an IBM or Dell or Macintosh PC in your home or workplace right now.

Golf equipment is no different. On one hand, you could make a strong case that every investment cast, cavity back, offset iron model, no matter whose name is in the cavity, is a clone of the original Ping iron design. That's fine as far as it goes, but unfortunately, in the golf equipment industry there has been a very dark side of cloning in which unscrupulous companies have arranged for models to be made which copy every detail of a heavily marketed clubhead, right down to coining a name that may even phonetically sound like the model name of the original design.

Unfortunately, most of these knockoffs have been sold in the component clubmaking segment of the golf industry, where the quality custom clubmakers exist. The effect has been such that most golfers associate ALL component-made golf clubs with cheap knockoffs, assuming that all are far lower in quality than the heavily marketed brand-name clubs. Such knockoff heads are usually made by low-quality foundries that are not skilled enough in their production operations to attract business from serious quality-minded golf companies. Lofts, lies, and headweights are usually far outside the tight production tolerances delivered by the quality foundries. To save money, their metals are often a mixture of remelted scrap with a bit of new material thrown in. These companies and their customers damage the reputation of all the quality-minded component manufacturers who see custom clubmaking for the quality of the fit, because most golfers choose to lump every one of the component companies together into one barrel of bad apples.

The fact is, there are a few companies in the component clubmaking industry that DO care about and DO achieve high quality in their products. These companies subcontract the production of their heads to many of the same foundries that manufacture heads for the heavily marketed brand-name companies. These heads are made by the same people, on the same machines, using the same materials, with the same production standards as the ones that are made for any of the big heavily marketed brands of golf equipment.

Furthermore, companies such as mine, Tom Wishon Golf Technology, and The GolfWorks do our own completely original design work and frequently offer innovation that stands toe to toe with or even exceeds the brand-name manufacturers'. The reason you don't hear much about us is that we do not price our designs to make 300 percent gross profit, so we do not have multimillion-dollar marketing campaigns and tour player endorsement contracts. We are wholesale suppliers of the heads, shafts, and grips we design to the professional clubmakers who use our designs in their custom fitting work.

Where Do They Come from, Anyway?

Ever since investment casting took over as the predominant form of clubhead production, no golf club company makes their own clubheads. There is only one partial exception to this. Karsten Manufacturing Corporation, makers of the PING brand of golf clubs, owns their own investment casting foundry at which they manufacture their own stainless steel ironheads and putter heads. The production of their titanium and steel metal woodheads is subcontracted to quality foundries because they choose not to expand their foundry capability to do the more complicated task of making the woodheads themselves. Karsten Manufacturing invested in their own casting facility many years ago because a very significant part of their total corporate business has nothing to do with golf equipment. The company set up their own foundry to make the large volume of aircraft, medical prosthetics, and other commercial metal products that make up a large amount of their total corporate revenues. They knew the size of their entire diverse business could financially support a casting operation for the total number of different metal products they manufacture and sell.

Since the 1970s, Wilson and Lynx are two companies that acquired their own investment casting operation to manufacture their own heads. In both cases, the operation was shut down in a short time for lack of a profitable return on the foundry. If you're in the golf club business and you acquire or build your own foundry to make your own clubheads, what do you think the chances are you can solicit other golf club companies to have you, a competitor, manufacture their heads? You get the point.

Thus, you name the company, whatever its name or size, and their clubheads will be manufactured by independent, subcontracted foundries and factories that specialize in the production of golf clubheads—and the vast majority of that production is performed outside the borders of the United States.

Worldwide, there are approximately 75 different factories specializing in the manufacture of golf clubheads. Of these, 10 to 12 are considered to be high-quality factories with first-rate engineering and manufacturing capability. Another 15 to 20 after this are "pretty good," with the definition of pretty good meaning if the golf company contracting for clubhead production gets actively involved and monitors the production of their clubheads, the quality of the production will be good. The rest? They're all scrambling for scraps and hustling a living with little regard for overall production accuracy and quality.

The reason that the vast majority of the clubheads are manufactured overseas for even the big brand-name golf companies is of cost—both for the price of each head and for the cost of the production tooling molds/dies that are required to manufacture the heads. If you go back to the early 1990s, there still were a number of the golf companies that chose to subcontract the manufacture of their heads from U.S.-based clubhead specialty foundries. But two things happened. First, the quality of the top offshore foundries improved to the point that there were few U.S.-based foundries that could exceed that production quality.

Second, the big club companies in the United States saw the opportunity to increase their profit by expanding their marketing to pay for higher-dollar tour pro contracts, weekly tour pro incentive money,[2] and print and television advertising campaigns. Shifting to the overseas foundries allowed them to do that because all the U.S.-based clubhead producers charged more per head and more for the production molds and dies. Thus at present you can count U.S.-based clubhead foundries still in business on one hand, and you don't have to use even close to all five fingers to do it.

The big club companies that market their brand names so heavily would not make the switch offshore for their clubhead production unless the quality was there. While the major reason the U.S.-based foundries lost almost all their client companies to the overseas foundries was price, equally big reasons were service, experience, and quality.

The Future of Clubheads

If there is one thing I am not, it's a fortune teller. If I were, I'd be retired and playing my own designs on whatever resort course I could find with a beach, good hotel, and fine restaurants nearby! On the other hand, with 30-some years in this business and the fact that I have been fortunate to have contributed over 40 clubhead design "firsts" to the golf equipment industry, I'd like to think that I have some awareness in this area.

As I explained, several areas in which we designers were working or expanding our efforts have been closed off as areas of possible advancement by some of the recent rulings of the USGA to create a COR

---

[2] A key marketing element for golf companies is to publish the number of their club(s) in use on the PGA Tour. This count of how many of what club is played at which tournament is conducted each week on the PGA Tour by the Darrell Survey. Darrell Survey workers sit at the 1st and 10th tees of the second round of each event and write down every piece of equipment used by each pro, from the driver to the wedges, from the ball to the shoes. Several years ago it became common for the largest golf companies to pay pros $1,000 to $2,000 per week just to put their driver in the bag for the day of the Darrell Survey count. For the 80+ pros in each event who cannot command a six-figure+ endorsement contract, being able to bank another $1–2,000 a week is important, which is commonly paid whether they actually use the driver or remove a seldom-used club to allow the paid club to ride along for the one day of the survey count.

limit on clubface performance, as well as a limit to the size of the driverhead. While some of us can design and produce drivers with spring-face effect well beyond the USGA's ordained limit, such drivers will never see the light of day in the United States. In a sense, that's too bad because these clubheads have a built-in "regulator" to prevent them from ever bringing harm to the game, namely, the farther you hit the ball, the more accurate you have to be.

Rather than cry over spilt milk, some of the areas where I see further improvement in clubhead design occurring include:

Better Performing Fairway Woods: Because of their much smaller face size compared to drivers, fairway woods cannot develop the same spring-face effect as can the driver. However, there are some face design changes that will allow us to create a marked improvement in the ball speed generated by the 3-, 5-, and 7-woods and actually get their COR up there at the limit imposed for the drivers. Thus, I see longer-hitting fairway woods being a definite possibility in the near future.

Center of Gravity and Clubhead Mass Improvements: It has only been in the past three years that we've realized the true importance of the location of the CG in the clubhead. Very recently, clubheads with varied CG locations which will help golfers to overcome individual swing faults have begun to appear. I also believe it will soon be possible to change the orientation of the weight distribution, yet retain the same CG position inside the head. This will allow us to make clubheads that will be a little easier to hit more accurately and be able to deliver a little better distance from shots hit off the center of the face. In addition, I see clubheads of more varied CG location being developed for specific golfer types as a way to better fit the weight distribution of the heads to the playing ability of the golfers.

Adjustable Clubs: Heads which allow the golfer to move weight around for enhancing a draw or fade, or a low or a higher shot, are just beginning to appear on the market. I believe this area of club adjustability for achieving different ball flight or performance will continue, at least as long as most of these designs really "deliver the mail." Remember, it takes a large amount of mass movement in the head to create a medium-to-small change in ball flight. Heads that allow only a minor amount of weight movement will not deliver on their promise for truly significant ball flight change. Heads that allow a large amount of weight movement will demonstrate to golfers how helpful this technology can be by reducing the amount they slice or hook, or visibly changing the height of their shots as well. I expect to see a wide variety of adjustable options on clubheads over the middle 2000s which may include the ability to change weight distributions on irons, and change sole designs on irons, wedges, and putters.

Launch Monitor Enhancement of Head Performance: Let's face it. Many people who work in the retail shops and stores that sell golf clubs don't know a whole lot about real custom fitting. If they did, they wouldn't be working in such stores for $9/hour and being paid "spiffs" for selling the "right" (read high margin or overinventoried) clubs to consumers. Unfortunately, they know more about equipment than most of you (which is why I wrote this book), so that makes it real tough for you to determine if what they advise will get you into the right set, or whether you just helped move some inventory that was getting a little stale. What does this have to do with the future of clubheads?

Well, as the public gets more and more interested in having their clubs fitted via technology such as a launch monitor, you'll start to see more and more retail golf shops with such devices on their premises. But owning a launch monitor is not the same thing as knowing how to use it. Is it, indeed, being used to come up with accurate fitting recommendations for the customer, or is it just another "bell and whistle" for the salesman to use—and how can you tell the difference? You might start by looking around the retail store or pro shop to see whether there is any evidence that a qualified clubmaker actually works there. If not, you might want to ask, why not? I mean, let's say they run you through some snazzy new technology and get all sorts of high-tech recommendations for your clubs. You need to ask who will be building your clubs to those specifications. It's an important question. In my career, I have seen customers go through a retail "computerized club fitting" only to be handed a set of off-the-rack standard made clubs as if the fitting never happened. A second question you might ask is if they would give you the names of other golfers they have fitted so you can call these people to determine if they were pleased with the results.

Specialized Putter Design and Fitting: What better way to affect your score than to find a putter that allows you to actually make more putts?

Putter fitting is still in the stone ages and consists of little more than "Keep trying until you find one you like." Now that more is being done in putter fitting research, more refined guidelines for finding the best putter specifications for loft, lie, length, and headweight are coming. This will allow golfers to improve their putting by matching the putter head, shaft, grip, length, loft, lie, and swingweight to precisely the way they stroke the putt. Because precise putter fitting will require the putter to be built to YOUR individual requirements, it will likely become the territory of the professional clubmakers.

Real Custom Club Fitting: Recently I read the results of a survey about custom fitting of golf clubs compiled by the leading golf industry data-gathering company. The survey was put together from responses filled out by some 2,000 consumer golfers with handicaps from the low single digit to the low 30s. What was amazing for me to read was just what most of these golfers believe constitutes a "custom fitting" session.

Many felt that hitting clubs at a "Demo Day" on a driving range or going through a company's fitting cart parked on the range was what custom fitting is all about. While sampling clubs on a Demo Day or choosing the lie angle of your irons and the flex of the shaft from a fitting cart are better than just taking clubs off the rack inside the store, this approach to club buying is not even close to what real custom fitting is all about. Think of this as trying on shirts or slacks picked off-the-shelf in a fitting room vs. real custom fitting being similar to going to the tailor's shop. At the tailor, all your measurements will be taken, you would choose the fabric and style, and the tailor would cut and sew each item of clothing expressly for YOUR individual physical characteristics. In a real custom fitting of golf clubs, measurements of your swing and physical parameters would be taken, and your set would be hand built from a wide assortment of clubheads, shafts, and grips precisely to meet YOUR individual swing, strength, and size.

The main reason I see real custom fitting being more prevalent in the future is simple—it may very well be the last untapped area in equipment technology for golfers to obtain golf clubs that truly do result in better shotmaking and lower scores. The USGA's rules governing equipment regulations have closed almost all the possible areas for us to use real physics to design clubheads and shafts which really do offer visible increases in distance and improvements in accuracy. What's left is real custom fitting. Fortunately that is a huge thing for golfers. Since no more than 2 percent to 3 percent of all golfers have ever been truly custom fitted for every aspect of their clubs to be able to maximize their performance, that means there is a chance for real game improvement out there to be had. But only if you find an experienced clubfitter to lead you through the process.

Notes: For those who think I am kidding, the 21 variables in a golf club are as follows. I can vary:

1. Clubhead loft angle
2. Clubhead lie angle
3. Clubhead bulge (woods only)
4. Clubhead roll (woods only)
5. Clubhead sole angle (irons only)
6. Clubhead face angle (woods only)
7. Clubhead hosel offset
8. Clubhead material composition and design
9. Shaft flex
10. Shaft torque
11. Shaft weight
12. Shaft spine alignment
13. Shaft flex profile
14. Shaft material composition and design
15. Grip size
16. Grip weight
17. Grip material composition and design
18. Club length
19. Club swingweight/Moment of Inertia
20. Club total weight
21. Set makeup

GETTING THE LEAD OUT

Frequently you will see golfers with lead tape on their clubheads. When you ask why it is there you will get answers ranging from: It makes the ball easier to draw or fade; to: It allows them to hit the ball higher or lower. In fact, neither will occur. The lead tape it would take to alter the launch angle or direction of the shot is far more than you would ever want to see put there. Let's look at the math.

To alter the launch angle or direction of the shot of an existing clubhead would require a minimum of 25 grams or more of weight. Typically, lead tape is available in half-inch-wide strips, and a 4.5-inch-long strip will weigh 2 grams. That means it would require almost 34 inches of tape to achieve a 15 gram addition. You'd not only be lucky to even SEE your clubhead after all that tape got stuck on, you'd be lucky to be able to pick it up off the ground! So if you think a strip or two of lead tape on the sole will increase the height of your shots, on the top will lower your flight, on the heel will combat a fade, or on the toe will fight a hook, you are whistlin' Dixie.

The only, and I mean ONLY, use of lead tape is to increase the swingweight of the club. So if you have a sense that your clubs are a little too light feeling, if you feel that you can't tell where the clubhead is during the swing from a control standpoint, if you are fighting being quick with your tempo or all of the above, then for sure this is what lead tape on the clubhead is for.

To give you a guideline for such use, a 4-inch-long strip of half-inch-wide lead tape placed anywhere on the head will increase the swingweight of the club by one swingweight point—i.e., from say a D1 to a D2. Because 99.9 percent of all golfers cannot feel an increase of one swingweight point, if you do wish to experiment with a higher swingweight on your clubs, you need to start with at least a two-swingweight-point increase and go up from there as you hit balls to judge the change in headweight feel.

Where to put it? Anywhere you want, because any addition of less than 42 inches of lead tape won't change the direction or the height of the shot. Most convenient is to put it on the sole or on the very back of your woodheads, or in the middle of the cavity on the back of your irons.

Chapter 4—A SHAFTING YOU'LL LOVE

Of Pipers—Pied and Otherwise

While teaching a seminar on clubfitting to a group of PGA professionals a number of years ago, I posed a couple of questions as a prelude to speaking about shaft selection.

"How many of you think the shaft is the most important component of the golf club," I asked. Almost immediately most of the hands in the room shot up. Then I asked, "How many of you think the clubhead is the most important part of the club?" The rest of the hands shot up, although it was a vast minority compared to the pro-shaft voters.

With all the votes cast, and apparently no one willing to hold out for a vote in favor the grip, I continued, "All of you who feel the shaft is the most important part of the club: send me your favorite shaft, I'll install a clubhead and send it back with a guarantee you won't be able to hit it as well as you do now. And I'll make the same offer to those who feel the head is the most important part. You send me your favorite clubhead, I'll put a shaft in it and guarantee you won't like your shotmaking results."

The point I was trying to make to the pros is the same one I want to make to you. *There IS no one most important part of the golf club.*

If you have a "favorite club," it has earned that distinction because *everything* about it, the head and its specifications, the shaft and its design, the texture and size of the grip as well as the assembly features of length and swingweight/Moment of Inertia are right for how YOU swing and play the game.

That is not to minimize the importance of the shaft, it's only to put it into perspective. The golf shaft is, I believe, one of the most fascinating design and research areas within all of golf. Why? Because it is without question the least understood and the most confusing component of the club.

Ever hear the saying "The shaft is the engine of the golf club"? Actually, that's not quite true. The shaft is really more like the drive train. YOU are the engine. All the shaft does is transfer your power to the clubhead and dictate a small part of your shot trajectory and a yet smaller portion of your accuracy. Yet, because many golfers don't have access to the facts, there are a tremendous number who switch shafts each season, looking for THE shaft that's going to salvage their game.

Consider the pros on the PGA Tour. Many of these guys change shafts in their clubs more than they change grips! First, they NEVER use the stock shaft that comes with the club that YOU buy off the rack (so much for "Play the same club the pros use").

The major shaft manufacturers all have sales reps that are at every event on the PGA Tour. During the Monday-to-Wednesday practice rounds, they buzz around like bees to honey, trying to get the pros to try their latest shaft design. Why? Because the shaft companies know full well that the pros are the Pied Pipers and the golfers, excuse the analogy, are the "children of Hameln" who will follow.

Ten years ago it was the Grafalloy Pro-Lite that was the hot shaft on tour. Then it was the purple-and-gold UST Pro-Force. Now it's the various models of the Fujikura Speeder, Graphite Design YS, and Aldila NV. While the Pro-Lite and Pro-Force are both still being made, their sales are but a shadow to their past because the mantle of "hot shaft" has now passed on to the Fuji, YS, or NV shafts.

What happened to these "hot shafts" that sold millions of units when they were at the height of their popularity? Did they suddenly become junk and/or the new shafts become that much better? Have the pro swings changed so that these shafts no longer work? No, it's just that a different flavor has found its 15 minutes of fame on tour. Wait another year and there will be yet another flavor (or three) that will catch the limelight and drive golfers to spring for yet another reshaft of their driver.

Why do the pros switch shafts so often?

Sometimes it's because of the endorsement money the pros get to play a new shaft, although, to be honest, shaft endorsement money is a rarity on the professional tours. The shaft companies just don't make the profit margins necessary to pay many players to use their designs. That's become nearly the exclusive province of the big club companies that make way more than the proverbial lion's share of the profit in the golf business.

No, the main reasons the pros change shafts so often are that they are human and that they can try out any shaft they wish, free of charge. Like you or I, every pro goes in and out of "slumps" in their ball striking. In the search for their swing, often they will blame the slump on their clubs and make a switch as a form of hunting for the combination that will magically bring back their A-game. With a new shaft, they might perceive a different "feel" that gets them back on track. With a new shaft, they get a breath of fresh air that can take them along until the next time they fall into a slump.

The other reason the pros switch shafts so often is because they can. Their endorsement contracts usually specify that they only have to play a certain number of their sponsoring company's *clubheads*. No pro would be dumb enough to allow the contract to include the company's branded shafts—you know, the ones they put in their clubs "on the rack" to sell to you—in that endorsement deal because they don't fit the pros' typical swings. In addition, every week on the PGA Tour brings a caravan of company trailers, manned with technicians who are like pages to the knights. Any of them can make a shaft switch in minutes.

No, the pros change shafts because they believe it's worthwhile at the time and because they can do it so easily. But I am not sure if they understand the role they play in leading amateur golfers to think of their shafts as some kind of magic wand. You see, shafts are kind of like snakes. They come in different colors and markings, and you can't tell just by looking at them which ones will be poisonous or friendly.

Shafts can be made with an almost infinite variety of flex, torque, and weight features, which combine to create a wide variety of bend and twist characteristics in your clubs. But here's an interesting point I will share with you.

Sand the fancy paint job off the graphite shafts, rip the labels off the steel shafts, toss them all in a pile and there is no way anyone, short of a shaft designer, could tell which shaft was which; and, even then, it would only be after they take a lot of time-consuming measurements, many of which require the use of a number of complicated looking electronic machines. Therein lies an interesting point about golf shafts.

They can be designed to a whole variety of bending, twisting, and weight variations, but no golfer can possibly know how they will perform until they hit a club with that shaft installed. This keeps a certain segment of the golfing market enamored with the thought that the "magic shaft" is right around the next page on the calendar.

Science and Magic Meet Form and Function

"The Magic Shaft!!" The mere thought conjures up the idea that the shaft must ultimately control the performance of each shot—and woe betide the golfer who ends up with the wrong shaft. Your game will go in the tank, and you will be almost as helpless as a beginner taking his or her first lesson. Heck, I remember myself being enamored with that misguided thought as well.

Back in my early days in clubmaking I was also working as a club professional. One day I borrowed a friend's brand-new persimmon driver with an Aldila #9-flex graphite shaft. (Just to tell you how confusing it was, in this model of graphite shaft, Aldila made flexes numbered from 1 to 15!) This was the early 1970s, and graphite shafts were new on the scene, so we all were fascinated with the possibilities. This #9 flex driver was SO PERFECT for me that it was not a matter of going deep and in the fairway—it was more like, "You want the ball on that sprinkler head next to the fairway bunker out there at 290?" Bam, it was there!

So I feverishly ordered an Aldila #9 flex shaft, duplicated the length and swingweight of my friend's driver, and started making travel plans for Tour School that fall! I could not believe it when I put my driver with the same shaft, same head, same specs into play and could not hit anything but ugly snipes off the tee. And THAT began my lifelong quest to understand the golf shaft.

How much does the shaft contribute to the execution of each shot? I hate to tell all you shaft fanatics this, but the answer is: a lot, but not as much as the clubhead. When it comes to ordaining the ball speed, launch angle, and backspin, the three elements that determine how far and how high every shot will go, the clubhead is far more important than the shaft.

The shaft has two primary and one minor roles, other than connecting the grip to the head. Number one, it's the chief controller of the total weight of the golf club (i.e., how much your club weighs in ounces or grams). Number two, the way the shaft bends forward just before impact can have a *slight* but visible influence on the ball's launch angle. Number three, in graphite shafts there is a matter of the twisting of the shaft and how that may have a slight effect on shot accuracy. And that's it! From a pure performance standpoint, that's all the shaft does.

There *is* one more thing. This function has nothing to do with pure ball-flight performance, but it's extremely important when it comes to the golfer's perception of a shaft being good, so-so, or "poisonous." Namely, some golfers can perceive a "FEEL" in their shafts and place a high degree of importance upon it. It works like this: The shaft will feed back how much it bends during your swing and how solidly or not the ball was hit by the clubhead. Have you ever hit the ball off the toe or heel and felt that yucky sensation? It's the shaft that delivers that feeling to your hands. Hit the same off-center shot with a totally different shaft and it might feel different—at least to golfers who have the sensitivity to perceive and process such feedback.

On the other hand, the shaft is also responsible for delivering the message of that dead-center, on-the-button, feeling of the perfect shot as well. Hit the ball dead center on the clubface with a shaft in the clubhead that is way too stiff, and the shot feels "dead." On the other hand, ever hit your wife's clubs? Once you get past a little more whippy feeling in the shaft, I bet you noticed they felt very solid when you hit the ball right on the button, possibly even more solid than YOUR clubs feel. It's the shaft that did that, by bending more than your shafts normally do and thus delivering a different sensation back to your hands and brain. The more bending of the shaft in the swing, the more solid is the feeling of impact—the less bending of the shaft, the less solid the shot will feel. So much for you guys who insist on playing stiff or extra-stiff shafts!

Then there is the feeling of the actual bending of the shaft itself during your swing. Most golfers don't have the sensory acuity to feel differences in how much and at what point the shaft bends. But for those who do, the feeling of when, how much, and where in the swing the shaft bends can be the difference between "It's magic" and "Get that thing outta my hands."

To most tour players and single-digit amateurs, even some middle handicap players with a lot of playing experience, the shaft is all about feel first. Secondary to these golfers is the shaft's contribution to the height of the shot and the total weight of the club.

"Feel" is what makes shaft fitting so complicated and creates tons of golfers who are ever open to trying the next "flavor" that comes down the line. The problem is that feel is a *qualitative* thing and not something that can be measured as a degree, inch, gram, or ounce. We're getting there in terms of a way to predict and quantify the feel of a shaft, but we're not quite there yet.

We who design and test shafts are very aware that if feel makes the difference between acceptance and rejection, we had better gain the ability to measure and predict it. We need to find a way to design "feel" into a shaft. Meanwhile, there are things about shafts that CAN be qualitatively measured and used to "predict the magic."

That's what I want to tell you about in this chapter, so that you can take some of the trial and error out of shaft selection and, in the process, end up with the best shaft for your game.

A Weighty Matter

Let's start with shaft weight. Shaft weight is important because the total weight of the golf club has a big influence on how fast you can swing it; and, as you know, how fast you swing the club has a lot to do with how far you hit the ball.

Total golf club weight is simply the sum of the weights of each of the three major parts. Headweight + shaftweight + gripweight = total club weight (see fig. 4.1). This is not to be confused with swingweight, which is the ratio of how much weight lies in the last 14 inches of the club versus the weight in the rest of the club. We'll talk about that later.

The shaft contributes more than the head and the grip to the total weight of the club only because it is offered in the widest range of weight of all the three components of the golf club. Take a driver for example. The driverhead will usually weigh somewhere between 195 grams and 215 grams. The exact number depends on the shaftweight, swingweight, and the length you went for in the final product. That's a 20-gram difference, from high to low, for 98 percent of the driverheads on the market today. (In each individual iron it will be about half that range because golfers don't generally use as wide a variety of shaft lengths and shaft weights as they do with the driver.) Most grips are even closer to each other in their weight. Only when a golfer goes for a humongous-sized grip will the weight of the grip jump out of its narrow high-to-low range of about 10 grams and have a little more effect on the total weight.

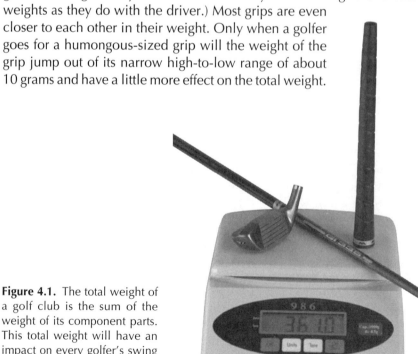

Figure 4.1. The total weight of a golf club is the sum of the weight of its component parts. This total weight will have an impact on every golfer's swing speed, tempo, and timing.

So that leaves the shaft. Shaft manufacturers can make a steel shaft that weighs up to 130 grams or a graphite shaft that weighs as little as 40 grams. That's a range of 90 grams, or a little over three ounces. Perhaps you can now see how the total weight of the golf club is most influenced by the shaft that is selected. The equation is simple: You want lighter clubs, go with lighter shafts, and vice versa (see fig. 4.2).

So, from a performance standpoint, what's the big deal about shaft weight and total weight? Well, it's like the difference between a feather and a sledgehammer. On paper, the lighter the total weight of the club, the faster you should be able to swing it. The heavier, the slower. And when you talk distance, you are talking swing speed, first and foremost.

If you could increase your driver swing speed by just 2 mph, you would see a distance increase of about 5 yards before the ball hits and rolls—providing you still can make a solid sweet spot contact with that 2 mph higher swing speed. This is the main reason that graphite shafts hold the potential to allow golfers to hit the ball farther.

Graphite as a material is far lighter than steel. At present, the steel shaft makers are busting their chops to create a steel shaft that will weigh less than 100 grams. They will likely never make a steel shaft that weighs less than 90 grams. Yet some graphite shafts are as light as 40 grams, and a TON are available in the 55–65 gram range. In terms of allowing you to swing the club faster, you have three choices: graphite, graphite, or graphite.

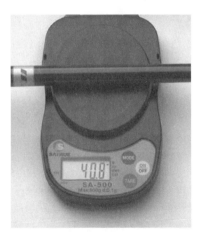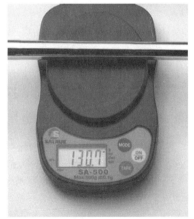

Figure 4.2. Shafts can vary by as much as 90 grams in weight (>3 oz.). Shaft weight is a larger factor in the club's total weight than either the clubhead or the grip.

That's the good news. Now here's the bad. *You have probably already achieved whatever gains in swing speed you're going to achieve from the weight of the shaft that's in your driver already.*

With the big stick and possibly your fairway woods as well, you're probably already playing with clubs that have a very light total weight. Over the past 3 to 4 years, the market share of graphite shafts in drivers has grown to something like 85 percent of all the drivers sold each year. Most all of the premium club companies use stock graphite shafts that weigh in the area of 60–70 grams in their drivers and fairway woods. In other words, if you have graphite shafts in your woods now, you probably don't have much room to drop down significantly lighter yet in total weight to get a measurably higher swing speed for more distance.

The only reason that graphite shafts are a little less predominant in fairway woods than drivers is the cost factor. Most golfers are more than willing to spring for the higher cost that a 60 gram graphite shaft adds to a driver. However, multiply that by 2 or 3 for the rest of the woods, and well, sometimes that's a little tougher to get by the family CFO.

In the irons, only about 20–25 percent of all sets are presently sold with graphite shafts, with price being completely responsible for that much lower market share. Loosely translated, you have a lot better chance of getting a driver and two fairway woods approved by the boss than nine graphite-shafted irons! Now, SHE might have all graphite clubs in her bag, but that's justified. Because the parameters for fitting total weight include golfer strength and swing speed, she probably has a much greater need for playing with graphites in both the woods and irons than you do. Nevertheless, if you're looking for more distance, and if the feel of your steel shaft irons has been getting a little heavy on the back nine or in the last half of your large bucket of balls, you too might want to consider going all graphite. The extra distance is there to be had, with more ease and comfort in swinging the irons as a nice side benefit. And if you still pack and walk, you'll lighten the load in your bag by a full pound when you convert from steel to graphite in all your irons!

If you want to know whether you have a chance to gain more distance from a move to a lighter graphite shaft, there's a pretty simple test you can do at home. First, let me say that if you still have a steel shaft in the old #1, you are pretty much a lead pipe cinch to make the switch to light graphite in the driver and increase your swing speed. If you already have graphite in your driver, you can at least go through the motions of this test to see whether there's a chance.

If you have a reasonably accurate scale in the house, lay the driver across the plate on the scale so it balances. If the scale says 12.25 ounces

(347 grams) or higher, you could change to a 55–65 gram shaft and you might be able to squeeze another mph, maybe two, out of the club. If your current driver weighs less than 12 ounces, sorry, you probably won't be able to find a new graphite shaft that would be lighter by enough weight to make a difference in your swing speed. In that case, however, all is not lost for the driver distance seeker.

Remember what I said in Chapter 1 about driver loft? Chances are good you are one of the 90 percent not using the right loft in your current driver to maximize your distance potential, so there is definitely still hope for your dreams of more distance. For a real chance to increase your swing speed from a switch in shafts, the new shaft will have to be at least an ounce (28 grams) lighter than the one you currently have. So, remember. If you weighed your current driver and it tipped the scale at 12.25 ounces or higher, you have a shot at moving into a 45–55 gram shaft and gaining enough swing speed to see a little shorter second shot into the greens. At that point the question will arise, how much are you willing to pay for that increase in distance? You can take it as a solid rule of thumb that the lighter the shaft the more expensive it will be.

Why would there be no real swing speed increase if you shifted to a shaft that would be, let's say, half an ounce (14 grams) lighter than what you have now? The answer is simple and learned only from years of design and fitting experience. *Small-to-medium changes in shot performance and ball flight require big changes in the golf club.*

And the reason for THAT is because the human body has an amazing ability to adjust to changes made in your golf equipment. Thus, for a shaft weight change to impact on the body's ability to swing the club measurably faster, I have found in my fitting experience that the decrease in the shaft weight has to be significant—in the area of one ounce (28 grams) lighter.

There is one other possible proviso you need to know about shifting to a lighter shaft. If the shafts in your current clubs are either too heavy or too light for your strength, swing tempo, and swing mechanics, AND the swingweight balance in the club is not matched well to your swing tempo, you're probably hitting the ball off-center more than you should because of this double whammy of misfitting. In that case a change of shafts to whatever weight is right for your strength and tempo, accompanied by the right swingweight balance in the club for your swing, could bring you a much higher percentage of on-center hits. From that, you could gain distance in pretty significant chunks. So it is very important to be fitted in the right shaft weight WITH the swingweight that is best matched to your strength and swing tempo.

So who's going to figure this out for you? I can give you a little starting point for selecting the right weight of the shaft and best swingweight to go with it, but ultimately it should be an experienced clubmaker who would take measurements, observe your swing, and work one on one with you to make that final determination for what weight shaft and which swingweight to go with it. However, here are some guidelines for you to follow.

Shaft weight selection is pretty much all about golfer strength and the tempo or rhythm of the swing. No rocket science here, just the logic that golfers who are physically less strong, not that quick with their swing tempo, and less athletically inclined are all going to be better off with golf clubs that have a very light total weight (i.e., much lighter shafts). The weaker, the smoother, and the less athletically inclined the golfer, the lighter the shafts should be. That same lightweight shaft in the hands of a much physically stronger golfer with a faster swing tempo will, in all likelihood, cause him or her to swing TOO fast, destroying tempo and lowering the probability of hitting the ball consistently solid and on-center.

I know. I know. I just heard some of you say, "but I'm pretty strong, used to be a good athlete and I want more distance too. You're telling me I have to stay with steel shafts?"

No, I am not saying that at all because, fortunately, there is a way to "trick" a light graphite-shafted club into giving you a heavier perceived weight *feel* by building the club with a higher swingweight. This will prevent it from making you swing too quickly and suffer from the dreaded "heelers."

When I have used the term "swingweight balance of the club," what I mean is either the swingweight or the Moment of Inertia of the whole club itself. More will be said about all this important stuff later, but for now, if you know what swingweight is, then fine, I got the point across. If swingweight is foreign to your golf vocabulary, here's a quick summary before we get back to the shaft weight fitting.

In basic terms, swingweight is a way to express the feeling of the clubhead's weight when you swing the club, although I still love the old Scottish clubmaker's definition: "It's the heft of the club, laddie, the heft!" If you can really sense that the head feels heavier when you swing the club, the swingweight is probably higher than if the head feels pretty light out there on the end of the shaft.

Without going into the convoluted world of swingweight too deeply in the middle of a shaft discussion, swingweight is simply the measured weight in the golf club as it travels about one fixed point. A special scale that has been used since the 1920s to measure golf club swingweight defines that point. It records the weight balance of your clubs using a letter/number designation. The higher the letter and the higher the number with it, the heavier the clubhead will feel. Period. Swingweight is not really an expression of real weight as much as it is a comparison of how the weight in your clubs is distributed.

The club companies build virtually all their men's clubs to a standard D1 or D2 swingweight—D1 with the R flex shafts, and D2 for the S flex shaft clubs. Women's clubs are generally all built to a swingweight in the low-to-middle C-range. If you are worried about the weight difference of that one swingweight point, don't be. Pull a dollar bill out of your wallet, tape it on your clubhead and you have increased the swingweight by 1 point. Can't feel the difference? That's all right, neither can 99.9 percent of the other 27 million golfers in the country.

If you are physically less strong or a little less athletically inclined, and you have a smoother swing tempo, your light graphite-shafted clubs would be okay for you in a D0 swingweight for men and about C4 for women. If you are of average strength and tempo, think about D2 swingweight and ladies, about C6 with light graphite-shafted clubs. If you are physically strong with a faster tempo, do not swingweight a set of clubs made with very light graphite shafts under at least D4 (men) or C8 (women), or you may start experiencing a lack of control with your swing tempo and a higher incidence of off-center hits.

The reason having a high swingweight is important for the high strength/fast tempo golfer is that it will help keep your swing tempo and timing more under control. High swingweights with very light graphite shafts for lower-strength, smoother-tempo golfers do not usually work well because the combination makes the clubs more "laborious" to swing.

In short, if you are physically strong, have a faster swing tempo, and are more aggressive in your swing, you can still use light graphite shafts in your clubs. But you'll likely do a LOT better with the clubs if they are ALSO built with more "heft" (i.e., a much higher swingweight) to create a more head-heavy feel. Then too, as much as I have been talking about the very light 55–65 gram graphite shafts, there are a large number of graphite shafts designed in the weight range of 70–85 grams as well. Physically strong, and/or quick-tempo players may find that a slightly heavier graphite shaft in this weight range may very well be the ticket to more distance. Remember, with most steel shafts weighing 115–125 grams, a drop down to a 75–80 gram graphite shaft is still a good drop when it comes to the possible effect of increasing your swing speed.

Another Way to Take Flight

The other major contribution of the shaft is its effect on the launch angle of the shot. The only problem is that this shaft effect usually works only for golfers with better-than-average swing fundamentals. So, if you are considering a shaft change in your clubs to alter the height of your shots and you have a really crummy swing, I am sorry to tell you that the shaft will not do much to change or affect the height of your shots.

But don't worry if you are cursed with poor downswing mechanics. For golfers with definite swing flaws, vast improvement through better fitting certainly does not stop just at the trajectory contribution of the shaft. For less skilled golfers the changes will focus on clubhead specifications like loft plus the face angle, of course, the shaft from the standpoint of its weight, and then on the assembly specifications of length and the swingweight balance. If you know you have serious swing flaws, do not feel bad because, really, in those above fitting areas alone, you can and will experience a tremendous amount of improvement. And again, custom fitting IS very helpful for less skilled players. Don't ever think that you have to "get better" before you are ready for custom fitting!

To understand how the shaft can have an effect on the height of the shot is really pretty easy, as long as all you think about is how the shaft bends in the last part of the downswing before the clubhead hits the ball. Any other bending the shaft makes before that has very little to do with the performance of the shot. All the various ways the shaft bends as a result of your swing will have an effect on the "feel" of the shaft, but will not have any effect on the flight of the ball.

The contribution of the flex of the shaft to the flight of the ball all comes from the shaft bending forward just before the clubhead hits the ball. No matter what the golfers try to do in their swings, whenever they actually hit the ball, the shaft will be flexed forward a little before the clubhead hits the ball.

The stronger the golfer, the later the golfer's release of the wrist-cock, the faster the golfer's swing speed, and the more flexible the shaft, the more the shaft will bend forward before the clubhead hits the ball. And the stiffer the flex of the shaft, the less this forward bending of the shaft happens before impact. Now, let's address some specific myths that many golfers (and even golf equipment industry people) have about the way the shaft performs in a typical golf swing.

Three Myths

Myth Number One: The first myth to erase is that the shaft flexes back and then forward like a buggy whip to catapult the ball down the fairway.

Golfers like to call this the "loading and unloading of the shaft." But that's really misleading because it makes you think that the shaft flexes and "unflexes" in the same direction. And the shaft does NOT do that in the swing. The bending that occurs right when you start the downswing does not flex back on the same plane when you hit the ball because we rotate the club around our bodies when we make a full swing. So the bending that happens in the very beginning of the downswing occurs in a totally different direction of bending from the final bending forward of the shaft just before the head hits the ball. So there's no way the shaft can flex back and forth like a buggy whip to "slingshot" the ball.

Myth Number Two: The second myth is that the clubhead sometimes (usually? often? always?) will "lag behind" just before impact with the ball.

As we swing the club back down to the ball, we have a wrist-cock angle. (The wrist-cock is the angle between the shaft and the arms, and it has to "unhinge" and straighten out at some point before hitting the ball.) This unhinging of the wrist-cock is called the "release." Here's a fascinating point that most people in golf don't know: When we release the wrist-cock on the downswing, the arms begin to slow down and the clubhead begins to speed up. The reason is that the arms give up their energy to the club at the moment of unhinging the wrist-cock. Arms lose energy; arms slow down. The club gets energy; club speeds up.

That release of the wrist-cock also applies something called centrifugal force to the club. That centrifugal force combined with the arms slowing down and the club speeding up causes the shaft to begin to bend forward. And because the arms DO slow down when the wrist-cock is released, the shaft HAS to bend forward before hitting the ball.

The only possible way the clubhead could lag behind the shaft is if the golfer could keep their arms accelerating faster than the club on the downswing, and that can't happen unless the golfer never unhinges the wrist-cock on the downswing.

If you want to see what I mean, next time you are hitting balls, just try to hit the ball without unhinging your wrists! You want to know the closest shot in the game to doing that? It's Tiger Woods's famous long iron "stinger" shot! You know, the one where he hits a 2-iron about 8 feet off the ground? To hit that shot, Tiger holds the wrist-cock release so long with his hands in front of the clubhead that the 2-iron head loft at impact would be about 6 degrees, plus the shaft never gets to bend forward very much at all to increase the launch angle.

As far as you and I and the rest of us mere mortals are concerned, as long as we have a wrist-cock that we unhinge before impact, there is no way that the head will lag behind with the shaft bent backward at the moment of impact with the ball.

Myth Number Three: The third myth to bury is that the forward flexing of the shaft just before impact (which some people mistakenly call "buggy-whipping" or "kicking") increases the speed of the clubhead. It does not. Here's why.

The only way a shaft could act like a spring and slingshot the ball would be if it could bend back and spring forward in the same plane or direction. But the golf shaft is not like a buggy whip or a fishing rod. With those two objects, we move them so that the flexing back takes place on the same plane as the flexing forward. In those cases the spring back of the flexing will contribute to the speed of the tip end of the whip or the rod. When we swing a golf club, we rotate our bodies which also rotates

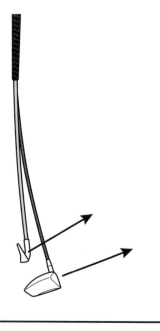

Figure 4.3. After the wrist-cock angle is unhinged, the shaft begins to bend forward. How much the shaft bends forward before the club hits the ball determines the shaft's effect on the height of the shot.

the shaft around. This means the shaft bends back on a different plane from the one on which it bends forward, so it can't pick up bending speed from its initial flexing. A buggy whip and a fishing rod can do that because they bend forward on the same plane on which they were flexed back.

So the shaft may contribute to the height of the shot by bowing forward before impact, which increases the loft of the clubhead when it hits the ball (see fig. 4.3). There are a number of shaft models that are designed to offer a choice of low, medium, or high trajectory for the shot. Shafts which are designed to have a higher flight pattern will be more flexible, usually in the bottom half of the shaft so that the forward bending of the shaft can be greater. Conversely, shafts designed to hit the ball lower will be made so the bottom half of the shaft will be stiffer.

Sometimes It IS the Archer, Not the Bow

The golfer's swing, however, has a *huge* influence on how a shaft will perform, or even if the shaft will perform at all as it is designed.

I just described to you how a shaft is made to bend forward roughly at impact to offer a difference in the height of the shot to the golfer. But that can only happen if the golfer can hold the unhinging of the wrist-cock until later in the downswing. On the other hand, there are many golfers who unhinge the wrist-cock very early in the downswing. Their first swing movement to start the downswing is usually done with a "grab-bing" or "pulling" of the club with their hands instead of beginning the downswing with the shoulders or hips.

When the golfer unhinges the wrist-cock very early in the down-swing, it causes the shaft to bend before the club has been rotated back to get in line with the target. Thus, the shaft bending they create from their early unhinging of the wrist-cock happens in a direction of bending that won't be in line with their target. That means golfers with an early unhinging of the wrist-cock won't see a height difference between differ-ent shaft designs—they pretty much end up hitting all shaft designs of the same flex to the same shot height because they use their shaft-bending force too soon before impact with the ball.

In addition, golfers who unhinge the wrist-cock very early in the downswing will almost always allow the wrists to flex forward before the club hits the ball. When this happens, the clubhead will pass the hands before impact, which then increases the loft of the head when it hits the ball—and the ball flies higher no matter what. With this type of impact

Early
Release

Figure 4.4. If the golfer un-hinges the wrist-cock angle too early on the downswing, it is common for this early unhinging to continue to cause the wrists to flex for-ward before hitting the ball. This type of swing move will usually hit the ball high with all types of shaft designs.

position in the swing, no matter if the shaft is a low or high flight design, all shots will be hit high (see fig. 4.4).

How much can the shaft influence the shot trajectory for players who have the correct swing mechanics? That depends on how strong you are, how late you can hold your wrist-cock release, and how stiff or flexible the shaft has been designed. Even if you are Tiger Woods hitting a driver with a woman's flex shaft, the shaft cannot bend forward any more than the distance between the CG of the clubhead to the center of hosel. As you guessed, it's physics at work again.

True, Tiger will hit the ball sky-high with L-flex shafts, but that will be more because of his 185 mph ball speed than bending the shaft that much more forward. His launch angle with women's shafts, however, will only be increased by about 2–3 degrees over the launch angle he gets with his own shafts. But when his shot takes off on a launch angle that is 2–3 degrees higher, that 185 mph ball speed will keep the ball traveling upward on that higher angle for so long that the actual height will be much higher off the ground (see fig. 4.5).

Ironing Out One More Detail

By the way, so far we've only been talking about the shafts in your woods. Iron shafts are different. Not only are they shorter but they are almost always designed with a larger tip-end diameter than the wood shafts. Because of these differences, iron shafts are much stiffer than wood shafts, which make iron shafts far more limited in their contribution to the launch angle of the shot.

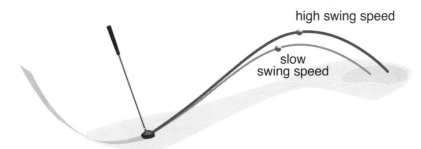

Figure 4.5. If a high–swing speed golfer hits a very flexible shaft, the ball will take off at a slightly higher angle but will achieve a much higher flight due to the higher ball velocity.

The much stiffer iron shaft puts up one helluva lot more fight to prevent itself from being flexed forward. Because iron shafts are bigger around down at the tip end and shorter than wood shafts, they are much stiffer and require a lot more force than any golfer has to bend them as much as a wood shaft. And there is one more difference to add.

Because iron clubs are shorter in length AND heavier in total weight than the woods, you can't swing them as fast and thus you can't put as much bending force on the iron shafts. So the combination of stiffer shafts and slower swing speed means that no matter what you do, you cannot get your iron shafts of the same letter flex as your wood shafts to bend forward and help increase the height of your shots as much as you can with the shafts in your woods. They just won't bend that much. But that's okay; that's what the increased lofts on your ironheads are there to do (see fig. 4.6).

Figure 4.6. Because iron shafts are shorter and larger in diameter at the head end, they cannot bend as much in the swing as the longer and smaller tip-diameter shafts in wood clubs. This means wood shafts can influence the height of the shot more than iron shafts.

Pushing the Speed Limit

It has become a common practice among shaft manufacturers to publish a recommended golfer swing speed for each of the flexes of the shafts they design and manufacture under their shaft company brand. We're not talking about the shafts made by these companies which end up being the stock shaft in a big golf club company's standard made clubs. Those shafts are "proprietary" to each club company, and the companies that make these shafts are not allowed to print or say anything about them.

There are a number of shaft manufacturers that design, manufacture, and market shafts under their own brand names. Most of you are aware of companies like Aldila, Royal Precision, True Temper, Grafalloy, UST, Graphite Design, Fujikura, and Penley, just to name a few. Some of you are aware of the actual models of shafts that are designed and promoted by these companies: e.g., Aldila NV, Royal Precision Rifle, True Temper Dynamic Gold, Grafalloy Blue, UST Harmon Design, Graphite Design YS, Fujikura Speeder 757, Penley Stealth, and so on.

The shafts designed and promoted by each shaft company under their own brand are all listed in each of the shaft companies' Web sites and in their printed catalogs. Among the information available will be something called a "swing speed rating" for each flex of each different shaft model. I'm pleased they do this because I had the pleasure of starting this concept of predicting a golfer swing speed requirement to help guide golfers in their search for the flex that would best match their swing.

My 1991 book, *The Modern Guide to Shaft Fitting*, was the golf industry's first published study of shafts in which real quantitative information was used to compare shafts. Within this book was the first attempt to use hard test data on shafts to predict a golfer swing speed rating for fitting the flex of a huge assortment of different shafts.

If you take the time to dig into some of the shaft companies' Web sites or catalog information, you will find a listing of the shafts that would look like the following example from the Aldila Shaft Company Web site (see table 4.1).

In table 4.1 you can see that the company offers a point of reference using both driver swing speed and driver overall distance as a way for golfers to determine what flex would match closest to their needs. Not all shaft companies provide this type of information, and thus golfers are left a little more in the dark and certainly open to making the wrong selection.

In addition, some of the more experienced custom clubmaking supply companies will provide swing speed recommendations for the branded shafts they distribute for the various shaft manufacturers. Most of these listings are good to use as a guide—I know because earlier in my career I created the swing speed rating systems for two of the largest custom

Table 4.1—Aldila NV series

	Driver Speed (mph)	75–90	90–100	100–110	>110
	Carry (yds)	180–210	210–240	240–265	>265
NV Series					
	NV 55	A	R	S	X
	NV 65, 75, 85		R	S	X
	NV 95, 105			S	X
	NV Hybrid 85		R	S	
	NV Hybrid 105			S	X

Note: An example of how one shaft company, Aldila, matches golfer swing speed to the flex of each of their shafts. Most shaft makers provide such information on their Web sites and in their printed materials.

clubmaking companies based on further research performed for and after my 1991 book on shafts.

An additional word about swing speed ratings for shafts. Wood shaft swing speed ratings are based on driver swing speed measurements, while the iron shaft ratings are based on a 5-iron swing speed.

Because irons are shorter and heavier in total weight than woods, golfers will generate a lower swing speed with the irons. Thus, it's important that in your hunt you use your 5-iron swing speed when searching through iron shaft swing speed ratings, and your driver swing speed measurement when perusing the wood shaft listings.

There are times when a golfer should opt for a shaft that has a swing speed rating that is lower or higher than the golfer's actual swing speed. For example, the original concept of awarding a swing speed rating to a shaft is based on the general premise that as the golfer's swing speed increases, the force he or she generates to elicit the bending force on the shaft increases as well. Usually this is true. However, it is certainly true that due to differences in swing tempo and the time of unhinging of the wrist-cock on the downswing, two golfers could have the same swing speed but generate different amounts of bending force on the shaft. Let me give you an example.

Let's say Tom and Chad both have a swing speed measured with the driver to be 90 mph. However, Tom, who has a little more excitable personality, really "pours on the coal" when he starts his downswing, while Chad, being a little more mellow, has a distinct pause between the end of the backswing and the beginning of the downswing. Tom has a fast, aggressive downswing tempo, while Chad's tempo is very smooth. Tom releases the wrist-cock later in his downswing while Chad unhinges the wrists earlier. Yet both have the same 90 mph swing speed.

In truth, Tom would be better off looking for shafts that are ranked in the swing speed category of 95–105 mph, while Chad should look for shafts in the 80–90 mph swing speed rating. How so? The higher the swing speed rating for a shaft, the more stiff the shaft will be, and vice versa. Thus, because Tom exhibits many of the swing characteristics that combine to cause more bending force in the shaft, he needs to have a shaft that is a little more stiff than what his swing speed would otherwise indicate. And Chad, being the polar opposite in his swing to Tom, would be better off with a shaft that is a little more flexible than what his swing speed would ordinarily lead you to believe he needs.

This is precisely how clubmakers who are experienced in shaft fitting perform their shaft fitting recommendations. They will start with a swing speed measurement of each golfer, but then, after observing the golfer's swing movements and tempo, they may decide to modify their original swing speed–to–shaft flex recommendation based on the manner in which the golfer actually applies the bending force to the shaft in the swing.

CHAPTER 5—BECOMING FLEXIBLE

A Term with a Lot of Flex in It

The contribution of the shaft to the height of the shot is related to the flex, or rather, what we now call the *flex profile design* of the shaft. Shaft flex is one of the most confusing and complicated aspects of a golf club. Why? After all, since the shaft is a hollow tube that tapers in shape from grip end to head end, a shaft designer has two primary things he can vary in its design: the diameter of the shaft and the thickness of the walls of the shaft. The larger the diameter and the thicker the walls, the stiffer the shaft; the smaller the diameter and thinner the walls, the more flexible the shaft.

Simple, eh? But wait. The plot thickens when you think of how many different places over the length of a shaft the designer could change its diameter and wall thickness to elicit a difference in the flex. For this reason there literally are an infinite number of flex designs that are possible in a shaft.

Most golfers only think of the flex of their shafts as a single letter printed somewhere on the shaft. You know, L for ladies, A for senior, R for regular, S for stiff, and X for telephone pole. And what a circus that is! Because there are no standards for shaft flex in the golf industry, an R-flex equals an R-flex except if the R is made by another maker of Rs, in which case R might not equal R at all. And Yogi Berra didn't make up that babblespeak, the shaft industry did!

Think of it this way. Every other design specification of your golf clubs is described by a real quantitative numerical measurement of something. Loft and lie on the clubheads are measured in degrees, and degrees are REAL. So if the loft of one head is measured at 10 degrees and another one is 11 degrees, you know the exact difference between the two and the probable difference in terms of shot height, backspin, and distance. Same thing with length, which is measured in inches. Let's say you have two drivers, one built to 45 inches and the other at 44 inches. Any questions about how much longer one is than the other? And the same thing goes for the other specifications on the club like total weight, shaft weight, and so on. They are real, agreed upon, quantitative measurements.

But flex has always been described to golfers with a letter. And compared to degrees, inches, and grams, letters mean nothing—at least they don't give you a real comparative sense for how stiff an R-flex is and how much difference in stiffness there is between an R- and an S-flex shaft. Is it one letter, since the two are side-by-side in the alphabet? Then how much difference between an L- and an A-flex? See what I mean? (See fig. 5.1.)

I bet if you asked 100 golfers whether an R-flex in one brand of club was the same as an R-flex in another, most would answer: "Sure they are, because they are both Rs." Sorry. Not only do the letters mean nothing in terms of how stiff the shaft is, but each shaft company is completely free to decide how stiff they want their R or S or whatever letter flex to be.

You can read how one attempt to standardize flex in the golf industry failed in "What IS Standard Anyway?" at the end of this chapter. It explains why, if you are choosing a shaft for your clubs and you want an S-flex because that's what you've always had in the past, you will have

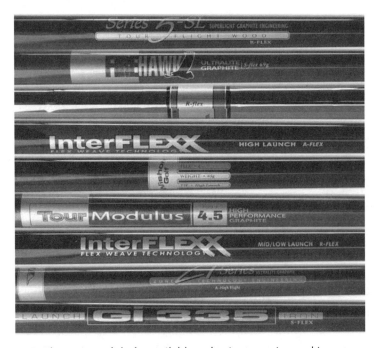

Figure 5.1. The variety of shafts available today is staggering and is one very good reason why golfers should rely on the expertise of professional clubmakers.

no idea how stiff that S-flex in the new shaft is just by looking at the label or the printing on the shaft. One thing is true, at least most of the time—within the SAME COMPANY'S CLUBS in the SAME MODEL OF SHAFT, you can assume with reasonable accuracy that the flexes do increase in stiffness from L to A to R to S to X, even though you will have no idea by how much. Heckuva way to run a system, isn't it?

This is another reason I became so interested in shafts and have done so much shaft analysis and research in my 32 years in this crazy business. I recognized the confusion, discovered no one could answer my questions, and I figured I had to find it out for myself.

I will never forget back in 1972 when I first realized this and started my real "quest" for definitive information about shaft flex. In the golf course pro shop where I worked at the time as a club pro and did my clubmaking work, we kept all of the single drivers displayed vertically on a shelf, heads down with the shafts leaning back against the wall.

We had about four different company brands of drivers in stock. All were shafted with True Temper's popular Dynamic steel shaft design because, back then, that was the most popular shaft golf companies used in their clubs. We had all of the Dynamic S-flex drivers lined up side-by-side, then the Dynamic Rs.

One morning as the sun first popped in through the window, it happened to shine on the drivers in such a way that the little changes in diameter on the steel shafts called step-downs were reflecting the sun's rays. I happened to look up at the drivers when the reflections off the shafts caught my eye. All of a sudden for some reason it hit me that the position of the step-downs on the shafts were not located in the same place on each driver that was built with the same Dynamic S-flex steel shaft. Hmm, I thought, all of these are the same shaft, same flex, and yet the step-downs on these shafts don't line up. Wouldn't that mean that each is a different stiffness?

Not realizing I was about to open a can of worms, I picked up the phone and called True Temper Corporation, makers of the Dynamic steel shaft. Eventually I was passed on to a technical person so I could ask, "What is your definition of how stiff your Dynamic S-flex shaft is to be in a driver?" A long pause followed from the other end of the line. Soon the technician came back, not with an answer but with a question, "Um, how stiff do you want it to be?"

Well, now I was really confused because I thought this was a "cut-and-dried" situation, so I explained what I had observed from the different step-down positions on all these different drivers built with the same shaft. The technician then very casually said, "We make the Dynamic S-flex shaft and sell it to all the club companies, but they make up their own minds how they want to install it in their drivers."

So I asked, "Well, how do I know which installation of the Dynamic S-shaft makes the flex correct"? To which the True Temper shaft technician ended the conversation by saying: "You just try them out and pick the one that feels the best to you." Now wasn't *that* a scientific solution for how to fit a shaft?

As it has always been, each shaft company has their own method of defining the stiffness of their shafts using equipment that actually turns out numerical measurements. So do some of the golf club companies. But no one openly shares that information with you, me, or anyone else. Try calling one of the big club companies and ask them how they measure and define their shaft flexes. Good luck. I have called a few, only to be told: "That's proprietary information we can't share with you." Loosely translated that means "You might be a competitor trying to fool us to find out information that we don't want you to know."

There are several empirical ways to measure the stiffness of a shaft, but the two predominant methods are called deflection and frequency testing. Both center around applying a known weight or force on the tip end of the shaft to measure how much the shaft bends. The less the shaft bends under the force, or the faster the shaft flutters (oscillates) up and down, the stiffer the flex of the shaft (see fig 5.2).

Fortunately, there are more and more shaft manufacturers who are providing information to match golfer swing speed with the flex of each model they design. If you took the time to scan through the swing speed–to–shaft model and flex charts that most shaft makers display on their Web sites, you would see that they do often list a little higher swing speed recommendation for the same flex of one shaft model as another. So the shaft makers are aware of the fact that differences they create in one shaft model vs. another might require a little different golfer swing speed to be properly matched with the right shaft flex. Without a swing speed recommendation for shafts, it becomes very difficult for any golfer to really have his or her swing characteristics fitted to the correct shaft flex. And unfortunately, most of the big club companies do not provide their retailers with swing speed recommendations for any of the stock shafts they install in the standard made clubs carried in all of the pro shops and off-course golf stores.

I would bet the farm that there is no one in the world who can tell me how many different shaft models and flexes within each model are made in the golf equipment industry today. I have probably tested more shafts in my career than any human in the history of the game, and I

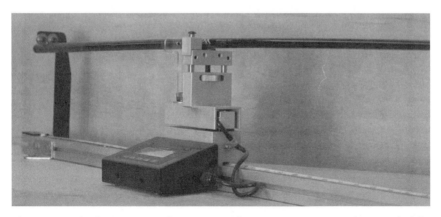

Figure 5.2. The frequency analyzer *(top* and *center)* can measure the speed of the oscillation of a shaft to note its stiffness, while a deflection machine *(bottom)* measures the amount of force required to bend a shaft a certain amount as another means of empirically measuring shaft stiffness.

know I couldn't come within several hundred of the correct answer! Suffice it to say your choices in shafts among all the clubs made today are absolutely mind-boggling. So here's what you need to know about shaft flex to make at least a dent in ending some of the confusion.

- From a pure shaft performance standpoint, 90 percent of you are going to be better off with a shaft that is more flexible than what you think you need.

Let me put it this way. If you happened to end up with a shaft that is too stiff for your swing speed and your swing mechanics, the ball will go a little shorter in distance because it will probably fly a little lower; you might have a tendency to see the ball fly over to the fade side of the target; and your feeling from hitting the ball on the center of the face will be a little more "harsh," as if the club felt like it vibrated a little more in the hands.

On the other hand, if you happened to end up with a shaft that is too flexible for your swing, the ball might fly a little higher and from that, possibly a little farther; it might cause a fade shot to fade a little less or a draw shot to draw a little more; and the feeling of an on-center impact on the clubface will be softer or more solid-feeling to your hands. Of the two, choosing the second choice is a no-brainer.

- Unless you work with a professional clubmaker to make your shaft selection, you will have to do a lot of trial-and-error test hitting of all sorts of shafts before you come up with a decision.

You might be able to guess that you want to have an R- or an S-flex for example, but because the R from one company can be very different in stiffness from the R of another, you have no other alternatives but to: (a) do trial-and-error testing to see for yourself how stiff or flexible that new R- or S-flex shaft really is compared to your old one; or (b) listen to a retail salesperson who 9 times out of 10 won't know enough about shafts to really help ensure that you get the right one for your swing.

You might be measured for your swing speed in a retail golf store, but I am here to tell you that virtually NONE of the big companies that make the standard golf clubs stocked in the retail shops ever provide their retailers with a reference chart to indicate what swing speed matches up with which flex in each shaft model they offer. So the recommendation of the retail salesperson will either be a guess or based on which flex they have more of in their inventory.

A competent clubmaker will measure your swing speed, then observe your swing mechanics to look for things like your tempo, how you start the downswing, and where in the downswing you release your wrist-cock. The clubmaker will then ask you some questions about how you want to see the ball fly and other performance goal queries to determine what you want to achieve that could be associated with the shaft's performance. He or she will then reference the files of shaft information that he gets from his suppliers, or from research on shaft testing that they or other clubmakers have done and made available to each other. He will also have more precise lists of what swing speed matches well to what shaft flex for what shaft design. After that, he will make a recommendation and possibly build a test club for you to hit to obtain feedback. The clubmaker may also have a launch monitor which can be used to actually measure the launch angle contribution of the shaft as you swing the club. And in the end, the clubmaker will come up with a far more accurate recommendation of which shaft is likely to perform and feel best to YOU.

- There is the letter flex of the shaft and then there is the distribution of the shaft's stiffness over the entire length of the shaft (called flex profile or bend profile). Both must be considered in the shaft flex fitting to optimize shaft performance for your game.

Shaft designers can and do make their different model shafts within each letter flex to have different bending characteristics in different areas of the shaft. This is done primarily to offer golfers a little different option for the feel and the height of the shot. Perhaps you have read about shaft models that are offered in "high flight," "mid flight," and "low flight" versions. What this means is that the shaft designer has changed the distribution of the stiffness over the length of the shaft to allow the shaft to bend forward more before impact (higher flight), bend forward a little less (medium flight), or bend forward not much at all before impact (lower flight).

For example, if a golfer with a medium-to-late wrist-cock release on the downswing needed to play a shaft that would fly the ball higher to maximize carry distance, the shaft would be designed to be of the overall stiffness to match his swing speed and tempo, but would likely be more flexible in the tip half of the shaft. Increasing the flexibility of the tip section will allow the shaft to bend forward a little more before impact with the ball, and thus increase the trajectory and height of the shot (see fig. 5.3).

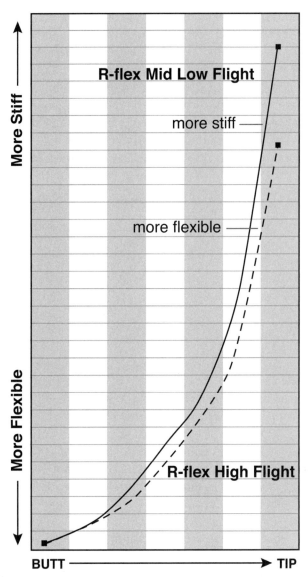

Figure 5.3. The two curved lines on the graph represent the stiffness measurement for two different shafts of the same letter flex, each with a different bend profile to create a different height for the shot. From the graph it can be seen that the shaft represented by the lower curved line is more flexible in the tip half of the shaft than the other, and thus that two shafts of the same flex could hit the ball with different results of height.

Were the same golfer to need a shaft that would lower his ball flight a little, the shaft would be the same overall flex but designed to be stiffer in the tip half of the shaft. Stiffening up the tip half of the shaft would reduce its amount of forward bending and from that, keep the ball flight a little lower. Because there are so many different ways that a shaft can be designed to distribute its stiffness and thus change the shot height and bending feel of the shaft, here is another reason to seek a competent professional clubmaker who has good experience in shaft fitting.

No one knows everything there is to know about shafts, not even I, for all of the work I have done in shaft analysis and shaft research and design. But there are clubmakers who really are "into" shafts, and taking a little time to inquire and find such a clubmaker when you are searching for the right answers will return dividends in the form of better shaft fitting recommendations.

- Your swing speed is the first indicator for selecting the right shaft flex. But your swing itself, how much and where in the downswing it applies more or less bending force to the shaft, is a very important factor that has to be considered in the shaft flex fitting as well.

If you really never notice or you do not place much importance on the "feel" of the shaft's bending during the swing, you will be a good candidate for selecting a flex that, if anything, is a little more flexible than what your swing speed might otherwise indicate. If you do place a high level of importance on the particular "feel" of the shaft's bending movements, then without question you must match your specific swing movements to the design of the shaft's overall flex profile.

For golf swings that are more aggressive, faster in tempo, and with the wrist-cock release coming midway to later in the downswing—go with shafts that would be within your swing speed range but slightly stiffer in the tip section. You could also select shafts that have a swing speed rating that is slightly higher than your actual swing speed since these swing characteristics would bend the shaft a little more.

For golf swings that are much less aggressive, smoother in tempo, with the wrist-cock release coming earlier in the swing—go with shafts that would be within your swing speed range but slightly more flexible in the tip section. You could also select shafts that have a swing speed rating that is slightly lower than your actual swing speed since swing moves like this would bend the shaft a little less in the swing. (Later we will offer a step-by-step guideline for shaft fitting.)

Now, Don't Get Torqued Off

Most golfers who read a lot about equipment and are more particular about their shaft selection are aware of the term "torque" in a discussion of shafts. Mechanical engineers are, too, because they cringe in academic pain over the shaft industry's improper use of the term! But "torque" has been used to describe a shaft's resistance to the twisting forces placed upon it in the swing ever since graphite shafts made their debut in the 1970s, so 30+ years of tradition says we leave it alone and let the engineers continue to cringe.[1]

Because the USGA Rules of Golf say that all wood, iron, and wedge heads must have the shaft inserted in the heel end of the clubhead, virtually the entire weight of the head will be sticking out from the shaft. That means during the downswing, the clubhead could put a fair amount of twisting force (torque, in the proper use of the term) on the shaft. If the golfer has a very powerful downswing and the shaft is made with little resistance to twisting, the head could twist the shaft before hitting the ball and cause a shot that flies off-line.

Such was the case with the first fiberglass and then the first graphite shafts made in the late 1960s and early 1970s. Back in the mid-1960s, when fiberglass became the first composite material used to make a shaft, Gary Player jumped on a lucrative contract offered by the Shakespeare shaft company before he really spent much time playing with the black-colored fiberglass shafts. When Player discovered the shafts had poor resistance to twisting and caused some pretty errant shots, he killed two birds with one stone and solved his problem by putting his old steel shafts back into his clubs but painted them black to look like the finish on the fiberglass shafts he was supposed to play! That allowed him to keep the contract and still play the shafts with which he was most comfortable!

Some of you who have played since the early 1970s, may recall that graphite shafts went through the same performance issue as well. The initial graphite shafts had very little resistance to twisting, which created some pretty scary looking shots! It was not until the 1980s, when shaft makers discovered how to change their method of manufacturing to give

---

[1]The term torque actually refers to the force of twisting that may be put on an object. However, the golf shaft industry has used the term to describe the designed ability of a shaft to resist the force of torque as described by a special test, for which again there is no standard in the golf industry!

their shafts much better resistance to twisting, that graphite established a permanent foothold in the shaft industry. Steel shafts, on the other hand, never went through this problem because steel has an inherent built-in resistance to twisting by virtue of the properties of steel when formed into a tubular shape. The reason that composite material shafts like fiber-glass and graphite experienced early torquing problems is that these materials are really a bundle of little fibers all held together parallel to each other by a high-grade form of glue.

Early composite shafts were made with these fibers all running straight up and down the shaft so that the shafts could be made with enough stiffness and strength to withstand normal use in a golf club. However, because all of the fibers in the early composite shafts were only aligned up and down the shaft (called "zero-ply" layers), there was very little resistance to twisting. Thus, when graphite shaft makers discovered that wrapping some of the layers with the fibers aligned at an angle to the shaft (called angle-ply layers) would increase the shafts' resistance to twisting, graphite found a permanent home in the shaft industry.

A Matter of Degrees

A shaft's resistance to twisting is rated by a test each shaft manufacturer performs in which the shaft is clamped with a weight hung on an "arm" that sticks out from the tip end. The number of degrees that the shaft twists when this specific weight is suspended from the test apparatus is measured, and each shaft is rated by its degree reading from the test. The lower the number of degrees, the more resistance the shaft has to twisting.

Currently, graphite shafts are made with torsional stiffness between 1.5 degrees torque to 8 degrees torque. Steel shafts will display a much more narrow range of torque than graphite. Their range will be between 2 degrees and about 3.5 degrees because their torque cannot be changed once the diameter and wall thickness of the shaft are established by the requirements of the steel shaft's flex and weight design.

With graphite shafts, because the torque is controlled by the number of "angle-ply" layers wrapped around the shaft, it is possible to make almost any combination of flex plus torque together in the same shaft. Thus, graphite can offer a wider range of design options in shafts than can steel (see fig. 5.4).

Some golfers believe the shaft's torque causes errant shots by twist-

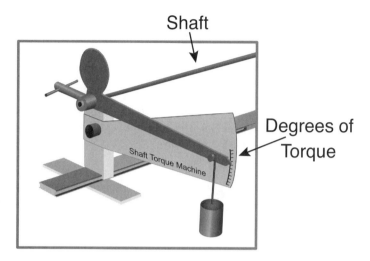

Shaft

Degrees of
Torque

Figure 5.4. The means of measuring a shaft's resistance to twisting involves hanging a weight on an arm extended from the tip end of the shaft and noting the number of degrees the shaft twists. The lower the degrees of twist, the more the shaft can resist twisting and the stronger and faster the golfer's swing should be to use the shaft. The higher the degrees of twist in the test, the less the shaft can resist twisting, which matches best to the golfer with a smoother, slower, and less aggressive swing.

ing when the ball is hit off-center on the face of the clubhead. The truth of the matter is that if torque becomes the culprit for a truly visible off-line shot, it does its dirty work by allowing the head to twist and change the position of the face BEFORE the clubhead ever hits the ball. And, almost always, this twisting will cause the face of the clubhead to turn open and thus cause a shot to push to the slice side of the target. Thus, if you hit a shot off the toe of the clubhead that hooks, even though you may feel the head twist, it was the "gear effect" action of the toe shot on the clubhead that caused the hooking spin on the ball, and not the twisting of the shaft.

I hope I have not planted a seed of fear that graphite shafts will hit the ball crooked because they twist. If so, then it's time to calm your nerves about torque and shot accuracy.

It's true that the early graphite shafts had a serious problem with torque. Those shafts, if measured on modern torque measurement equipment would be shown to have a torque measurement of 15–20 degrees!! Today, it is very rare to see a shaft with more than 6 degrees of torque. Those with such higher torque will almost always be women's flex shafts. Since the player expected to use such a shaft would have a much slower swing speed, her or his ability to twist the shaft would be far less, hence the less resistance to twisting in a shaft is also matched to the flex of the shaft.

To give you a point of comparison to this, there are many PGA Tour players using graphite shafts in drivers with 3.5 degree to 4.5 degree torque measurements. Thus, if you think that you need to have a 2 degree torque shaft to ensure accuracy in your shotmaking, it is simply not necessary. Playing with a shaft with a very low torque will increase the feeling of stiffness of the shaft. Thus, if the golfer does not have enough strength and a high enough swing speed, a shaft with only 2 degrees torque would end up feeling stiff and "dead," and that is even if the flex of the shaft were matched to the golfer's slower swing speed!

There really are only two things to keep in mind about shaft selection with torque in mind.

- If you are a golfer with a quick tempo and a fast, aggressive swing, stay away from graphite shafts with 5 degrees or higher torque and do not think shafts with a torque measurement of 3.5 degrees to 4.5 degrees will cause errant shots.

If you have a problem with accuracy, 99 times out of 100 it will be because the length of the club, the swingweight/balance/total weight of the club, or the face angle of the head is not well matched to your swing. Off-line shots that are caused by the golfer overtwisting the shaft do not tend to exhibit a curving flight—they are usually recognized by the ball tending to just "hang" over to the fade side of the target with little or no fade curve on the flight of the ball.

- If you are a golfer with a driver swing speed of 85 mph or less with average to smooth tempo and no real sense of aggression in the downswing, stay away from shafts designed with a torque measurement of 3 degrees or lower!

Even if the flex of a shaft is well matched to your swing speed and swing tempo, players with slower swing speeds (<85 mph) will find that shafts with torque measurements of 3 degrees and less display a very stiff and harsh feel, even when you make a great swing and hit the ball on the sweet spot of the clubhead.

Just remember these "two torque tips," and don't worry about shaft torque after that.

But . . . How Do You Feel?

Try this exercise. Turn on the faucet in your kitchen, put your hand under the stream and then try to put into words the definition of what you feel without using the word "wet." Think about it. You know the feeling, but you can't even begin to describe it without using the word "wet," can you?

For golfers who place an emphasis on the "feel" of the shaft during the execution of a shot, it's almost the same thing. Yet, for many golfers, the right shaft is ALL about "feel."

Let me give you a few examples of things I have heard from golfers with whom I have worked in my career who possess a fanatical sense of feel for the bending of the shaft. Phrases and comments used to convey a negative response to the bending feel of the shaft may include the following: "It feels too loose," "It feels too boardy," "The tip is just a little too late," "It doesn't feel like I can really control it," "Too much shaft for me," "Impact feels a little harsh," or "It's not right *there* when I want it to be." On the other hand, when the shaft falls right into the golfer's comfort range, I hear things like, "Man, THAT is solid," "I hardly felt a thing," "The ball feels real hot when it takes off," or "I know right where it is all through the swing." Talk about leaving an analytical clubfitter a little short in the way of definitive, empirical specifics!!

But that is what shaft feel is all about—listening to the golfer who has the sensitivity to detect bending differences in the shaft and trying to translate their often vague, descriptive feedback into specific recommendations for the overall flex and the flex profile of the shaft. While you may not be able to specifically describe the feeling of water streaming over your hand, some of us who perform in-depth research in this area are getting close to being able to empirically identify shaft-bending feel.

I am very pleased to have been the first to start measuring and graphing the shaft's flex profile. I can tell you it began as a result of pulling my hair out trying to get PGA touring pro Scott Verplank's shafts to all "feel the same" in each iron in the set I designed for him at the time of his comeback from elbow surgery. (See Chapter 13 for some of my Adventures in Clubmaking.)

While I have not fully completed my work on flex profile identification as I write this book, I look forward to doing so. When it's complete it will be possible for golfers who are "very picky" about the feel of their shafts to use graphs to compare the way shafts bend over their entire length, and from that be able to know if a new shaft being considered will possibly display the same feel as one the golfer formerly played and liked.

In the meantime, for all golfers who place a premium on the bending feel of the shaft, there are a few simple tips I can offer to guide your search.

When a shaft elicits comments like, "too loose," or "too whippy," or "I don't feel I can control it," it might be easy to say that the shaft is too flexible. But you have to know that there are generally two types of "too flexible" that you have to dig into before you know what to do.

First, a shaft can be too flexible in the tip section or too flexible overall in the whole shaft. If the shaft feels too flexible the second you start the downswing, this would indicate the overall flex of the shaft is not stiff enough. In such a case, you would want to move to the next-stiffest letter flex. On the other hand if the shaft does not feel too whippy until later in the downswing, closer to the moment of impact, this would tend to indicate the shaft's overall letter flex is probably okay, but that it is too flexible in the tip section. Thus, you would be better off staying in the same letter flex of the shaft, but selecting a model that was designed to be a bit stiffer in the tip section of the shaft.

On the other side of the bending-feel coin, when a golfer offers feedback such as, "too boardy," "dead-feeling," "the ball just wants to hang," these are all indications that in some way, the shaft is too stiff. In most cases when a golfer indicates these feelings, the remedy is more often one full letter flex code softer in the stiffness of the shaft rather than moving to a more tip-flexible version in the same letter flex.

If the golfer says the feel of impact is "okay," or "reasonably solid," but the ball flight is either a little too low, or they have to "make a little more aggressive swing" to be able to make the club feel good, then the overall general flex is okay, but it's likely too stiff in the tip section. At the end of the day, shaft fitting for bending feel is still more trial and error based on listening to feedback—at least until I get around to finishing my work on analyzing and illustrating shaft flex profile!

To Reshaft or Not, That Is the Question

Ever been to a PGA Tour event and noticed that the shafts in the pros' clubs are not the same as the shafts in the clubs you see on the racks in the pro shop or off-course golf stores? Well, you're seeing a classic example of the reason for custom clubfitting.

The stock shafts that the big assembled club companies put in their standard made clubs are created or chosen on the basis of what each company thinks "average golfers" need to have. In no way do those shafts have the flex profile design that matches properly to the pros' swings, so the pros all have their endorsement contract clubs reshafted with shaft models that either: (a) the pro is familiar with from having used it before in another club; or (b) strikes the pro's fancy as being new and able to deliver the "magic!" That's what all of those vans are for that you see parked near the driving range at each tour event during the Monday-to-Wednesday practice round days. Daylight to dark, the technicians in the caravan of trailers following the tour from week to week switch shafts for the pros more than any other club adjustment imaginable.

- Please think twice before you head out and reshaft your clubs with the "hot shaft" you hear is being used by the pros.

Shaft fitting is so much about matching the golfer's swing character-istics to the weight and flex profile design of the shaft. Unless you have similar swing fundamentals to the pros, the shafts with which they play are not likely to be the best match for your swing. Most tour players have the ability to swing in excess of 110 mph, have a powerful downswing move at the ball, and have a late release of the wrist-cock; and if you froze their swing at impact, you would see a straight line all the way from their shoulder through their hands to the clubhead, with their head well behind the ball. All of these swing characteristics lend themselves well to shaft designs which are stiffer overall and in varying levels of being stiffer in the tip end of the shaft as well. Hence, in varying degrees that is how most of the shafts you see and hear being used on the PGA Tour are designed.

So while it might qualify as a status symbol to pull your driver out of the bag installed with the latest hot shaft from the tour, be honest in evaluating your swing characteristics before you pull the trigger on such shafts, even if you wind up playing a shaft that is "one flex softer."

On the other hand, reshafting your current driver or clubs is fine, because the "universal" shaft design chosen by each club company will not fit each and every golfer and golfer swing type. If you are considering new shafts in your clubs, as I mentioned before, the only place you're going to have a good chance of being matched up properly will be at the shop of a skilled and experienced clubmaker.

Professional clubmakers are used to working with a wide variety of products. For one thing, their suppliers carry hundreds of different shafts.

If he or she has been working in clubmaking for a number of years, the clubmaker will not only have the experience to know the differences between shaft models, but will probably have feedback from other golfers already fitted with the shafts you are considering. Thus the clubmaker will be more used to observing your swing characteristics and using experience to recommend the right shaft. Besides, not many retail golf shops offer the service of reshafting clubs, since their preferred business is selling new standard made clubs.

To Steel or Not to Steel

One of the most common questions I hear from golfers is whether they need graphite shafts or not. Sometimes the question is almost posed with a sense of fear similar to when you hear the service manager at the garage tell you it's going to cost a thousand dollars to get your car in tip-top shape! Yes, most graphite shafts cost more than most steel shafts, but let's take a look at the whys and wherefores on shaft material decision-making, and then you can decide for yourself.

The number one reason graphite shafts exist is to create shafts of the lightest weight possible. Lighter shaft means lighter total weight of the golf club, which means less effort to swing the club, a higher possible swing speed, and from that, more distance.

You can hardly find a steel-shafted driver in any of the golf shops these days because the driver is all about distance, and so are the light graphite shafts. Drivers are obviously the longest club in the bag, so a lighter shaft can afford a little more ease in swinging, whatever length you end up with in the driver.

In short, the only way you should consider using steel in the driver and fairway woods is:

- If you are well above average in physical strength *and* you prefer a high total weight in the club to help prevent your already quick tempo from getting any quicker.
- If you have already tried graphite WITH a high swingweight in the driver or woods and still felt the total weight of the club was just too light to allow you to control your tempo and swing timing and rhythm. Otherwise, with the variety of different weights of graphite shafts available, consider graphite in the woods for sure.

- If you have tried graphite and you simply prefer the impact feel that steel delivers.

For the irons, let's take it from the opposite side and talk about which golfers are the best candidates for graphite shafts.

First and foremost, irons are about accuracy. While we all hate to hit a lower-numbered club from the 150 marker than we are used to, the cure is not necessarily a new shaft. Distance in the irons can also be dialed up a little by small decreases in loft, done by your clubmaker bending the hosels of the irons a bit.

Golfers who should consider moving to graphite in the irons would include golfers who:

- are below average in physical strength,
- have noted a recent loss in strength and body flexibility,
- have lost distance with their irons,
- notice the irons feeling heavier and requiring more effort to swing on the back nine or after hitting 20–30 balls with the irons on the driving range,
- experience minor hand, elbow, or shoulder discomfort from the feeling of impact with the ball.

If you are not in the market to buy a complete new set of graphite-shafted irons and prefer to change to graphite using your current ironheads, you must keep two things in mind.

1. Iron shafts just don't bend as much in the swing as do wood shafts.

Staying away from all the complicated explanations as to why, that means that you should consider choosing one flex letter softer in the graphite iron shafts than you used with steel shafts. The increase in flexibility could help make the ball fly a little higher and thus allow you to carry the ball a little farther than before. And take my word, one flex softer in iron shafts is NEVER going to make the shafts feel too whippy—again, because iron shafts simply do not bend as much in the swing as do wood shafts.

If your swing tempo is on the smoother side with less of an aggressive tempo, pick graphite iron shafts that weigh in the range of 60–70 grams. If you tend toward a more aggressive or quicker tempo, pick graphite iron shafts that are in the range of 70–80 grams. In either case, if your switch to graphite in the irons is away from steel, even an 80 gram graphite shaft will make your irons at least 30 percent lighter than they were before. You do remember what a lighter shaft can do, right? Hint—it starts with the letter 'D'!

> 2. If you are reshafting your current irons with graphite, be absolutely sure that the clubmaker or shop doing the reshaft adds weight to the clubheads, i.e., reswingweights the irons, as a part of the total job.

When you remove a steel shaft and replace it with a graphite that weighs 40–50 grams less, the swingweight balance of the club will be too light for you to swing consistently unless weight is added to the head. Way too often in my career I have seen or heard a graphite reshaft blow up in the face of the golfer because the swingweight of the clubs was not reestablished for the new, much lighter, shafts.

Fitting the Puzzle Together

Okay, so you say, "All that stuff you've said about shafts is fine and dandy, but how the heck am I supposed to know what shaft is right for ME?" Good question.

First, out of the 2,000 or so different shafts made today (all right, that's *my* educated guess for the total number), there are likely something like 150–300 of them that would perform well and properly fit any given golfer. For some golfer swing types there are even more that will satisfactorily do the job of transferring the energy of the swing to the clubhead and the feeling of impact back to the golfer.

The reason for such a high number is that so many shafts are designed so close to each other in their specifications. Shaft makers identify certain golfer swing types and design their shaft selections to match those different categories of swings.

So, in general:

- Shafts designed for good ball-strikers are going to be medium stiff to pretty stiff in the overall flex, and the same as well for the tip section of the shaft.
- Shafts for most average male golfers are going to be medium stiff to flexible in both the overall stiffness and the tip section design.

- Shafts for slower swing speed players such as seniors and women will be both softer in overall flex and tip section stiffness.

The colors and the names on the shafts might be different, but from a pure design and performance standpoint there really are a ton of shafts out there today that are virtually clones of each other in terms of their flex profile design. Yes, there are variations on the three basic schemes of shaft design, but that is primarily for increasing the shaft company's sales options, as well as for the pros and then the golfers who simply have to experiment to find that shaft with the "right feel."

But this raises an interesting question. If you have two shafts with the same weight, same torque, and flex profiles that are almost identical, would you not be talking the same performance, no matter the material and labor, and ultimately the price?

Cost and Quality: Getting What You Pay For

I know that one of the burning questions among golfers is why shafts vary so much in price, and do you get what you pay for when you spend more for a shaft?

In general, among steel shafts you do; with graphite shafts *sometimes* you don't. Let me explain.

When it comes to steel shafts, cost differences are all about the manufacturing expertise and machinery used in forming the shaft, combined with the cost of the steel alloy from which the shaft was made, with a fair amount of labor thrown in as well.

The steel shafts you see on sets sold in Kmart or Wal-Mart are usually "seconds" with slight manufacturing defects and blemishes, or they are intentionally made by the steel shaft companies to be lower-cost "second-grade" shafts club companies require for use in such low price clubs. These shafts will have wider variations in straightness, wall thickness, weight, and, as a result, in their flex as well. They may have fewer "step-downs" on the shaft which means a lower cost in their manufacturing. They are, as advertised, low-cost because their lower price is required for use in sets of 3 woods and 8 irons that retail for less than $300. In other words, in this case, you get what you pay for.

Some of the new very lightweight steel shafts, those you see that weigh in the area of only 95–105 grams, can be made only by using more expensive steel alloys with adjustments in the shaft-forming process that require more attention and care to shape the higher strength steel into the "tubes." Hence, the higher price of shafts such as the True Temper TX-90 and Royal Precision Air-Lite is easily justified.

In between are the first quality semi-lightweight to standard-weight steel shafts (115–130 g weight range) such as Dynamic, TT Lite, Dynalite, Rifle, etc. Rifle steel shafts from Royal Precision cost a little more because making a steel shaft with a constant straight taper on the outside of the shaft (i.e., no step-downs) is a more expensive process of manufacture than making shafts with graduated changes in diameter called step-downs. Dynamic Gold and Dynalite Gold cost more than their "non-Gold" versions because someone has to weigh all of the Dynamics and Dynalites to group them into the little "sub-flexes" in which each shaft is offered.

In graphite, is there ever a difference in price and quality! Much of this happens because there is far more graphite shaft–making capacity in the world than there is demand. It costs a fortune to equip a company to make steel shafts. It only costs a small fraction of that, however, to buy the equipment to make graphite shafts. So there are a whole lot of graphite shaft makers who are all competing for the business.

And you know what happens next. He who writes the check calls the shots.

When a golf club company beats a shaft vendor senseless to get the lowest price possible, a common act which I have witnessed more times than I care to recall in my career, something has to give. In other words, the shaft maker is not in business to lose money, no matter how much he gets squeezed by the club company. So here's what happens.

About one-third of the cost of a graphite shaft is tied up in the labor and production procedures, the other two-thirds in the cost of the raw materials. Then there is an old adage in the graphite shaft business that goes, "lower torque and lighter weight cost money."

So if you see graphite shafts that are used in 3 wood + 8 iron packaged sets that sell at mass-merchant retailers for $399 or less, you are looking at shafts that have torque between 5 and 7 degrees, weight over 70 grams, and a much wider plus/minus tolerance in each of the shaft design specifications, including weight and flex.

Graphite shafts that weigh less than 60 grams, and/or have lower than 3.5 degrees of torque, rise dramatically in price. To achieve such low weight and torque specifications, the labor, engineering, initial raw material, and discarded material costs are all much higher. In other words, if you see a 45 gram graphite shaft with 2 degrees of torque, swallow hard, you will pay a pretty penny for that exotic shaft!

The Business of Shaft Making

The business of shaft manufacturing is one of the more interesting parts of the golf equipment industry. I mentioned previously that there are far more shaft makers, at least graphite shaft makers, than there is demand to fill their total capacity. Steel shaft makers don't have this problem because there are at present only six different companies in the world with the production capability to manufacture steel shafts. Graphite shaft makers? Well if you picked the number "100" out of the air that might not be too far from how many companies there are in the world today with the ability to manufacture a graphite golf shaft.

The vast majority of the volume in shaft making comes from what is called "private branding." This means the shaft companies get the vast majority of their business making the stock shafts that are installed in the standard clubs you see displayed on the racks in pro shops, off-course golf shops, sporting goods stores and mass-merchant retailers (i.e., Kmart, Wal-Mart, Target, etc.) Depending on the golf company and the intended final retail price-point of the standard clubs, these stock shafts might be designed to be different and unique (i.e., proprietary for use only by the one golf club company that provided the requirements for the design), or may simply be a stock shaft that the golf club company simply puts their name on.

There is no question that the lower the price of the standard made clubs sold through these traditional retail outlets, the lower the price and quality of the shafts. If you are talking about mass-merchant dealers, the graphite shafts in these clubs are sold to the clubmaking companies for a VERY low price. They have to be extremely low cost because any 11-club set retailing for $400 or less to the end user must have a wholesale price that allows the golf company to make 20–30 percent profit, and the mass merchant retailer to make at least a 40 percent+ profit margin.

Most of the graphite shafts that are made to be installed in the standard brand-name clubs sold in pro-shop and off-course golf stores are a medium-cost shaft. That's all they need to be because in large part, these shafts will weigh 60–70 g and typically will have a torque measurement not less than 4 to 4.5 degrees.

Most of these shafts are labeled only with the golf company's brand name. However, sometimes you will see a shaft that is labeled both with the golf company's name as well as that of the shaft manufacturer. This is done when the golf club company believes that the shaft company name is well respected and will add a perceived value to the shaft. In such cases, the golf company will usually pay more for that shaft because of the co-branding nature of the marketing.

In the 1980s and early '90s, it was common for the big golf club companies to use the shaft company's name on all their clubs and not to create their own branded shaft. With steel shafts that are marketed to the "better player" market, you still see this today, with companies using shafts labeled with the "True Temper Dynamic Gold" or the "Royal Precision Rifle" names. The reason again is perceived value from the target market. Better players are more familiar with the Dynamic Gold and Rifle steel shafts. The golf company knows this and is well aware using such shaft brands in their clubs will enhance the sales appeal of their irons.

In woods, you don't see this practice much anymore, and the reason is one of profit. Each shaft company produces shafts under their own brand name, and those shafts cover a wide spectrum of golfer types. But virtually none are used in any of the large club companies' wood clubs. Instead, virtually all the golf club companies choose to install a "private brand" shaft made by these same shaft companies in their stock clubs. The reason is twofold.

One, marketing in today's world is all about brand recognition, so the golf companies want to promote their own brand first and foremost to the public. Second, the shafts carrying the shaft company's name have a much higher cost than what the large club companies are willing to spend. Remember, those stock shafts in the big companies' clubs have to help ensure profit margins that are high enough to support their huge marketing programs.

But that's the way it is. The shaft business today is largely a buyer's market because of the old supply versus demand rule of business. The only way that the shaft makers can really "make it" is: (a) to do a LOT of volume, meaning millions of shafts, at the lower prices, or (b) promote their own branded shafts heavily on the professional tours so as to create a "reshaft and custom club" demand for their higher-priced, higher-margin shafts.

Approximately 10 or so of the shaft makers are very successful in competing in this brand-name shaft business, often called the "after-market" of the shaft industry. The more successful and well-known companies in this segment of the business are Aldila, True Temper, Royal Precision, Grafalloy (owned by True Temper), Graphite Design, Fujikura, and UST. Fringe players in this group who do not come close to the self-branded volume of these previous seven companies, but who have small but dedicated bands of followers are Penley, Harrison, and A.J. Tech. The rest of the 90 or so shaft makers have to depend strictly on private brand business from the many and diverse golf club assembly companies. As you can imagine, the competition for the large golf companies' big-volume shaft business is fierce, and price undercutting as a business practice is a way of life. There are not many industries in which it is more difficult to build a successful and profitable company, but the experienced and reputable ones do a very good job.

WHAT IS STANDARD ANYWAY?

Some of you who may work in technical or product related careers may be very aware of an organization called the *American Society for Testing and Materials*, otherwise known as the ASTM. This is the organization that sets the standards for product composition or measurement within all industries in the United States.

Well, the ASTM tried to get involved with the golf equipment industry a number of years ago, but because the industry members could not agree on a uniform set of standards, the ASTM gave up! I know, because I was a member of the ASTM committee charged with setting up standards for test procedures for measurements such as the flex and torque of golf shafts. With such standards it would then be possible to accurately compare the published specifications of a shaft made by one company to a shaft made by another.

After three years of trying, the ASTM had to cease their attempt to establish standard methods of measurements for golf shafts because the shaft manufacturing companies refused to agree on how to conduct such tests. In short, some of the companies wanted only to do it "their way," with compromise being a foreign word. *As a result, whether it comes to the clubheads, the shafts, the grips, or the assembly of golf clubs, no standards exist for measurement within the golf equipment industry.* Every maker of golf equipment is free to determine their own means of measuring any one of the 21 different specifications that make up a club.

What does that mean to you? It means that when you shop for clubs, you don't know if the loft of the 5-iron for example is 25, 26, 27, or 28 degrees. Or if the length of that 5-iron is

37.75 inches, 38 inches, 38.5 inches, or whatever. While lofts may be engraved on the woodheads, they almost never are on the irons, and no club on the planet made today clearly labels the length.

Of the companies that engrave a loft number on the bottom of their drivers, there are some that make the actual loft to be intentionally different from what they say it is on the sole—and we're not talking about minor +/- tolerances. We're talking a driver that says 10 degrees on the sole but is *always* made to be 11.25 degrees. I know this because I have had the chance to measure many, many drivers, and when you see 15 of the same 10 degree loft driver all measure the same 11.25 degrees on the nose, that's way too much of a coincidence.

So, I called this particular company to ask about this, and I received a gobbledygook response telling me they had a "special manner" of measuring loft and not to worry about anything, etc. The manner in which this company associate handled my question would have made a professional politician proud. On the other hand, since I know that far too few golfers use enough loft on their drivers, in the end I guess I have to applaud this company for "forcing" golfers into a club that will perform better for them.

The clubs and their specifications are what they are as determined by each club company. Heckuva deal, isn't it?

So, how does that mess you up? Let's say you're in the market to change your irons and the 5-iron in your current set has 26 degrees of loft and is 38.5 inches long. You have no idea if the loft of the 5-iron in the new set is the same. Sure, you could take your current clubs with you to lean side-by-side each similar numbered iron to check length, but loft is more influential on distance than length. Thus, you could walk out the door with the new set, head to the golf course and wonder what the heck is going on when you can't hit the 5-iron as far as you used to.

There are no standards in clubmaking, there are no standards for how each company measures whatever specifications they choose, and you're supposed to be able to play to the best of your ability with each club you buy.

Chapter 6—Spines and Grips and Stuff

Gettin' Some Spine

One of the most interesting recent developments in clubmaking is a practice called "spine alignment" or "spine matching." Not many golfers know about it, but it is a technology in shaft fitting that has the possibility of improving your on-center hit percentage, particularly with the woods. Here's the deal.

The Rules of Golf don't say a whole lot about the shaft. One thing that is written into the rules, however, is that the shaft "shall exhibit similar bending properties in all directions." That means no matter which way you rotate the shaft, it is supposed to bend exactly the same way under the same force. Now, this sounds like a logical requirement since shafts are all supposed to be completely round in the first place which, by the way, is one of the other requirements for a shaft in the Rules of Golf. If the shaft does exhibit the exact same bending properties in all directions it is said to be a "symmetrical" shaft. If it doesn't, it is an "asymmetrical" shaft.

It turns out that, no matter the shaft company, it's really difficult to make a perfectly symmetrical shaft. Oh, it can be done, but thanks to the fact that so many shaft companies get beat to death for lower prices, almost all shafts made today have some degree of asymmetry. The term "spine" was generated to refer to the shaft having planes of bending that are stiffer or more flexible on the same shaft (i.e., NOT similar in bending properties in all directions). What everyone doesn't agree on is whether the asymmetry is enough to result in off-line shots when you make a perfect swing.

The catch-22 in this is you don't know for sure if a shaft is causing mis-hits from its asymmetry unless you pony up the cash to have the shaft checked by one of the various "spine alignment" processes that now exist in the equipment industry. Once the desired spine is found, it is marked and from that a "stable" or consistent plane of bending is located. When the clubmaker builds your club, he will epoxy the shaft in place with the stable plane of bending in the 3 o'clock/9 o'clock position (aimed at the target) I mentioned back in Chapter 4 when I was explaining how the shaft bends in the swing. The result is supposedly a shaft that is much more consistent in its bending characteristics as it carries the clubhead forward to strike the ball.

You'll find golf equipment pundits who pooh-pooh the whole thing, taking the approach of "Much Ado About Nothing." But you'll also find substantial test data that say there might be something to it. In the somewhat rare case of a really badly asymmetric shaft, if realignment to a more stable 3 o'clock/9 o'clock plane is not done, the shaft would be very unlikely to allow the clubhead to hit the ball straight and on center. I've seen it, because I was deeply involved in the first real commercial testing of shaft alignment back in 1997.

However, I don't want to leave you with the impression that you have a bag of clubs with shafts that are wobbling all over the place every time you hit a ball. Things in the shaft manufacturing business have changed since spine aligning was invented.

Today, most of the higher-quality graphite shaft makers include a special test that is performed on every shaft to find a stable plane of bending before the shaft is painted and logoed. Thus, a normal installation of the shafts with the logo either straight up (12 o'clock position) or 180 degrees reversed from that will ensure that the stable plane of bending will be aimed at the target. (The problem here, in another little catch-22, is that there's no way of knowing whether your shaft was made by a company that performs this check or not unless you get hired to work in the golf equipment business!)

So, amid this vagary there are two reasons for golfers to consider one of the various forms of shaft spine alignment checking.

- If you know the length and the swingweight of a club is right for your swing and athletic ability, and you feel that there are times when you make a really good swing at the ball and you hit the ball off-center or you see the ball fly a slight to a medium amount off-line, this is a possible symptom that your shaft would be suffering from "shaft asymmetriosis."
- Reason two, if you are a total golf nut, total equipment nut, and you want to cover every single possible base to be sure your clubs are exactly right. In this case, having your shafts all spine checked would erase all possible chance that one or another of your shafts could be "infected."

If neither one is a problem with you, then forget it as long as your shafts are made by a reputable shaft company or shaft designer.

The process of shaft spine alignment checking is primarily the domain of custom clubmakers. There are licensed processes such as SST PURE® and PEAKED PERFORMANCE™ that some clubmakers offer. In addition, there exist a number of like-minded and interested clubmakers who have banded together through an internet forum called SpineTalk to discuss this phenomenon. These clubmakers share information and techniques as well as spine analysis equipment ideas to be able to do a very credible job of checking and realigning shafts to their most stable plane of bending.

How to Avoid Being Given the Shaft

Intimidated? Maybe a little gun shy? A little hesitant about making that shaft decision now that you know more than you ever wanted to? I promised myself I would not leave you hanging with only a chapter full of "19th Hole Trivia" facts. So, it's time to put this together in as simple an explanation as I can.

If you just want to buy a standard set and be sure that you end up with a shaft that is okay for your game, I can make that pretty simple.

Don't buy the clubs from a shop or store that can't at least measure your swing speed and show you how they are matching your swing speed with the selection of the shaft. Based on the stock shafts that are installed in the big companies' clubs as standard, follow this swing speed to a shaft flex chart for making your selections. If they won't provide their retailers with such flex fitting guidelines, then I will. This is a guideline only, based on the average stiffness measurements of the stock shafts installed in standard made clubs today (see table 6.1).

Almost all the stock graphite shafts that are installed in the larger companies' men's flex woods and labeled with the company's name will be pretty similar to each other—65–75 grams in weight, 4 to 5 degrees in torque, with the flex profile of the shafts designed to be not too stiff overall for each letter flex and not very stiff in the tip section. In fact, quite a number of the larger club companies have been putting softer flex shafts in their woods for several years and labeling them a flex higher. Why? Because they know the ego-driven propensity for so many male golfers to choose a "Stiff Shaft" when they really would be much better off with a "Regular."

Table 6.1—Swing Speed and Swing Tempo vs. Shaft Flexes in Standard Made Golf Clubs

Driver Swing Speed (mph)	Swing Tempo	Shaft Flex	5-Iron Swing Speed (mph)	Swing Tempo	Shaft Flex
<60	fast	L	<50	fast	L
<60	medium	L	<50	medium	L
<60	slow	L	<50	slow	L
60–70	fast	A	50–55	fast	L
60–70	medium	L	50–55	medium	L
60–70	slow	L	50–55	slow	L
70–80	fast	R	55–60	fast	A
70–80	medium	A	55–60	medium	L
70–80	slow	A	55–60	slow	L
80–90	fast	R	60–65	fast	A
80–90	medium	R	60–65	medium	A
80–90	slow	A	60–65	slow	L
90–100	fast	S	65–70	fast	R
90–100	medium	R	65–70	medium	R
90–100	slow	R	65–70	slow	A
100–110	fast	X	70–75	fast	R
100–110	medium	S	70–75	medium	R
100–110	slow	S	70–75	slow	R
>110	fast	X	75–80	fast	S
>110	medium	X	75–80	medium	R
>110	slow	S	75–80	slow	R
			80–85	fast	S
			80–85	medium	S
			80–85	slow	R
			85–90	fast	X
			85–90	medium	S
			85–90	slow	S
			>90	fast	X
			>90	medium	X
			>90	slow	X

Note: Accurately selecting the right flex for your clubs is a task that requires knowing your swing speed and swing type.

Unless you have a pretty specific requirement for the bending feel of your shafts, the stock shafts in the brand-name OEM clubs will perform reasonably well for a reasonably wide range of average to less-skilled golf swing types.

How do you know whether you need to move out of the company's stock shaft and into something different? Well, I mentioned one reason already, that being if you are "picky" about getting THE shaft for your game, and you have a preferred bending feel in your shafts. Other reasons to chuck the stock shaft and go for a specific shaft fitting are:

a. If you have a medium-late to late release of the wrist-cock on the downswing. That means if you videotape your swing and you see that the unhinging of the wrists begins when the club is at or below your belt, you have a medium-late to late release.

b. If you have reasonably good swing fundamentals but you hit the ball higher than most golfers with whom you play and you are uncomfortable with your high shot trajectory.[1]

c. If you tend to start the downswing very quickly and abruptly, as if before you finish the backswing.

d. If you have a more aggressive downswing tempo, and

e. Any combined factors together of a, c, and d.

Otherwise, follow table 6.1 for picking your flex among the stock shafts in the brand-name company's clubs and you'll be okay.

Now for you "picky players," you golfers who keep the shaft makers busy coming up with all their different shafts each year, here's the deal.

Go find a local professional clubmaker who has had a number of years' experience in studying this crazy world of golf shafts.

---

[1]An excessively high trajectory caused by poor swing fundamentals cannot be changed simply by the selection of a shaft made with a low or mid-trajectory flex profile design. If your ball position is off the left heel to off the middle of your forward foot, if you know that you deliver the club to impact with a straight line from your forward shoulder, down the arm, and down the shaft to the clubhead, and you still hit the ball higher than you are comfortable with, then yes, you are a candidate for a lower flight shaft design. But if you break the wrists forward before impact, thus letting the clubhead pass the hands before impact with the ball, or if you have a ball position at the left toe or more forward, your high trajectory is caused by these swing and position errors, so a shaft with a lower flight trajectory would not make any difference.

Yes, there are a number of the big-name companies who will build special orders for their clubs with different shafts offered through their custom department. But you need to know for sure what shaft brand, model, and flex is the right one for you before you order. They won't fit you; they will just install the shafts that you tell them to install from their list of different shaft options. So you have to know what exact shaft is right for your swing and feel requirements BEFORE you place a custom order with a large manufacturer of clubs.

I'm not going to tell you that every clubmaker is a shaft fitting expert either. Some do not yet have the depth of experience, while others are so into shaft design technology that their wives would probably tell you they need to "get a life." If you are really serious about the shaft, however, that's the person you need to find.

You certainly should talk to the clubmakers in your area and ask how they fit the shaft to the golfer. In short, a clubmaker with a good amount of shaft fitting expertise will follow most of these steps and perhaps add a few more of their own. For example:

- They'll measure your swing speed once you hit a few balls to get warmed up. If you are being fitted for both wood and iron shafts, the clubmaker will take separate swing speed measurements with the driver or 3-wood and then with any of the irons to separately address any differences between your wood and iron swing as well as the differences in the wood and iron shaft designs.
- The clubmaker will carefully watch, or even videotape, your swing to note such shaft-specific things as your swing tempo/ rhythm, how you start the downswing, when and how you unhinge your wrist-cock release, and your lead arm position at the moment of impact with the ball.
- You will be asked a bunch of questions about things like: what you liked or disliked in previous shafts you have played; whether you are interested in steel or graphite, and your own opinions of why; whether your current clubs feel too heavy, about right or too light; what ball flight and/or feel you want to achieve in the new shaft; what trajectory you have with your current shafts and what you want to achieve for the shot trajectory in the new shafts.
- How much money you want to spend!! This is not to tell the clubmaker how much to soak you, but is just one way for the clubmaker to start eliminating possible shafts from consider-

ation. Remember, there are many shafts out there that do not vary a lot in design from each other but do in price.

- The clubmaker may have test clubs for you to hit to try the shaft(s) being recommended. Or the clubmaker might take the approach of building you a test club to obtain your feedback over a number of ball hitting sessions on your own, after which the final decision will be made based on your input.

- Certainly not all experienced shaft fitting clubmakers have a launch monitor. Many do; more will in the not too distant future as the price of these sophisticated analysis units keeps coming down. If the clubmaker has a launch monitor you would be tested during the fitting with some of the shafts the clubmaker is considering as the recommendation for your clubs. Points the clubmaker would reference would be ball speed, and for sure the launch angle of the shots you hit with the test or trial club(s).

Now That You've Been Shafted, Get a Grip

If there is any part of the golf club that is most often overlooked, it is the grip. The heads and the shafts get lots more attention, so the grip is known as the "Rodney Dangerfield" of the golf equipment business.

Most golfers initially select grips as an afterthought; we rarely, if ever, clean them; and most will wear them down until they look like something that would be used to rake cobwebs off the ceiling. Yet few things about the club are more important because of one very important point . . . the grip is the golfer's ONLY contact with the club.

One of the golf companies recently conducted an experiment in which a number of golfers were asked to hit five shots in succession with each of three clubs. The clubs were exactly the same in all respects except one had a brand-new grip on it, the second had a clean but worn grip, and the third was not only worn but had not been cleaned in years (it even had a bit of sunscreen on it). The golfers using the new grip hit the ball an average of seven yards farther than those using the clubs with the worn grip and 13 yards farther than those with the dirty grip and the sunscreen.

It makes sense if you think about it. The grip is nothing less than the point that joins two amazingly complex machines: the golf club and the golfer. You can buy all the $500 drivers you want, but if you get the grip wrong, you might have wasted your money.

Basically, the grip needs to allow you to control the club without excessively tightening your hands. When you tighten your hands, you tighten your forearm muscles. When you tighten your forearm muscles, you develop "alligator arms," and your swing becomes short and cramped as opposed to long and fluid.

The earliest grips were made of leather with a cloth "listing" underneath to make the grip thicker. Leather strips, about an inch wide and 30 inches long, were cut and wound in a spiral around the butt end of the shaft. The two ends were secured by tacks, and the strips were further pressed into place with a device called a grip roller.

If this sounds as if it would result in a grip that is much thicker than the modern one, you'd be right. In fact, the old versions were closer in thickness to a tennis racket handle than to a modern grip. In some ways, however, this was okay because in those days they tended to play with the grip much more in the palm, while today golfers are taught to hold the grip more with the fingers. With a palm grip, you need a much thicker shaft grip to maintain control and comfort with the club.

Grips pretty much remained unchanged until the early 1900s. Wound-on rubber was tried for a time but soon lost appeal because, when it rained, your clubs tended to become unguided missiles.

During this period, two other types of grips were tried. The Cawsey grip was a one-piece grip, made of leather that could be slipped on the end of the shaft. The grips were sewn down the back, which created a ridge (now called a rib) that helped the golfer to line up his hands better to the face of the club. Primarily because of the expense of making these grips they didn't last long on the market, but providing a raised area on the bottom of the grip to help with the golfer's hand grip remains with us today in the "ribbed grip."

An improvement on the Cawsey grip was developed by Bussey, a company that made cricket bats as well as golf clubs. It was similar to the Cawsey grip in that it was one piece and sewn together down the back. It was an improvement in that the leather was very thin, it was made from a soft suede leather, and it had grooves cut all around its circumference that gave the golfer a better hold of the club. In many ways, it was a clear precursor to the modern grip.

Rubber grips began to appear in the late 1940s and were actually molded to the shaft. Thus, the club companies had to install big vulcanizing ovens that would literally cook the rubber on the shaft.

The modern grip, however, did not develop until after World War II. In the 1950s rubber and other materials became more available, and the one-piece, slip-on grip almost completely supplanted the leather-wound grip. Not only were they much easier to apply and replace, but they were much cheaper as well.

There was also a third advantage. Manufacturers soon realized that by varying the compounds used in the rubber, they could create a wide variety of textures. Today, the golfer is presented with a bewildering selection of grips in all manner of sizes, grip designs, textures, and even colors.

How to cut through that bewildering variety is our next subject.

Size and Texture

There has been a variety of measurement systems devised to fit you with the right-sized grip. Some are based on laying your hand over a printed template, some are based on your golf-glove size, and some are based on the proximity of the finger tips on your upper grip hand to the base of your hand when you take your upper hand grip on the club. None has really proved satisfactory, because we're faced again with that unmeasurable factor of fitting called "feel."

What it boils down to is this: *Find the grip that feels the best to you when you place it in your hand.* As a result of that principle, this is the way my friend Tom Grundner, a very fine clubmaker himself, prefers to do a "grip fitting."

First, Tom will give the customer a series of grips mounted on the ends of some cut-off shafts. They will be exactly the same grip (texture), but each will be a different diameter size. He will tell them to ignore the texture and fondle, caress, and grip each one until they come upon one whose size simply "feels right" in their hand. That tells him the correct size for that customer.

He would then lead them to a grip display rack and show them all the grips he has that are in their preferred size. Each one is a different texture, however. He will ask them to handle the grips until they find one that, again, "just feels right" to them.

That is the grip the golfer should use on their clubs.

Grips can be installed by a competent clubmaker to almost any size deemed to be comfortable by the golfer. I will never forget fitting former NBA great David Robinson from the San Antonio Spurs. The first thing I thought when we shook hands and I felt his hand completely engulf mine was what fun the guys in the production department were going to have installing these grips! Fifteen wraps of buildup oversizing tape per grip, and "The Admiral" was a happy camper with his new clubs. Unfortunately he went back to San Antonio and told his buddy George Gervin about this, and the next week the guys had to do the same 15 wraps all over again times 13 clubs for "The Ice Man!"

Generally, there are seven men's size categories of grips, each with a known (and agreed-upon in the golf industry, for once!) decimal size diameter attached to it. These decimal size diameter measurements refer to the actual diameter of the grip at a point 2 inches down from the end of the grip. They range from 1/64-inch undersize, to standard, to 1/8-inch oversized. Any competent clubmaker can fit virtually any size grip out of any size shaft-grip combination. Following is a table of the common grip sizes available and their diameter as measured 2 inches down from the end of the grip (see table 6.2).

When you go to many golf stores, however, the selection unfortunately narrows, as does the knowledge of how to install grips to precise diameter sizes. In general, you can get "Ladies," "Standard," "Midsize," or "Jumbo" grips, although whether the store has them in the texture or model you want is a separate issue. Because most golf retail stores do not employ qualified clubmakers, you tend to be stuck with what's available as opposed to what is right for you.

I believe that, if you have to err in one direction or another, err toward the larger size. Most golfers will be better off with a slightly oversized, rather than a slightly undersized, grip, if for no other reason than that they will tend to hold the club a little more relaxed. There is a belief among some golfers that if the grip is too large, it can promote more of a fade or slice. In my fitting research I have found if the grip is completely comfortable to the golfer, this is not going to happen. And believe me, comfort reigns supreme in the fitting of the grip size to the golfer.

Just as there exists a chart for measuring the golfer to guide him or her to the right club lengths, there also is a chart of hand and finger length measurements which can be used to help identify a suitable grip size for every golfer. That chart follows, but remember, if a grip other than what this hand-and-finger-length chart ordains happens to feel more comfortable to you, by all means go with comfort first in your grip size selection (see table 6.3).

Another area that is truly in the realm of the subjective in grip fitting is that of surface texture. There are a number of general categories: smooth rubber, wrap-style rubber, full-cord rubber, half-cord rubber, urethane wrap-style, urethane smooth surface, and real leather wrap.

The smooth rubber grip has what it implies: a smooth surface made of rubber usually with little molded markings to enhance traction. A wrap-style rubber grip is a rubber grip molded to look and feel like the spiral

Table 6.2—Common Grip Size Options

Men's Grip Size (inches)	Diameter at 2 in. (inches)	Women's Grip Size (inches)	Diameter at 2 in. (inches)
1/64 undersize	0.885	1/64 undersize	0.840
Standard	0.900	Standard	0.855
1/64 oversize	0.915	1/64 oversize	0.870
1/32 oversize	0.930	1/32 oversize	0.885
3/64 oversize	0.945	3/64 oversize	0.900
1/16 oversize	0.960		
3/32 oversize	0.990		
1/8 oversize	1.125		

Note: The proper fitting of grip size involves custom building the grips to a precise diameter.

wrap pattern of a leather grip. Thus, the hands and fingers will feel the grooves between the wrap surfaces. In addition, rubber grips may be manufactured from two different rubber hardnesses in the same grip to offer a different feel to each separate hand. This unusual new development in rubber grips makes it sound like "Rodney" is working hard for a little respect!

A full-cord grip has little linen or cotton strings embedded lengthwise in the rubber the full length and circumference of the grip to increase the friction level and help absorb hand perspiration. A half-cord may be made in one of two ways. First, with no cord on the top, or "12 o'clock surface" for an all-rubber feel to the thumbs but corded on the bottom, or "6 o'clock" half of the grip for absorption of hand moisture. Or the half-cord is made with far fewer strings embedded all around and up and down the grip so the golfer feels less of the cord fibers than in a full-cord grip.

The urethane grips are in essence an imitation of the old leather grips, but with the material of the grip made from a foam-backed urethane compound. Such grips may be wrapped or smooth in style and are usually characterized by their tackier surface feel. Finally, while they are rarely seen today and are REALLY expensive, real cowhide or calf leather grips are still available for golfers who prefer that feel as well. However, good luck on finding a clubmaker who is skilled at the wrapping technique for real leather—these clubmakers do exist but generally are recognized by the amount of gray in their hair!

Within each of those categories are a zillion degrees of surface hard-

Table 6.3—Hand and Finger Measurements vs. Grip Size

Hand Measurement (inches)	Middle Finger Length (inches)	Grip Size (inches)
<5-3/4	2 to 3	Junior
	3 to 4	Junior +1/64
	>4	Junior +1/32
5-3/4 to 6-1/2	2 to 3	Ladies Standard
	3 to 4	Ladies +1/64
	>4	Ladies + 1/32
6-1/2 to 7	2 to 3	Men's -1/64
	3 to 4	Men's Standard
	>4	Men's +1/64
7 to 7-3/4	2 to 3	Men's Standard
	3 to 4	Men's +1/64
	>4	Men's + 1/32
7-3/4 to 8-1/4	2 to 3	Men's +1/64
	3 to 4	Men's +1/32
	>4	Men's + 3/64
8-1/4 to 8-3/4	2 to 3	Men's +1/32
	3 to 4	Men's + 3/64
	>4	Men's + 1/16
8-3/4 to 9-1/4	2 to 3	Men's +1/16
	3 to 4	Men's + 5/64
	>4	Men's + 3/32

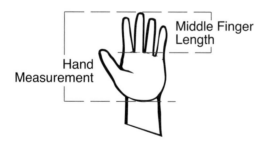

Note: Finding the correct grip size can also be done by measuring the two dimensions shown above and comparing those measurements to the grip size listings in the chart.

ness and types of texture design. Which you pick is completely up to you. As with size, the only test that's important is the "fondle and hold test." In other words, with apologies to the 1960s, if it feels good, play with it.

That being said, you also need to keep in mind that, as with every other aspect of the golf club, there are trade-offs whenever you make any selection. For example, you can pick that nice squishy soft-feeling grip but in all likelihood it will wear out more quickly than one made of a firmer compound. You can go for that nice smooth surface grip, but it could tend to be harder to control in the rain. Or you can opt for that slightly more expensive cord grip. They give you a super gripping surface, they absorb hand perspiration, and they wear like iron, but those little strings have a nasty habit of shredding golf gloves, not to mention the occasional patch of skin.

The point is that, even with those trade-offs, it is well worth your time to choose your grips carefully, take care of them properly (see Chapter 10), and install fresh ones them as frequently as you can afford. They are the ONLY thing that connects you to the club.

LOSING STIFFNESS

It is a common myth among golfers that shafts will lose stiffness over time due to constant flexing from years of ball-striking. Not so, and any number of tests have been performed to prove it.

The only way that a shaft can change performance and need to be replaced from wear and tear is (a) if it is bent, "kinked," badly rusted, or pitted (steel shafts only, of course); or (b) it is cracked, or a section of fibers of the graphite "de-laminates" from the surface of the shaft. If you happen to remove the grips from your steel shafts and note a bit of "rust-dust" on the inside of the shaft, don't worry, it won't have any negative effects on the shaft. The nickel/chrome plating on steel shafts is typically not done on the interior of the shafts, so moisture entering the shaft through the "vent-hole" on the end of the grip can cause some surface rusting on the inside of the shaft over time.

A common malady of graphite shafts is something called "bag-rash." Graphite shafts are finished by painting and sometimes clear urethane coating over the paint. Over time, as the shaft rubs against the dividers in the golf bag, the paint finish will rub off and leave the bare surface of the graphite shaft exposed. This is no different from a scrape on the fender of your car—you hate seeing it but the car (and the shaft) will continue to perform as designed.

Shaft companies are not in the practice of offering the service of "refinishing" their shafts. Thus, if the "bag-rash" spot bothers you, the solution is to use automotive touch-up paint in a color close to the rest of the shaft's finish to cover it up.

IF YOU CAN'T STAND THE HEAT, GET OUT OF THE TRUNK

Will my graphite shafts be damaged if I leave them in the trunk of my car in this heat? Good question, since the trunk of the car in summer in desert and Gulf Coast climates can reach as high as 175 degrees, and graphite shafts are held together with epoxy resins, which do have a temperature at which they can and will let go. But don't worry about your clubs.

Here's how you can tell whether the temperature inside your car trunk has damaged your shafts. If you pull out your clubs and the heads fall off—it's time to worry. You see, the temperature at which the epoxy on your heads breaks down is far LOWER than the temperature at which the graphite shafts will be affected.

SPLIT-SIZING GRIPS

Almost all grips are tapered; that is, they are bigger in diameter at the top than they are at the bottom. That's pretty much the way it has always been.

For most people, that's fine. For some, however, it is not. Many people find the lower portion of the grip to be too small for their hands. This can cause them unconsciously to regrip the club before, or worse, DURING the swing.

One solution to this potential problem is to have your professional clubmaker (you DO have one, don't you?) custom install your grips so the lower half of the grip is larger than what you have been used to feeling.

Generally, oversize grips are created by applying extra layers of tape on the shaft prior to applying the grip. When the grip is finally slid on over the tape, it is forced to expand because the shaft now has a wider diameter. If the clubmaker layers the buildup tape equally over the length of the grip, the whole grip increases at the same rate.

But if the clubmaker applies more layers of buildup tape to one section of the shaft than another, when the grip is slid on, that portion of the grip will be thicker. This is called "split-sizing."

Actually, this practice of split-sizing grips is somewhat new, having derived from a time-honored research technique called: "Hey, I wonder what would happened if I do it like this." Many golfers who have tried this form of grip sizing, however, really do like the feel and note a tendency to not loosen the lower hand and "regrip" the club as much during the swing.

As with most areas related to "feel" in golf equipment, you never know until you try it.

CHAPTER 7—IT'S A MIRACLE

Putting It Together

We've looked at the clubheads. We've looked at shafts and grips. Now it's time to put them together into a whole that is greater than the sum of its parts. But let me make this qualification. The whole will be greater ONLY if the assembly of the head, shaft, and grip result in a finished club that is built to the right length and the correct swingweight. The head, shaft, and grip can each be perfectly selected for the golfer's fitting needs, but if the length and swingweight are not right for the golfer as well, the chances of hitting the club consistently solid and on center are less than your chances of winning big in Vegas.

Another part of putting it together is deciding exactly which clubs you're going to put in your bag. No, I don't mean the brand or model of the clubs; I mean what mixture of clubs. In clubfitting this is known as your "set makeup." Believe me, set makeup is just as important as any individual fitting specifications for getting the most out of your equipment.

Set Makeup and the 24/38 Rule

If you are like most golfers, you bought your clubs at a golf store where they sold you a set consisting of a driver, 3-wood, 5-wood, and eight irons (3 through pitching wedge). The putter and any additional wedges were extra.

Why those clubs?

The answer is tradition. Traditionally, a set of irons consists of eight clubs, which is currently interpreted as 3-iron through pitching wedge. But that common set composition forces most of you into buying a set that has at least two clubs most golfers, in all probability, cannot and will never be able to hit.

The story starts with the "Vanishing Loft Disease" we discussed in Chapter 1. You'll remember, since the 1960s the club companies have been tinkering with the loft and length of clubs—gaining distance by lowering the loft angles and lengthening the shafts—in order to say their clubs "hit farther."

There is a rule among custom clubmakers called the "24/38 Rule" and it goes like this: The vast majority of golfers simply do not have, and never will have, the ability to hit consistently an iron that has a loft angle of 24 degrees or less and more than 38 inches in length. To do so requires a swing precision that the average golfer rarely has the opportunity to attain.

If this were the 1960s and you were buying a set of clubs, the 3-iron would be right on the edge of the longest iron you could reasonably expect to hit—24 degrees of loft, 38 inches in length. In 2004, however, because of loft creep, your 5-iron is now the 24/38 cutoff club. So what are you doing buying a 3- and 4-iron? For that matter, why are the club companies SELLING you 3- and 4-irons when they know the 24/38 rule as well as anyone?

The answer is tradition. That and the fact they don't want to reduce the basic 8-club iron set they sell to the retailers for fear of suffering an instantaneous drop of 12.5 percent in revenues. Heck, either a #4 through a gap wedge or a #5 through a sand wedge sounds pretty good to me for the set. That still keeps the sale at eight clubs, and I guarantee you it will be eight irons far more golfers will use than the typical eight irons most have and will buy these days.

When you buy a set of clubs from most golf equipment retailers, and certainly any custom clubmaker, you can and should specify which irons you want in the set. So, if you are going to buy eight clubs, why not make them 5-iron through pitching wedge, plus a gap wedge and a sand wedge instead of the 3- and 4-irons?

The USGA rules say you can put up to 14 clubs in your bag. Fortunately, they don't tell you which 14 you have to use.

If it hasn't come through loud and clear so far, I admit to having many strong opinions about golf equipment. But each one came about from the things I have learned in my 32 years of clubmaking, clubfitting, and design experience. One opinion up there at the very top of my list is that most golfers completely underestimate the importance of proper set makeup and how it can immediately impact your ability to score—lower if you choose wisely, but higher if you don't.

Playing with a Full Deck

Sure, I agree—nothing impacts scoring like being able to putt well. Get around 18 holes in fewer than 30 putts, and you will score better. OK, so there are times when we might really be punishing ourselves and one-putt for a double-bogey, but day in and day out, if you get around in 28 or 29 putts you will usually head home from the course with a smile, a hug for the spouse, and an extra pat for the dog.

When we talk set makeup, however, we are talking about the other 13 clubs, the ones that are there to get you to the dance floor. If, via common sense, the set makeup is well matched to your playing ability and the shotmaking requirements of the courses you play, your one-putts will more often be for par or birdie and certainly not for the dreaded double.

Set makeup is all about common sense, which unfortunately is not as common as it should be among many golfers. Too often wishful thinking overcomes common sense when it comes to selecting the right clubs for your bag. Here's why set makeup is SO important to better scoring in golf.

A pitcher can throw a perfect game, a quarterback could complete every pass in a game, a round-baller can shoot 100 percent from the floor or the free-throw line, but in golf I seriously doubt we'll ever see a golfer make birdie on all 18 holes and post a score of 54! Golf is all about minimizing errors because the holes don't have a "bad day" like a hitter, a wide receiver, a cornerback, or the defender trying to stop the shooter from getting to the hoop.

Lower scoring in golf is tough because it's all up to you and what you can do with your 14 clubs to minimize errors. You hit the tee shot in the short grass more often; you have a better chance of hitting the green in regulation. You keep the approach shot out of hazards, bunkers, and tall grass and hit it closer to the green more often, your chances of getting the ball "up and down" are far more likely. You hit it 30 feet from the hole instead of 60; the challenge of two-putting is far easier. You pitch it or chip it inside 5 feet instead of leaving it 15 feet from the hole; you have a much better success rate in one-putting. Common sense, right?

Then why do I see so many golfers pass up a 7- or 9-wood, or eschew the use of hybrid clubs, and buy sets of irons with a 3- or 4-iron? One reason might be embarrassment at what their playing partners will say when they see a bouquet of head covers sticking out of the bag? But the main reason, I suspect, is a lack of knowledge of what is going on with those clubs, and THAT is what this book is here to correct.

Why do some golfers persist in using the old #1 with a single-digit loft angle, when a much higher loft driver or even a 3- or 5-wood is far more consistent off the tee? All too often, it's wishful thinking that the next drive will, all of a sudden, signal an end to their previous tendency to hit only one out of six shots with the face square and impact on center. I call this the "slot machine" approach to golf because, as with the slot machines in Las Vegas, in the long run the individual will never win.

Why do some players try to hammer a sand wedge too hard to get to the green instead of using a club that would fill in the space between their loft-challenged pitching wedge and a normal-loft sand wedge? Why would people not use a 60-degree wedge to help stop the ball better when they know their greens tend to be firm or are raised well above the surrounding fairway?

I think that much of it comes from (a) the golfer's lack of awareness of how set makeup can minimize mistakes; (b) what the golf stores stock and what the salesperson (usually incorrectly) tells them they need; and (c) yes, probably some embarrassment at what others might say about what's sticking out of their bag.

When you see a set of cavity-back irons, a hybrid club, or multiple wedges in a player's bag, you are truly seeing common sense and set makeup wisdom in action.

When I lived in Austin, Texas, my home course was Austin C.C. Tom Kite was also a member and would practice there frequently between tour events. One day he came over to where I was hitting balls on the range. Much to my relief, he wanted some help with his new irons instead of commenting on how bad I was hitting the ball! Tom had signed a new endorsement contract with Titleist and wanted his new irons bent to a 5 degree loft increment between clubs instead of the normal 4 degree spacing. The reason? He wanted to eliminate one of the irons so he could add a fourth wedge to his set makeup.

Tom told me he had analyzed his previous year on tour and discovered some of the shots he had lost could possibly have been saved if he had had an additional wedge with a specific loft and sole angle different from the other three he carried. Since 14 clubs is all anyone can pack, to make room for the fourth wedge he decided the club to cut was one of his regular long irons. And he knew the only way to do that was to change the irons' loft increments to 5 degrees. That way, with one fewer numbered iron, he could cover his approach shot distance needs and have the space in the bag for the other wedge. All I had to do was to help Tom decide what the actual lofts would be on each of the irons to make sure his distance requirements were covered, and then the bending adjustments would finish the job.

In short, he knew the wisdom of set make up—to carry the right complement of clubs that would cover all his distance needs and minimize his chances of making errors and losing shots.

For golfers who don't have the ball striking ability of a Tom Kite, the set makeup choices normally center upon replacing hard-to-hit clubs with clubs that are easier to hit but will travel the same distance. It is probably the most overlooked and underutilized game improvement decision that most golfers make when it comes to their clubs. Read through the following guidelines and if any apply to your game, swallow any self-imposed embarrassment and start using some common sense. Your reward will be lower scores.

1. If your swing speed is 90 mph or less, if you hit your current 9, 10, or 11 degree driver on a medium-to-low trajectory, and if you hit the driver off center two or more shots out of five, go get fitted with a driver with more loft and built to a shorter length with the swingweight adjusted for that shorter length.

   If you don't do that, leave the driver in the car and use the longest fairway wood you hit with confidence off the tee. Losing 15 yards but being in the short grass will be better in the long run for your score—and will eventually convince you to go get fitted with a shorter length and higher loft driver.

2. Find the longest iron in your bag you can hit solidly on center four out of five shots.
   - If that is the 7-iron, start using a 7-, 9-, and 11-wood or suitable hybrids in the place of the 4-, 5-, and 6-iron.
   - If that is the 6-iron, use fairway woods or hybrids up to the 9-wood.
   - If that is the 5-iron, use fairway woods or hybrids up through the 7-wood.
   - If that is the 4-iron, consider a 7-wood because with your ability you will probably hit a solid 7-wood as far as a good 3-iron.
   - If the longest iron you hit consistently well is the 3-iron,

resign your day job and start practicing, my friend. You might have a future in professional golf!

3. If the loft difference between your PW and SW is 6 degrees or more, please, do yourself a favor—buy a gap wedge that you know has a loft halfway between the PW and SW. If you don't know the lofts of your PW and SW or what the lofts of any of the gap wedges are, get to a clubmaker who can accurately measure and bend iron lofts. If you are just buying a gap wedge without knowing the actual loft, you're just guessing and you might still end up with an unwanted spread in yardage between two of the wedges and two other wedges, which hit the ball about the same distance.

4. Consider a 60 degree lob wedge if any of the following apply:
   - The greens on the course you normally play are firm and don't hold shots that well.
   - Your greens are small.
   - Your greens are raised up higher than the surrounding fairway.
   - Your greenkeeper delights in "tucking" pin placements on your greens.
   - You struggle with consistently hitting your SW as high as you want.
   - You constantly struggle with stopping the ball on the green with any of your existing wedges.

5. Most sand wedges are made with a 55 or 56 degree loft as standard. You may want to consider a second SW of 58–60 degrees loft if any of the following apply:
   - Your greens are built much higher than the sand traps.
   - Your greens superintendent delights in growing the rough 2 inches or taller close to the green.
   - Your well-hit sand shots roll too far once they land on the green.

When talking about replacing long irons with higher lofted fairway woods that hit the ball the same distance, there is another option. There are tons of different hybrid clubs made to all sorts of length and loft specifications. This variety creates confusion in trying to determine if hybrid clubs are a true replacement for long irons or whether they are simply a "narrow-body fairway wood" in disguise.

Way too many golfers have been lured to the hybrids as an alternative to replacing the conventional long irons only to discover that they just bought a club that duplicates the distance of an existing fairway wood. This still leaves them without a replacement for their impossible-to-hit long irons.

There is a very simple test you can perform to determine if the hybrids you might be considering will adequately replace your long irons in distance. Bring the long irons you are hoping to send to pasture with you to the golf shop. Sole each long iron and the hybrid you envision as its replacement side by side so you can compare their lengths.

If the hybrid is the same length or one-half inch longer, you're OK, as long as you know the lofts are the same on the two clubs.

If the length of the hybrid is an inch or longer than the long iron you want it to replace, or if the loft is two or more degrees less, you will be defeating the purpose of the club change. The hybrid will probably hit the ball longer so you STILL won't have a replacement for the long iron you want to dump.

This isn't rocket science, folks, but you do need to match the loft and length of each hybrid to each specific long iron in your bag. What do you do when you find that all the hybrids in the golf shop are longer and stronger than the long irons you want to replace? Let your fingers do the walking through your yellow pages and look for a competent custom clubmaker to build a hybrid (or hybrids) for you that will have the same length and loft as the long irons you want to get rid of.

Going to Great Lengths

With the logic and common sense of your set makeup now firmly cemented in your golfing brain, the next factor in putting it together is the length of your clubs.

I have the utmost respect for some of the big companies that make standard golf clubs. I came very close to playing my trade for one of the largest before I finally decided to get down to brass tacks and start my own company. The engineering capability of some of the large companies is extremely good and the quality of the clubheads they design and monitor through the manufacturing process is excellent. But I did not want to put my skills to work for any company whose mantra is to make standard built golf clubs because I believe so strongly in the need for custom fitting for ALL golfers.

When the big club companies make their woods to one (overlength) standard, they are doing 90 percent of all golfers a disservice. Irons? Not so bad there with regard to standard lengths (other than that there is no defendable reason for irons with graphite shafts to be one-half inch longer than those made with steel shafts). As long as golfers exist from under 5 feet to over 7 feet tall, with arm lengths, swing styles and athletic abilities covering an even wider spectrum, one standard length cannot fit all.

It's like having a shoe store with 100 different styles of shoes—all in the same size. I don't care if that size IS the national average, it still doesn't make sense. Why, then, would it suddenly MAKE sense when you are talking about golf clubs as opposed to shoes?

I know. You heard this earlier in this book, but I'll say it again. Club length is supremely important when it comes to hitting the ball solid, on center, and to the maximum of a golfer's individual potential for distance.

Remember. The average driver length on the PGA Tour is 44.5 inches. The average handicap of a PGA Tour player is something like 5 shots better than scratch. Since the major manufacturers and even fringe players in the assembled club business all make their drivers 45 inches to 45.5 inches, how can you possibly expect to play your best with driver lengths that are longer than what the best players in the world use?

Look at it this way. If the PGA Tour professionals could consistently control a 45- to 46-inch club, that's what you'd see in their bags. They can't, so they don't even try. Now, what is it again that makes you think YOU can?

Finding the Right Length

Okay, fine. So most golfers today are using clubs that are too long to allow them to play their best. How do you know what the right length is for you? Most people assume that if they are over 6 feet 2 inches or shorter than 5 feet 8 inches, they might need "inch-over" or "inch-under" length clubs. Nothing could be farther from the truth.

The length of your clubs is not determined by your height; it is determined by the length of your arms in relation to your height, and then massaged from there to the final length by your swing plane and ball striking ability! But always remember this fitting credo about club length . . .

The proper length for all golfers is the longest length that the golfer can hit SOLID AND ON-CENTER the highest percentage of the time.

My clubmaking compadre, Tom Grundner, once fit a professional basketball player with a set of inch-UNDER length clubs. No question he was tall (about 6 feet 11 inches), but his arms (Tom swears) hung down to about his ankles. (A slam-dunk was almost a flat-footed exercise for this guy!) But because of his ARM LENGTH, he needed shorter clubs.

The way a clubmaker determines proper length is by first measuring the distance from the golfer's wrist to the floor and referencing that dimension to a chart developed over years of fitting research to guide the initial club length recommendations. Fitting length is not done through a fingertip-to-floor measurement, but wrist to floor. The reason is the wide variance people have in finger length. The wrist measurement is a more reliable measurement to indicate arm length. The size of your hands or length of your fingers is only relevant to grip fitting and not club length (see table 7.1).

So proper length fitting starts with a length recommendation based on the golfer's wrist-to-floor measurement. But this is just the beginning. After the initial length from the wrist-to-floor measurement is determined, there are other factors that have to be considered before making the final decision. The first of those is the golfer's swing plane.

Table 7.1—Wrist-to-Floor Measurement for Initial Club Lengths (inches)

Wrist-to-Floor	Driver Length	5-Iron Length
27 to 29	42	36.5
29 to 32	42.5	37
32 to 34	43	37.5
34 to 36	43.5	38
36 to 37	44	38.25
37 to 38	44.25	38.5
38 to 39	44.5	38.75
39 to 40	44.75	39
40 to 41	45	39.25
41 to 42	45.5	39.5
over 42	46 and up	39.75 and up

Note: A wrist-to floor measurement is used as the initial guideline for determining club lengths for the golfer that will match well with their height and arm length for comfort. To make the measurement correctly, wear flat-sole shoes only, stand comfortably erect, shoulders perfectly level, arms hanging relaxed at the sides. The measurement is made from the major wrist crease on the dominant hand to the floor in inches plus any fraction.

The Plane Truth about Club Length

The customary definition of swing plane is the angle of your lead arm in relation to the ground when you swing the club all the way to the top of the backswing. A right-handed golfer's lead arm is the left, and vice versa for the left-handed player. Many of you know this as an upright versus normal versus flat swing plane. If you take a look at the examples in the photo, you can more easily see what I am talking about (see fig. 7.1).

Unless you are gifted with exceptional athletic ability, golfers with a more upright swing plane will have a more difficult time controlling a longer club length than golfers with a flatter swing plane. This is because in an upright swing plane the club travels at a steeper angle down to the ball. Add to an upright plane a swing move where the golfer shifts the club "over the top" and swings down from the outside to the inside on their swing path, and you have another problem that gets in the way of being able to control a longer length.

So who swings the club "over the top" and outside/in to the ball? Almost every slicer who has ever played the game, that's who. Am I saying if you slice the ball, then you're probably not doing yourself any favors with a longer club length? Right.

Swinging to the Beat

The next swing element that plays a huge part in the decision for club length is the golfer's swing tempo or rhythm. I'll bet you can figure this one out before I explain it. The faster the golfer's swing tempo, the more frenetic and violent the swing, the more difficult it will be for the golfer to control a longer length. Why? Because the faster the swing, the less time the golfer has to get a longer club into the position it needs to be on the downswing to ensure a solid, on-center hit.

Another thing—and you might want to brace yourself for an additional bit of bad news here. These swing factors are all cumulative in their effect on club length.

In other words, if you have an upright swing plane, swing "over the top" with an outside/in path to the ball, AND have a fast tempo—a longer club length will be the kiss of death to your golf game. If you have a smooth tempo with a flat swing plane and want to try a longer length, okay, give it a try. You have a swing that might (repeat MIGHT) give you a chance of controlling a driver with a longer length.

Figure 7.1. Flat, normal, and upright swing planes *(top to bottom)*. The more upright the swing plane, the more difficult it may be for the golfer to handle a longer club length.

Whether you will be successful with a longer length is also a matter of the third length-fitting factor—your athletic ability.

Golf IS an Athletic Endeavor

Golfers who are good athletes, with good hand/eye coordination, and who are also skilled ball strikers are always going to have an easier time controlling a longer length club. That is not to say that they will NEED or WANT to use longer lengths in their clubs. I am just saying they will have an easier time of it.

All of us know or have seen people who are good ball strikers. They seem to have an almost magical ability to hit the vast majority of their shots solid, on center, and with consistent trajectory and accuracy. These players gained this skill partly because they have the athletic ability necessary to perform the hundreds of kinetic movements of the golf swing in the proper sequence and with the proper timing. Hence, better athletes tend to be good ball strikers and will always have a better chance to handle longer lengths in clubs.

As for the rest of us, if you are a beginner or have not yet reached the point where 90 percent of your shots get in the air, please, err on the shorter side in your clubs. Indeed, many very experienced clubmakers will build beginners' sets by making them one inch shorter than what the wrist-to-floor length chart prescribes. They may then make the club-to-club length change in the woods to be three-quarter inch rather than the usual one inch, and might build the irons with a three-eighth-inch length change between clubs instead of the usual one-half inch. Doing that simply makes for a more controllable set of clubs and if there is ANYthing a beginner needs (not to mention the rest of us), it's something that will make the clubs easier to control.

A-R-G-G-H!! Drivers!

Let me digress a bit here on the issue of driver length because it is a particularly sore point with me.

As you've probably already gathered, 90 percent of the drivers sold in shops are too long for most players. If you follow the simple procedures outlined in this chapter you will know whether your current driver is longer than your best-fit length. If it is, get it cut down and reswingweighted to the shorter length, and don't be shy about doing it.

Even better, head out and get custom fitted for a new driver with both the right length AND best loft for your physical makeup, ability, and swing. Trading off accuracy for distance is simply not worth it.

Let's start with the issue of distance since so many golfers believe longer lengths automatically mean longer shots. You probably think you can get more distance with a longer shaft, right?

In a test conducted and documented by one of the companies that also specializes in fitting research, drivers ranging from 42 to 46 inches were put to a test on a swing robot that DOES have the athletic ability to swing longer clubs and hit them on-center. Here are the data (see table 7.2). Read it for yourself.

But wait. The plot thickens.

There is another reason for having a shorter club. It appears that, in the hands of real people (as opposed to a swing robot), the shorter club might very well hit the ball not just with more accuracy, but farther as well.

Do you remember our discussion in Chapter 2? For every quarter inch by which you miss the sweet spot on your club, you lose about five yards in distance. Miss it by a half inch and you lose 10 yards; three-quarters inch, 15 yards, and so forth.

Conversely, if you can gain enough control of the head to hit the ball even a quarter inch closer to the sweet spot, you will gain back all the yardage you think you are losing by using a shorter shaft. This, by the way, is the reason most people do end up hitting shorter-length drivers farther. They're simply hitting closer to the sweet spot more often because the shorter club is easier for them to control and thus improve shot consistency.

Table 7.2—Effect of Driver Length on Distance

Driver Length (inches)	Swing Speed (mph)	Ball Speed (mph)	Carry Distance (yards)
42	90	133.0	209.7
43	90	133.2	210.1
44	90	133.5	210.5
45	90	133.6	210.7
46	90	133.8	211.0

Note: The above information shows how futile it is to play with a driver that is too long. Finding the correct length for the individual golfer will *always* result in game improvement.

Earlier I told you a very important fitting maxim about length . . .

The proper length for all golfers is the longest length that the golfer can hit SOLID AND ON-CENTER the highest percentage of the time.

If you are hitting a 45-inch driver so that your on-center hit percentage with this driver length is well below 50 percent, your longest length to hit solid and on-center the highest percentage of the time may be as much as 2 inches shorter. To other golfers with a little higher on-center hit percentage, that longest length to hit most solid might be only 1 inch shorter.

As I said earlier, wrist-to-floor dimension is only the start for coming up with the best length for your game. It has to be tempered with considerations of your swing plane, swing path, and ball-striking ability to end up finding the longest length that you can hit solid and on-center the highest percentage of the time.

Let me digress. There are golfers who may never be able to hit a driver. Well, that is, a driver in the sense of defining a driver as a LARGE woodhead with a loft of 14 degrees or less built to a men's length of 43 inches or longer. Who might be candidates in this? Many golfers with a wood club swing speed under 70 mph, golfers with mostly an "arm swing" who do not generate much of a body turn in their swing, and any golfer who psychologically can't bear looking at a head the size of a grapefruit on the end of the shaft.

You see, most golfers don't know the original name for the driver. In the 1800s that club was called the "Play Club" because its only function was to put the ball "in play." Then along came some marketing genius who decided that calling it a DRIVER was a more manly way of describing it, and we've been swinging out of our shoes ever since.

Remember my original definition is simply whatever club you use off the tee to hit the ball the farthest AND straightest you possibly can, as often as you can. Nothing has changed since the early days of golf, however. Its purpose is STILL to put the ball "in play" not "out-of-bounds."

Would you like to know how to determine which club is ACTU-ALLY your driver? It's simple. Go to a driving range and create an imaginary fairway in front of you—let's say it's the red flag on the right and the blue flag on the left, or whatever you can use as a reference that's about 40 yards apart. Now, start hitting balls.

The longest club that you can use to hit 7 out of 10 balls between those two flags is your driver! It might say "driver" on the bottom, or it might say "3-wood," or "5-wood," or even "5-iron," and I don't care what the distance is on your shots. Whatever club gets you 7 out of 10—THAT CLUB IS YOUR DRIVER—at least in a world where common sense replaces wishful thinking.

Don't believe me? Just play nine holes someday with that club as your driver and see what happens. You might be . . . no, let me change that . . . you WILL be surprised. On the other hand, I am also a realist. I know most of you won't actually make that club your real driver, which is why I am spending so much time telling you about reducing driver length and increasing driver loft.

Club companies these days routinely sell drivers off the rack for men with 8 to 11 degree lofts and 45-inch lengths. They have to KNOW that no more than 10 percent (if that) of all golfers have the swing skill for that length and the swing speed for that loft—yet they sell them that way anyway because they are afraid if they don't, their competitors will. For some golfers, all it takes is to make one good impact out of 20, and they are singing the praises of their new 45-inch miracle club all over the place; and NO club company wants to miss out on sales.

If the distance from your wrist to the floor is less than 40 inches and you're not a good ball striker, then a 45-inch driver is too long. If your driver swing speed is 90 mph or less then you likely need more than an 11 degree loft. Simple as that.

Other Woods You Should Think About . . . at Length

OK, I've been hammering this matter of length on the driver to death. I admit it. But the driver is right there behind the putter as number two on the list of the most important clubs in your bag. You probably use the driver 14 times in an average round. I better say 14 *possible* times because that's the average number of par-4 and par-5 holes on most golf courses. So the driver is a very important club. If most of you do go shorter in length and increase the loft of your driver, I'll bet the number of times you gently pull the headcover back on and ease it back into the bag will begin to greatly exceed the number of times you jerk the cover back on and slam it into the bag.

Obviously, there are other woods in the bag. All lumped under the title of fairway woods, they too have suffered from "length increase-itis" over the past several years because of the big club companies' desire to deliver distance and log more sales. Actually, it's more accurate to say the disease that has afflicted the length of the fairway woods is not singular and has been a combination of "length increase-itis" and "length increment-orrhea."

It used to be, back when the driver was a mere 43 inches, your woods all decreased in length from each other by a nice, even separation of one inch. In other words, the 3-wood was one inch shorter than the driver, the 4-wood one inch shorter than the 3-wood, and so forth.

The 3-, 4-, and 5-wood also changed in loft angle by another nice even increment of three degrees. This was back when the woods you could buy were a driver, #3-, #4-, and occasionally a #5-wood. The 3-wood was 16 degrees, the 4-wood was 19 degrees, the 5-wood 22 degrees, and all the woods from driver to 5 were separated by one inch in length. How neat and symmetrical was that for ensuring a nice difference in distance between each wood?

Today, you have about as much chance of finding a 4-wood as you do of finding a good singer at the *American Idol* auditions. They hardly exist. The reason is that in their intense desire to deliver more distance to golfers to sell more units, the golf industry destroyed them.

There is one company that comes to mind still offering a 4-wood. But they happen to make their #4-wood option only one degree more in loft than their standard 3-wood and only one degree less in loft than their standard 5-wood loft. With 80 percent of the distance difference between clubs coming from the loft difference and the other 20 percent coming from the length spacing, this 4-wood doesn't have any real purpose. It exists only for golfers lamenting the loss of an even number on the sole of their woods, or maybe for a golfer who wants to carry a #4 and a #7 for a total of just two fairway woods to lighten the load. For that and that only, its existence is justified. It's fascinating that fairway wood sales today consist only of odd-numbered woods. But the problem is just like the letter flexes in shafts—the 3-, 5-, and 7-woods made by one company won't likely be the same loft and length as the same-numbered fairway woods offered by another.

Some companies change the loft between the 3-, 5-, and 7-woods by only 2 degree increments, while others will space the lofts of these woods three degrees apart. Some companies make the loft on the 3-wood to be 12 or 13 degrees, while others make the 3-wood with 14, 15, or 16 degrees. And that's just the loft we're talking about. You also have to worry about length for getting the distance spacing you want between the woods.

In length, because drivers have all grown to 45 inches or 45.5 inches for men, the 3-wood might be 44 inches, 43.5 inches or even 43 inches.

(Don't worry, ladies, there is a separate chapter coming up for your equipment counseling.) Then there is the incremental length difference between the fairway woods that is all messed up today as well. Some companies make the length change from the 3- to 5- to 7-wood to be only one-half inch, while others change the fairway wood lengths by an increment of one inch.

Then you have a few companies that no longer number their fairway woods and simply make them with loft numbers only engraved on the sole. Are you continuing to get the picture that this is one heck of an interesting industry?

Let me put it this way—if you walk into a golf shop and say, "I'm looking for new fairway woods," you have no idea if the new woods will have lofts and lengths that are compatible with your ability to control the club and whether they will work with your ability to get the ball comfortably in the air, much less know what distances you will get from each.

The reason fairway woods have all become lower in loft and longer in length is that same old story of marketing. Offer a golfer a club with which he hits the ball farther, and the chances are pretty good he'll buy it. And the chances of that happening is pretty good because the club companies know that most golfers only know their fairway woods by the numbers 3, 5, and 7, and not from an actual loft and length.

So the move to lower lofts and longer lengths on fairway woods is done to create artificial distance, which in turn was motivated by a desire to sell more clubs. I mean, how many of you would notice that the new 5- or 7-wood you just hit 15 yards longer than your old one really was an inch longer and had 2–3 degrees less loft on the face? All you'd notice is that "this 5-wood" hits it a lot longer than "the old one" and you'd be thrilled.

So what's the problem with that? After all, it IS a free country and the club companies are well within their rights to make their clubs any way they want. Unfortunately, here's what happens.

What do you do if this new long-distance 5- or 7-wood leaves you with a 30-yard gap between it and the longest iron you can hit consistently with success—let's say it's the 5-iron? Answer: you will be forced into hitting a 3- or 4-iron. And what's wrong with THAT? Reread the section earlier about the 24/38 rule. Because of loft and length creep, your 3- and 4-irons are now essentially unhittable clubs, at least in the hands of the average golfer. In short, you are left with NO options that will work, and a whole lot of options that won't. And you still don't have a club to cover that gap in distance.

You have again crashed into the grass ceiling. It is this kind of equipment-induced frustration that contributes to making this game harder to play than it should be, and a perfect example of the kind of thing that this book seeks to end.

On the other side of the coin, the problem with a set of fairway woods that only change by 2 degrees in loft and one-half inch in length is that you end up with clubs that hit the ball so close to the same distance you can't figure out what to hit when.

A further problem with a 3-wood that is 44 inches in length is that, remember, there are times when you're going to want to hit that long club off the deck. Believe me, if you think a 45-inch driver is tough to hit with the ball on a tee, you don't even want to think about hitting a length of 44-inch with today's lower 3-wood lofts with no peg under the ball!

You need the 3-wood loft to be compatible with your ability to get the ball well up in the air off the ground, at least a 3 degree change in loft between your fairway woods, and at least a one-inch change in length between your fairway woods to make sure they all hit the ball distances that are different enough to justify their individual existence. And that's if you swing the club 80 mph or faster.

If you swing the club under 80 mph and especially at 70 mph or less like many seniors and women do, if you do carry a 3-wood you need it to be no less than 16 degrees in loft, and you need MORE than 3 degrees of loft change between your adjacent fairway woods. The reason is the slower the swing speed, the less the distance difference will be between side-by-side clubs in your bag. Thus, if you are swinging the club under 80 mph, you would not want 3-, 5-, 7-woods spaced in a 2 or 3 degree increment. Going with a 3-, 7-, and 11-wood or a 5- and 9-wood would be much better for your game.

In all honesty, although I sit here and poke at the club companies for making all sorts of different fairway wood lofts and lengths, they are really not the ones to blame for this confusion. For that you need to turn to the retail golf shops, where most of their salespeople are not even aware of the fact that all the 3-, 5- and 7-woods in their store do not have the same loft and length. Because the club companies have the right to make their woods whatever loft and length they want, it becomes the responsibility of whoever sells golf equipment to keep you better informed and to help you make the best decision on what to buy.

I can tell you from personal experience that most retail salespeople do not have a clue as to the length and loft differences in fairway woods, as well as many other things you need to know about equipment to be able to make the best decision for a purchase. The reason is that very few of the retail shops take the time to really train their floor salespeople, and even fewer have professional clubmakers on staff. For those that do, my hat's off to them and by all means, please keep it up. For the majority that do not, it's time to get your act together and do it for the sake of the game, for the sake of your customers, and because that's how YOU'D want to be treated if the tables were reversed and you were contemplating spending hundreds of dollars.

So what length is right for you in the fairway woods? Well, let's go back to that wrist-to-floor dimension measurement and what it says your driver length needs to be. If your best fit for the driver is actually 45 inches (unlikely but possible), or if you insist on buying that 45-inch beauty you saw in the golf store, choose the 3-wood to be at least 1.5 inches shorter. If you occasionally struggle with consistently hitting the 3-wood well up in the air off the deck, make it 2 inches shorter. Then go with one-inch increments between the 3-, 5-, 7-, and 9-woods after that.

If your best length for the driver is 44 inches, start thinking of the 3-wood at 43 inches with a similar proviso of another half-inch off that if you struggle with that 3-wood off the deck from time to time. If hitting any previous 3-wood easily in the air was not a problem, to match with a 44-inch driver, make your 3-wood 43 inches. If it is a problem, go with 42.5 inches or even 42 inches.

Don't ever worry if your 3-wood ends up being two inches shorter than your driver. You gotta get that wood up off the ground to make it do its job of being the second-longest-hitting club in your bag. Once you nail down your 3-wood length, do your one-inch change between the 3- to the 5- to the 7-wood, and if you use one, to the 9-wood after that.

Really, no matter WHAT your best fit may be for the length of your driver, follow these same incremental length difference guidelines above for selecting your best matching fairway wood lengths. If you find your best driver length is all the way down to 42 to 43.5 inches, don't worry about it. Going down by one inch on the 3-wood is within your "safe zone" for swinging the club in control and getting the ball well up in the air off the grass.

Last point. I mentioned the 3-wood is supposed to be your second-longest-hitting club in the bag. If you are very adept at making contact on-center and getting the ball easily well up in the air with a low lofted 3-wood (13–14 degrees), there is nothing wrong with making it only one-half inch shorter in length than your driver. That way you can squeeze even more out of it for those long second shots or tight tee shot requirements. This is just another example of what the word "custom" in custom fitting is all about.

In the end, it all comes down to what we've been telling you all along—play the longest length that you can hit the most solid and on-center. Athletic ability and ball-striking skill rule supreme after a wrist-to-floor fitting guideline in the decision for what final length is best for YOU.

CHAPTER 8—THE DEVIL'S IN THE DETAILS

A Less Lofty Pursuit

Although our current emphasis in "putting it all together" is length, a word about 3-wood lofts is definitely in order.

For decades, the 3-wood was made with 16 degrees of loft. During the loft shrinking days of the irons, the 3-wood seemed to be somewhat immune in that it only moved down a little from 16 to 15 degrees. Not bad, as a 3-wood with 15 degrees is not much more difficult to get up in the air than one with a loft of 16 degrees.

Then about the time of the millennium, a "second" 3-wood with a loft of only 12 or 13 degrees began to appear from many club companies. You might have seen this when you happened to check out a fairway wood that read "Strong 3," or "3+" on the sole. That was the golf industry's "secret code"—a hint that you'd better be a very good ball-striker to get THIS baby off the turf, or else you should stay with the normal "3."

Today you see more "normal" 3-woods made with a loft of 14 degrees. That is a very tough loft for most golfers to get the ball into the air high enough to be able to carry as far as your swing speed can dictate.

So ask and make sure any 3-wood you are considering adding to "your family" has a loft and length that is compatible with your ball-striking ability and your best-fit length.

After that the loft of the 5-, 7-, 9-woods should increase by at least three degrees between clubs, and the lengths should decrease by one inch. In short, if your swing speed is 80 mph or more, when you get the 3-wood loft and length properly fitted for your swing and ball-striking skills, the other fairway woods will fall right in step if you use that "three degree and one inch" difference. You then won't have any gaps in distance between your shortest fairway wood and the longest iron you can hit consistently. This, in turn, means you will have a club you can swing smoothly for any distance you encounter in your play. And if your swing speed is less than 80 mph, one inch between fairway woods is fine, but the loft difference should be more than 3 degrees since slower swing speeds won't generate the distance differences you really need.

Weighing Out the Last Details

The strangest thing happened when graphite-shafted irons become more common in the golf industry. The standard sets of graphite-shafted irons suddenly became one-half inch longer compared to the steel-shafted version of the same iron model. I have had tons of clubmakers and golf pros ask me if there was something "different" about the performance of graphite shafts in irons that requires them to be built longer than steel-shaft irons. I mean, if the big companies all make their clubs that way; it has to be the right way to do it, doesn't it?

There is only one reason for this one-half inch increase in graphite-shafted iron lengths. Convenience. More specifically, convenience in the assembly of the clubs.

You see, there's a weird thing that happens to the swingweight of a golf club when you install a very lightweight graphite shaft. Those of you who have had existing clubs reshafted with graphite will know what I am talking about.

If you put a much lighter shaft into a clubhead, its swingweight drops like a rock; and a swingweight that's too low equals a bad club for all golfers. This leaves the golf companies with three choices.

First, they can create, order, and stock two different weight versions of each ironhead. This is inconvenient, not to mention more expensive.

The second option is not as expensive but is a lot more complicated. It involves designing ironheads with a "weight port" in them—in other words a way to add weight inside those heads that are destined for graphite shafts. Obviously, the big club companies would rather not do that if they don't have to because, again, this makes the irons more expensive to build and the clubheads rarely look as good cosmetically. To get around the weight port problem, club companies have come up with some ingenious solutions. For example:

Have you ever noticed a black "dot" on the sole of the woodheads made by some of the big club companies? It might be part of a word or logo on the sole or just a plain black "dot" sitting somewhere on its own on the sole. That's how some of the golf companies add weight to their graphite-shafted woods to get the swingweight of the club up to the proper level.

Today's hollow metal woods are all injected with a small amount of special "sticky glue" as a normal part of the foundry's production process. Its purpose is to act like flypaper to eliminate rattles by catching and trapping any loose metal particles inside the hollow metal heads.

With the woods, it's easy for the club companies to inject an extra quantity of this special glue as a way to increase the swingweight of the club. In minutes, the glue hardens to the consistency of taffy and the hole is filled with a black plastic plug. That's the origin of the black "dot" you see on the sole of your big company woodhead.

Because the body of almost all irons is solid, however, it's more difficult to add weight. The solution is the third option. Just make the graphite-shafted irons longer in length. Problem solved. Sort of.

If you make the length of ANY golf club longer, the swingweight will increase. You can test this for yourself. Place a weight at the end of a one-foot-long stick and hold the stick up by the nonweighted end. Now, place the same weight on the end of a three-foot-long stick and hold it the same way. In which case will the weight feel "heavier?" You got it, the weight on the longer stick.

So, do the translation. If you increase the length of a shaft, the head will feel "heavier" (higher swingweight) as a result. This phenomenon allows the club companies to use the same heads on both steel and graphite shafts. As long as they cut the graphite shafts a tad longer, the swingweight will come out the same.

The question is, do you WANT your iron shafts to be that "tad longer?"

Regardless of the weight, flex, torque, or type of material of the shaft, when it comes to YOUR game, the correct length is the correct length. Period. If your wrist-to-floor measurement plus a swing analysis says the 5-iron length should be 38 inches, then it should be 38 inches regardless what shaft goes into that 5-iron.

Sure, I'll be honest. That half-inch is not a lot for most golfers to adjust to, but that's not the point. Fitting length needs to be done on the basis of what's best for the golfer and not what's easiest for the manufacturer's assembly process.

Gimme a Little Space Here Please

In 90 percent of all standard made irons, the increment of length change between the numbered irons is one-half inch. Thank Japan and some Asian countries for the other 10 percent that do not change in length by one-half inch because of their predilection for the metric system.

By the late 1800s clubmakers had learned that a half-inch change in length coupled with a 3 to 4 degree change in loft angle means 10–15 yards difference in distance between each iron. Thus, as it has been and shall ever be, once the golfer's length for the 5-iron is determined, your irons will be made with a one-half inch change from club to club using the 5-iron as the base. There are some circumstances, however, in which this can and should be altered for the benefit of the golfer.

Let's say you are tall and you have a short arm length for your height, and your swing still has a way to go before you develop a level of consistency in your ball-striking. Being tall with shorter-length arms will likely mean a wrist-to-floor measurement indicating you need clubs that could be 1 to 2 inches longer in length. But, because you're still struggling with on-center hit consistency at your current skill level, longer clubs won't help that, to say the least.

Clubmaking credo time again: the longer the club, the harder it is to hit solid and on-center. An interesting thing in fitting players who do measure for longer-length clubs is that they are almost always more uncomfortable with their middle-to-short irons than they are with the longest irons in their set. This is because as the half-inch increment change in length keeps moving down through the set of irons, this type of tall height/short arm player has to crouch and bend over more to feel comfortable with the 7-, 8-, and 9-wedges.

Thus, it is not all that uncommon for experienced custom clubmakers to fit such players so the length of their longest iron is closer to standard. This keeps the longest iron short enough to improve the chances of on-center hits. Then the clubmaker might change the length increments from the normal one-half inch to either three-eighth inch or even one-quarter inch between all the irons down through the wedges. Reducing the length increment between the irons allows each higher-number iron to get progressively longer compared to the length they would be with a normal one-half inch progression. Thus, when the golfer gets to the 7-, 8-, 9-iron and wedges, these clubs will be much longer than standard and more comfortable to play.

What makes all this work is the most forgiving of all the design specifications that make up a clubhead—LOFT. As the clubs get higher in number, the loft increases, which makes each iron in the set progressively easier to hit, even though, in this case, the lengths are longer than normal.

By the way, the other candidates for changing the iron length increments from the typical one-half inch to three-eighth inch or one-quarter inch are seniors with many years of playing experience. Since they have probably developed decent consistency in the short and middle irons over their years of play, these players can gain back some lost distance due to age with a decreased incremental length difference from club to club. There will be more about that in Chapter 10.

And Not to Forget the Wedges

To finish up this discussion on club length, let's talk about the wedges for a minute. Wedge length is another club-fitting situation that generates many questions. This is because over the past 10+ years, wedge lengths have gone from being "all the same" to a conglomeration of variations from one company to the next. Before competition became so fierce for sales, it was s-o-o-o simple. The length of the 9-iron was the length of the PW and SW.

The problem is that today there are PWs that have the same length as the 9-iron and then there are PWs made one-half inch or one-quarter inch shorter than the 9. Some SWs today are made one-half inch shorter than the PW, so that means you could have a SW the same length as the 9 and PW, or a SW one-half inch shorter than the PW that is one-half inch shorter than the 9.

Did you follow that?

Then you have the now-popular LW (lob wedge) to consider. Some companies make their lob wedges to be one-quarter inch shorter than the SW; some the same as the SW. And don't worry, I won't try another sentence explaining all possible length relationships between the 9, PW, SW, and then add on the LW! (That sentence was even confusing to ME.)

So, let's get to the bottom line. If all the big companies say their wedges are the best, how can you know what is right for you?

Here's the deal. Whatever length is the most comfortable for you, that's your length for the wedges. No, there are no special wedge-only wrist-to-floor measurements here. Wedges are "scoring clubs" and scoring clubs are all about comfort and feel.

Please don't misunderstand me. I am not saying: "I don't care how long your wedges are" because there ARE some guidelines to follow for wedge length fitting.

- If you hit your PW with a full swing more often than you hit it with a three-quarter or half swing, then make it one-half inch shorter than your 9-iron and swingweight it the same as the 9. In other words, if you swing full with the PW, then you'll want that same 10–15 yard difference between your 9 and PW, and graduating it down from the 9-iron by one-half inch will do that.

- If the gap wedge (that sits between your PW and SW) is the first wedge you use to hit more three-quarter- and half-swing shots than full-swing shots, make the gap wedge the same length as your PW, and swingweight it +2 points higher than the 9-iron. The reason? Three-quarter- and half-length swings generate a slower swing speed than a full swing. The higher swingweight will allow you to feel the weight of the head more, which is better for your swing rhythm and timing for shots hit with less than a full swing.

- If you mostly make full swings with the gap wedge, then make it one-half inch shorter than the PW but make it the same swingweight as the PW and the other irons. Again, this is so you can still get the same 10–15 yards difference between it and the PW for your full-swing shots. For all golfers except a very few with "superb touch," the wedge that you use the most from sand should ALWAYS be built with a higher swingweight than any other wedge in the bag. The reason is twofold. One, the wedge will need a higher headweight to help create a little more momentum so it can get through the sand. Two, most shots hit with the sand wedge will be swung with far less than a full swing force. The higher headweight lets you "feel" the clubhead more and helps in developing the proper rhythm and timing to hit such shots more consistently.

- The length of the wedge used predominantly from the sand should be at least one-half inch shorter than the 9-iron. This is because for shots hit from sand, golfers will usually grip down on the SW and crouch more in their stance. (When I worked with Harvey Penick, he made it real clear never to use the word "choke" whenever talking about taking hold of the club further down the grip!) The SW can also be three-quarter inch to 1 inch shorter than the 9-iron if the golfer really likes to "sit down" or crouch when hitting sand shots. But, "one-half inch shorter than your 9-iron" is the general rule for SW length.

- If the lob wedge is used predominantly from grassy lies, the swingweight should be "in between" that of the PW and SW. However, if the lob wedge is your sand club, then it should have a higher swingweight as described before for the SW. For example, if your numbered irons are built to a D1 swingweight, the PW to a D3, and the SW to a D6, the lob wedge that lives more on grass would best be built or "lead taped" to a D4 swingweight. Again, this is to allow the golfer more head feel for shot rhythm and timing.

We Need Some Form of Balance

There are two ways to weigh a golf club. The first is the obvious one. You take a golf club, place it on a scale, and read how many ounces or grams it weighs. This is called the "total weight" of the club.

The second is called "swingweight." I know we covered this briefly earlier in the book, but (now that you know more) I wanted to cover it in a bit more detail because it is a very important part of matching your clubs to YOUR game.

Swingweight is not really a "weight" at all. It refers to the ratio between how much weight is in the front two-thirds of the club compared to the back one-third. It's really more like a way of expressing the club's "balance" (i.e., how the weight of the club is distributed). Let me explain it this way.

At one end of the shaft is the clubhead, which weighs a certain amount. At the other end is the grip, which also weighs a certain amount. In between, the shaft itself weighs something. When you grip a club and waggle it, the head end has a feeling of heaviness that stands out over and above the weight of the rest of the club. Some clubs feel as if they are very heavy in the head end, others can feel not so heavy. Comparing the differences in that feeling is what the industry calls "swingweight."

If golfers find the right swingweight in all their clubs, they will be able to sense the presence and location of the clubhead from the waggle, through the backswing, and into contact with the ball. If it's too light, the player will tend to swing too fast (almost never a good thing). If it's too heavy, the swing will be too slow or slightly cumbersome to make. Either way, if the swingweight is well matched to your strength, swing tempo, rhythm, and athletic ability, you will make swings that are more consistent and hit the ball more on center.

Swingweight is not really a subjective thing. There is a special scale the golf industry has been using since the 1920s to measure swingweight. This scale allows companies and people who build clubs to know how to assemble the clubs to achieve a specific swingweight goal. The grip end of a club is secured against the end of the scale, and the "teeter-totter" where it rocks up and down (i.e., the scale's fulcrum) is 14 inches down from the end of the grip. A slide weight can be moved back and forth along the beam of the scale until the club is balanced level in equilibrium. The slide weight will point to a letter-number designation such as C-6, D-2, or E-4. THAT is the swingweight for that club (see fig. 8.1).

The lower the letter-number combination, the lighter the head will feel when it is swung. The higher the letter-number reading, the heavier the head will feel. Most men's clubs coming from the factory are swingweighted from D-0 to D-2. Most women's clubs are built with a swingweight in the middle C-range. And the rule of thumb is ALL the clubs in the set are built to the same swingweight measurement, except the sand and lob wedges, which will usually be built to a higher swingweight than the numbered irons and PW.

There is no specific way of determining what swingweight is correct for any golfer, at least not in the way you can measure wrist-to-floor and come up with a definite length recommendation. Swingweight has always been a judgment call, based on the golfer's individual feel. Some golfers like swinging a club with a "heavy head" feel, a few others a light headweight feel, and many others have no idea what they like because they never have had the chance to experiment with different swingweights on their clubs to find out.

Generally, golfers of average to below-average strength, with slow, smooth, rhythmic swings (i.e., "swingers") tend to prefer clubs built to lower swingweights. Golfers with more upper body strength, with rapid, jerky, aggressive, quick tempo swings (i.e., "hitters") tend to prefer clubs

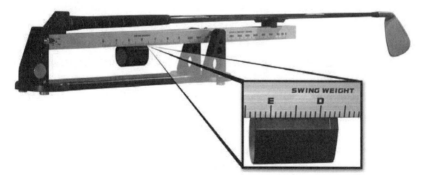

Figure 8.1. The swingweight scale used by almost every golf club company is designed with the fulcrum point 14″ from the end of the grip of the club, and with swingweight designations in letter and number increments, i.e., C9, D0, D1, etc.

with a higher swingweight. When in doubt, make the total weight of the club light and the swingweight a little higher than what is average.

The customary way to build the swingweight in a set is to make all the woods and irons up to the 9-iron to be the same swingweight. Then, if you choose, the PW can be up to 2 pts heavier than the 9-iron, the SW at least 6 pts higher than the 9-iron, and the LW maybe 4 pts higher than the nine. An allowable deviation from this in a well-made set would be about one swingweight point from high to low in the set, as in a spread from D-0 to D-1. In cheap sets you'll see a lot more deviation, as in a spread from perhaps C-8 to D-4. Sand and lob wedges can be an exception because the clubs all have different functions and are so often hit with a less than full swing.

How to find the right swingweight for you? One way would be to find any club you have that just "feels right" when you swing it. You might not know why it has always felt so good, but it does. There is a chance it has felt good to you because it has the right swingweight for your strength and swing tempo. If you have such a club, have its swingweight measured by a clubmaker and try adjusting your other clubs to that same swingweight—maybe doing one club at a time until you are sure.

The other way is a little more specific. It involves using special labels that stick to the faces of your clubs and show the impression of where the ball was hit on the face. This is the method many professional clubmakers use. They start with a light-swingweighted test club built close to the total weight of the clubs you are considering. As you hit balls, the clubmaker will note the point of impact on the face and keep adding weight to the head until you reach the swingweight at which you see your highest percentage of hits in the middle of the face.

Just keep in mind that the "heaviness" or "lightness" of the swingweight of the club has nothing to do with the actual weight of the head. The driver head for a D-1 swingweight installed on a graphite shaft and built to 45-inch length with a normal rubber grip will weigh about 200 grams (about 7 ounces). But if I put that same 200-gram driver head on a steel shaft and build it to the same length with the same grip, when you waggle this club you would think I stuck an anvil on the end of the shaft. I can make that 200 grams feel like anything you want by varying the shaft weight, the length, and even the weight of the grip. That's because the swingweight scale was designed to measure a ratio of weight over the length the club about an arbitrarily placed fulcrum point. The point of all this is that you should know what swingweight is right for you and have your clubs adjusted so they are all the same.

Getting MOI for Your Money

While swingweight is currently the standard method for attempting to match clubs within a set, there is another technology on the horizon that allows for swing feel matching of clubs on a genuinely scientific basis. It's called Moment of Inertia (MOI) matching. MOI matching truly poses a real opportunity to build all the clubs in the set so they require precisely the same physical force from the golfer to swing each club.

You might remember from Chapter 2 that the clubhead has a natural resistance to twisting (called the Moment of Inertia [MOI]), which can be increased, for example, by putting more of the head's weight out at the heel and toe ends of the clubhead. Well, it turns out that the club as a whole has an MOI as well. It is real science, it can definitely be measured, and it can be utilized to put together sets in which every club requires the same exact amount of physical force from the golfer to swing.

Swingweight matching doesn't do that because it arranges the weight in the golf club using a scale that has a fulcrum point set 14 inches down from the end of the grip. In a set of clubs made to the same swingweight, the MOI of every club usually decreases down through the set. That means the golfer has to use a different amount of swing force for each club. With MOI matching the clubs in a set, the potential truly exists for the golfer to develop a little higher level of consistency with each club in the bag. Granted, many golfers have developed very consistent ball-striking skills using swingweight-matched clubs, so the difference between swingweight and MOI matching may not be like night and day. But MOI matching has long been recognized by mechanical engineers as being a better way to match the clubs in a set. Instead of having to develop 13 swings, you need to develop only ONE SWING and use it for each of the 13 clubs. The 14th? Well the putter too can be MOI matched, but normally its MOI would be different from the MOI for the woods and irons because the putting stroke is so different from the full golf swing.

So, if it's such a great scientific way to match swing feel in clubs why hasn't it taken the golf industry by storm? That's a good question (even if I did ask it myself) with a very simple answer. It's pretty complicated to build MOI-matched golf clubs, and it only works correctly if THE RIGHT MOI for each golfer can be determined and then built into each club. Roughly translated, that means it is truly a custom fitting feature that cannot be "standardized" into one MOI measurement that works for all golfers. Take your favorite club to a professional golf clubmaker who has the equipment to measure MOI. There are not a huge number of clubmakers who do offer MOI matching yet because the technology is so new. But the number is gradually increasing. It doesn't matter which wood or iron it is other than being a club that has always "just felt right." You know . . . the one that every time you pulled it out of the bag you just "knew" you were going to hit the ball well. That favorite club is then hung on the arm of a special machine called a "period counter" where it is allowed to swing. The machine then electronically measures the swinging club's "pendulum period," which is a product of its length, total weight, and overall weight distribution balance.

These little info-nuggets are then fed into a computer with a few other static measurements of the club, a button is pushed, and presto-zippo . . . up on the screen appears all the information the clubmaker needs to build a set of clubs, each one having the same MOI as the original favorite (see fig. 8.2).

It's a technology that's catching on, partly because the equipment required to do MOI club matching was only recently developed for the golf industry. A few professional clubmakers have purchased the technology, with more becoming aware of its value in fitting all the time. People with MOI-matched clubs are raving about them. They say that if

Figure 8.2. Matching all your woods and irons to have the same Moment of Inertia has long been recognized as a superior way to ensure all clubs require the same exact force to be swung. Very recently, this technology has become available to custom clubmakers.

they close their eyes, switch clubs in the set, and take a full swing, they absolutely cannot tell the difference between clubs in terms of their swing feel.

That's pretty impressive. Will it show up on the big-name clubs in the golf shops anytime soon? Probably not, because, for one thing, it takes longer to build clubs that are MOI-matched to each other. The other reason is that MOI matching only works if the right MOI for each golfer's strength, swing tempo, and sense of swing rhythm is determined and then built into their clubs. In short, if a golf company's clubs were all built to ONE MOI, that MOI won't work for all golfers. So true MOI matching will remain a domain only of the professional custom clubmakers who invest in the MOI-matching equipment and learn how to use it.

The "Other" Weight of a Golf Club

We talked about swingweight a bit earlier. This time we are talking about the "other weight"—the total weight of the club. Golf club total weight is THE fitting factor when you are deciding between graphite and steel shafts.

The total weight is the sum of the individual weights of the head, shaft, and grip. A club with a lighter total weight can be swung faster than a heavier one. The main reason this is important is that each additional mph of driver swing speed translates into 2–3 more yards. It is one of the real factors that determine how far you hit the ball. Total weight also plays a very important role in the comfort you feel when swinging your clubs. Does the club feel too light, as if you can't control the timing and rhythm of your swing? Does it feel like just too much effort to swing the club back around to the ball? In both cases, that's total weight at work. In Chapter 4 we established that the total weight of your clubs is chiefly determined by the weight of the shaft used in the building of the club. The theory that "lighter shafts = more swing speed = more distance" assumes that you can swing the lighter club faster AND still hit the ball squarely on the sweet spot of the clubface. The problem is that a light total weight is nothing without the correct swingweight or golf club MOI for the golfer's strength and swing tempo.

Physically strong golfers, and especially those with a fast swing tempo on top of their greater strength, have a tendency to lose the feel of the head—its location in space—during their swing with a club that is too light in total weight AND too light in swingweight. Therefore, they tend to swing even more quickly and trash their timing and rhythm in the process. It's sort of like taking a four-foot-long stick with no weight on the end and trying to flip a light switch up or down. You'll quickly find that without some weight on the end you can't control the stick.

Once you've hosed your swing timing and rhythm, the probability of hitting a ball near the sweet spot starts to fade into the proverbial sunset. In all likelihood you will not only hit the ball with less control, but you will actually wind up LOSING yardage, depending on how far off the sweet spot you are hitting the ball. That is most certainly not what you wanted when you made the decision to go with a lighter total weight of your clubs in the first place.

Remember, the shaft is THE primary factor in the total weight of the golf club. While the headweight and grip weight play a role, compared to the weight of the shaft, they are only bit actors in this play. You want lighter clubs; you have to think lighter shafts. And, if you think lighter shafts, you have to think graphite.

Yes, the steel shaft manufacturers are doing a very good job reducing the weight of their designs. Steel shafts that initially all weighed the same 125 grams (4.4 ounces) now are being made in a little wider weight range between 100 and 125 grams (3.5–4.4 ounces). Fine. But, if you really want to lighten the load and "be all that you can be" in terms of swing speed, 25 grams (0.9 ounces) of shaft weight reduction is just a spit in the ocean. Hence the existence of graphite shafts where a huge weight reduction can be achieved.

Here is a little-known point of golf equipment minutia you can probably use to make an extra buck or two off your playing partners this weekend.

What club has the lightest total weight of all the clubs in your bag? Did you guess the longest one with the biggest head? The driver? If you did, you are absolutely right. Most golfers would not believe the longest club bearing the biggest head that hits the ball the farthest would be the lightest of all the clubs, so there's your bet to win a beer at the 19th hole next time you head out to play.

The average steel-shafted driver will have a total weight of about 375 grams, or 13.1 ounces. Change that standard steel shaft to one of the superlight steel shafts being developed today and the total weight drops to about 350 grams, or 12.33 ounces. That's a decrease in total weight of not more than 5 percent. In contrast, most of today's standard graphite-shaft drivers are built with a 65-gram shaft and weigh a total of about 315 grams (i.e., a svelte 11.1 ounces).

With some graphite shafts being made as light as 45 to 55 grams, these supershafts can allow a driver to be built that weighs less than 300 grams (10.5 ounces). Now, think of what I just said—the lightest steel-shaft driver on the planet will weigh about 12.33 ounces, while the lightest graphite-shaft driver can be made to weigh 10.5 ounces. That is a pretty hefty difference when it comes to: lighter total weight = more swing speed = more distance (see table 8.1).

What about the rest of the clubs in your set? From the driver with the lightest total weight, each of the fairway woods progressively increases in total weight, usually in a nice little bump up in 0.33 ounces from the driver to the 3-wood to the 5-wood and so on. The irons keep the total weight increase going, with the 2-iron being the lightest of all the irons. (I know: "Only God and Jack Nicklaus can hit a one-iron," so I did not even include one in the table!)

Each iron gets progressively heavier by about 0.25 ounces down through to the pitching wedge. Because the wedges can be an assortment of different weights depending on who built them and under what performance philosophies, the PW and gap wedge may also be close to the same total weight as the 9-iron, depending on the company making the clubs. But one thing's pretty much certain and that's the fact that your SW will be the heaviest of all woods and irons. If built with a steel shaft, it will push the scale at a robust 475 grams (or just over ONE POUND).

But the heavyweight champion of your bag is your putter, where a weight of just short of 19 ounces is not uncommon, with a total weight more than 19 ounces becoming very much IN these days among the off-the-rack manufacturers. If you're one of the sufferers of the dreaded "yips" like me and have turned to a long putter for relief, just pulling that monster out of the bag 18 times a round will burn a few extra calories for you because one of those puppies can be as heavy as a pound and a half!

If you take a moment to look at the chart of average total weights for each club (see table 8.I) you can see exactly what kind of weight you can drop by converting from heavier steel to lighter graphite shafts. But remember, as I mentioned earlier, for a change in shaft weight to show up as an increase in swing speed, you must drop the total weight of a club by a minimum of 25 grams (0.9 ounces), with 40-50 grams (1.4 to 1.75 ounces) being more realistic. A total weight drop for COMFORT, however, is another matter entirely. Most golfers will immediately notice a lighter, more comfortable feel in their clubs from a 25 gram (0.9 ounces) drop in the weight of the shaft. And that alone can bring about an improvement in your swing consistency and how well you hit the ball.

Table 8.1—Average Golf Club Total Weights

	Men's Clubs			Women's Clubs		
Club	Length (inches)	Graphite Shaft (ounces)	Steel Shaft (ounces)	Length (inches)	Graphite Shaft (ounces)	Steel Shaft (ounces)
Driver	45	11.25	13	44	11	12.5
3-wood	43.5	11.6	13.3	42.5	11.3	12.8
5-wood	42.5	11.9	13.6	41.5	11.6	13.1
7-wood	41.5	12.3	13.9	40.5	11.9	13.4
9-wood	40.5	12.6	14.2	39.5	12.2	13.7
2-iron	39.5	13	14.25	38.5	12.5	13.9
3-iron	39	13.25	14.5	38	12.75	14.15
4-iron	38.5	13.5	14.75	37.5	13	14.4
5-iron	38	13.75	15	37	13.25	14.65
6-iron	37.5	14	15.25	36.5	13.5	14.9
7-iron	37	14.25	15.5	36	13.75	15.15
8-iron	36.5	14.5	15.75	35.5	14	15.4
9-iron	36	14.75	16	35	14.25	15.65
Pitching wedge	36	15	16.25	35	14.5	15.9
Gap wedge	36	15	16.25	34.5	14.5	15.9
Sand wedge	35.5	15.5	16.75	34.5	15	16.3
Lob wedge	35.5	15.3	16.5	34.5	14.75	16.1
Putter	35	16.75	18.25	34	16.65	18.1

Note: Men's graphite shaft total weight averages based on 65 g shaft for woods, 75 g shaft for the irons. Men's steel shaft total weight averages based on 120 g shaft for woods and irons. Women's graphite total weight averages based on 60 g shaft for woods; 65 g shaft for irons. Women's steel shaft total weight averages based on 115 g shaft for both. Men's total weight averages based on 50 g grip, women's on 45 g grip.

Getting "Fitted"—The Ultimate Form of Putting It Together

There are many definitions of what constitutes "custom fit golf clubs" or a "custom fitting session." One of my colleagues in the clubmaking business perhaps described it best when he used the analogy of a car wash.

Let's say your car is looking pretty trashed out. At one level, you can hose your car down with water and squirt off the worst of the dirt. That's an improvement. Not great, but better than nothing. At the next level, you can get out the bucket and soap and give the car a good scrubbing. That's even more of an improvement. Or you can pull out all the stops and scrub it, rub it out, wax it, and detail it inside and out. Now you're ready for show time. The point here is that all the above can be described by car owners as "getting the car washed."

Getting custom fitted for golf clubs is much the same. There are several levels, and all can (and have) been used to describe "custom fit clubs." This is definitely an area where golfers do not have a real grasp on what constitutes a fitting session. In a recent survey conducted by Golf DataTech, the leading data-gathering company in the golf industry, many golfers felt that hitting clubs on a Demo Day at their local driving range constituted a custom fitting! Still others felt that filling out a few questions on a golf company Web site fit the bill for a real custom fitting.

The following is an overview of the various types of "custom fitting" sessions available in the golf industry today and what they actually accomplish. From this, you can choose for yourself what route to follow if you're thinking about taking the step to maximize your playing ability with the best equipment for your game.

Level One: A Level One fitting can be construed as the most basic approach to custom fitting. It has to be understood that such sessions are going to address only a few of the total number of fitting options. Basically, it would consist of the golfer hitting some shots with provided clubs, or answering a questionnaire on one of the golf club company's Web sites.

If you are doing this at a driving range, for example, most of the golf company carts will consist of a number of drivers of different lofts and shaft flexes, and irons built to different lie angles and flexes. The head and shaft model will be restricted to one each for the woods and irons. With a simple cart approach, you hit by trial and error to find the driver loft and wood and iron flex. There usually is a hitting board for checking the lie angle of the irons. For the Web site Q&A fitting sessions, the length and lie angle will be fitted by a height and wrist-to-floor measurement, with the shaft flex and driver loft fitted by your estimation of height and distance of your current shots.

No measurements of your swing speed are incorporated in either approach, and no decisions based on your individual swing characteristics are made other than if the lie angle is fitted by hitting balls from a board. The face angle is rarely a part of the fitting options, nor is an assortment of head designs or different shaft bend profiles and weights. If administered by a well-trained individual, which is never a guarantee, the fitting is better than buying straight off the rack, but it falls well short of a Level Two or Three fitting session.

Level Two: What distinguishes a Level Two fitting from a Level One is the use of a swing computer or launch monitor. There is one cart system from a major manufacturer that incorporates a type of launch monitor to obtain more information from the golfer for whom the fitting recommendation is made. In addition, some of the larger club companies are beginning to open fitting centers that are staffed by company personnel who use a better-quality launch monitor for analyzing the golfer. These are very limited in their locations as they are quite expensive for the companies to set up and staff. Another option from the companies are traveling launch monitor vans. A few of the large golf companies have such mobile fitting centers which travel around the country, stopping at retail stores or pro shops to offer golfers in each area a chance to book a session to be analyzed on a launch monitor. Because these mobile van/truck systems are expensive, they are limited in how many locations they can visit each year.

What makes this type of session a Level Two and not a Three is simply the limited options for fitting specifications the companies can offer. Head models are limited to each company's one or two designs. Face angle options are rarely available in the woods, lofts on the drivers and fairway woods are limited, and usually the shaft model options are limited to the company's own shaft designs. There are few golf companies that will offer a number of different shaft manufacturers' branded models.

Level Three: Now we're getting to the scrub-and-detailing version of custom fitting. This involves conducting an interview concerning the golfer's past tendencies and desires for shotmaking improvements from the new clubs; measuring the golfer for club length; electronically measuring the golfer's swing speed with both the driver and 5-iron and selecting shaft candidates from a list of many by weight, torque, flex and flex profile; selecting grips from a complete size and style/texture range; and building a single pilot club that can be tested and tweaked before building the complete set. This process (not including building time) will take at least three hours, spread over two or three visits.

Level Four: This level would consist of everything mentioned in

Level Three, plus a detailed analysis of the golfer's existing set and a careful analysis of the proposed set as it is being built.

Attention is paid to matching shaft frequencies or club MOI, swing-weights, loft and lie tweaking, grip buildups, spine aligning, dead weight, balance point, and so forth. Usually, several prototype clubs are built before the final set is done, and usually several follow-up visits are scheduled. This process, exclusive of the club building itself, takes about eight hours or so, spread over multiple visits. This is the rubbed-out, waxed, and detailed version of our car wash.

If you are lucky, you might be at a clubmaker's shop that has a computerized "launch monitor" or "MOI club matching" software that removes much of the trial and error from the process. These are devices that will electronically probe the output of your swing and provide the clubmaker with the data he or she needs to give you the best possible set of clubs.

Building a club that will provide the highest ball speed with the most optimal launch angle for your particular swing characteristics does this. Alas, these machines are expensive and not found in every clubmaker's shop, but thanks to good old American supply and demand, the price of launch monitors is coming down and allowing more and more clubmakers to put one into their shops.

Level Five: Theoretically there is a Level Five but, unless you are a PGA Tour pro, or the best friend of a big golf company CEO, you'll never see it. Custom designing a full set of clubs for a touring pro usually requires several visits by the professional, between which the designer and technicians will be grinding, shaping, testing, and "tweaking" every performance and shape aspect of the clubheads, shafts, grips, and the assembled specifications.

Most of the companies who pay tour pros to endorse their clubs will have several different variations of their "store models" for the pros to choose from. They may have a different sole shape, a different toe profile, a different topline thickness, a different amount of offset, or a variety of other little things that will be quite different from the "off-the-rack" clubs they ship to the golf retailers.

The clubs you buy in the retail stores are to the clubs the pros use as the Chevy Monte Carlo in your driveway is to the car Jeff Gordon drives in NASCAR races. For those who are still skeptical, let me describe exactly how a set of professional clubs is made.

In 1999 I had the pleasure of designing what tragically turned out to be the last set of clubs Payne Stewart played in competition. His set required four separate visits to my workshop over the course of six months.

Payne had just concluded a contract with Spalding that required him to play the company's investment-cast cavity-back irons, but he was most anxious to get back to playing with a forged carbon-steel design. I kept spare "raw forgings" from a Lynx set that I had earlier designed for just such projects as Payne's.

Payne's first visit was to find out what he liked to see in the various irons as he set up behind the ball. In other words, what kind of leading-edge shape, topline thickness and shape, toe shape, top-of-the-toe transition to the topline, the offset, how the bottom of the hosel should fan out into the blade (indelicately called the "crotch"), and many other subtle areas of each ironhead. Between visits one and two I ground, filed, bent, and formed each of Payne's preferences into each head in the set.

During visit number two, Payne stood right next to me as I reground and shaped each head to a nearly final form. Payne would insert a shaft in each head, assume an address position, look, look again, scratch his head and, in whatever way he could, express what was good, bad, or indifferent about each one. From this, I now had a much clearer picture of what he wanted and could final grind each head after he left. Matters like center of gravity positions were my responsibility to manipulate in accordance with the ball flight trajectory wishes that Payne had expressed.

During the third and fourth visits, the still-not-completely-finished heads were assembled with different shaft options. Payne hit shot after shot with each club, commenting only when he felt it appropriate to clarify his desires for the feel of both the clubhead and the shaft during the shots. Only when Payne gave final approval to each club was his job complete, and mine shifted into another gear.

All tour players require a minimum of two identical sets of clubs, one to travel with and one to keep in a safe place, packed and ready to ship. Should the nightmare scenario occur of their clubs being lost or even stolen, they can obtain a duplicate of their old set literally overnight. Because of that requirement, I also had to make templates for each head profile along with all sorts of measurements and photographs that would allow me to remake the backup set completely from scratch without having any of the original clubs to guide me.

All totaled, I probably spent somewhere in the area of 300 hours from start to finish on the two identical sets. It's something you should keep in mind the next time you see an ad implying you will be playing clubs that are "just like the ones the pros use." Trust me. You won't.

When It Really Becomes Magic

The idea of custom fitting is to have clubs in which the individual design characteristics of the clubhead, shaft, and grip are matched to your swing. Further, they are assembled to allow you to maintain essentially the same swing throughout the set, yet give predictably different distance and trajectory results because of the way each club is designed and built.

This is the essence of clubmaking and design. Unfortunately, that almost never happens because so few golfers ever do more in their search for their perfect golf clubs than drive to the local golf store or click on their computer.

The average golfer could lose five to six strokes by simply realizing that the golf club is not a "club." It is not something that is used to beat things into submission. It really IS a superbly designed, surgical quality, instrument—IF YOU TAKE THE TIME TO DISCOVER HOW IT CAN BE FIT TO COMPLEMENT YOUR SWING.

One swing, 14 controlled results—NOT 14 swings and 144 prayers.

Chapter 9—LADIES FIRST

Ladies First

In the many clubmaking and clubfitting seminars I have taught, there has always been one question from the group to the effect: "Can you tell us a little about how to fit women, seniors, and juniors?" And I have always responded with the same answer, "There is no such thing as gender or age when it comes to fitting golfers. There are only golfers with differences in their size, strength, and athletic ability. Both clubmakers and consumers need to understand that."

If you think of all women as "lady golfers," all seniors as "old people," and all juniors as "little kids," you could make the mistake of pigeonholing golfers into preconceived categories and make serious errors in your golf club buying.

When the golf industry creates a women's, senior, and junior golf club, they tend to make them "one way and one way only" for each of these segments of the golf market. Women's and senior clubs, for example, are made to one length and only offer one choice of flex—as if to say "you women and seniors are ALL THE SAME." At least within the standard made "men's" clubs you can choose from different flexes in the shafts and different lofts among the drivers.

There are women, senior, and even some junior golfers who can and should play with the same fitting specifications that you would find in men's clubs. And there are some men who can and should be playing with what are labeled by the golf industry as "senior," or "lady" club specifications.

To do the best in identifying the best golf clubs for women, seniors, or juniors, people in these demographic segments need to be thought of as simply "golfers" with their own unique characteristics of size, strength, and athletic ability which need to be evaluated free from any preconceived gender- or age-related notions.

Unfortunately, the golf equipment industry does not look at it that way when they create their standard clubs for each of these segments of the golfing population. Hence, mistakes are made in matching the best equipment to these golfers because too many incorrect assumptions are made about their needs.

For example, when a woman, senior, or junior comes into a pro shop or golf retail store to shop for clubs, the salesperson should not just automatically escort them over to the women's, senior, or junior club displays. They need to take the time to find out if THIS woman, senior, or junior is best served by the clubs built expressly for those segments of the market, or whether they require a less obvious solution. If they were trained to do this, they might end up steering these people to those sections of the store anyway, but they might also end up pointing them to the "men's clubs" section of the shop as well. Remember, golfers are golfers, each with their own combination of unique physical and athletic characteristics that all need to be addressed individually before making equipment decisions.

What Are These Clubs Anyway?

Being a designer, I will freely admit that organizing a golf club product line under the segments of "men's, women's, seniors', and juniors'" is a very logical and organized way to approach the task. After all, that's how the department stores approach the presentation of their clothing lines for each segment of their market.

But if you applied the golf industry's approach to equipment selection to the clothing industry, here's what you would see in your local department store. You would walk through the men's department and see the usual array of sizes and styles from small to XXX-large, but when you get to the women's department, you would see clothing offered in only two or three styles and only in size medium. The same thing is true in the senior department. The customer would only see limited styles and "one size" from which to meet their clothing needs.

In the average retail golf store, the regular men's clubs account for something like 90 percent of all the clubs in the store. Lofts on drivers are stocked from 8 to 12 degrees and flexes on both graphite and steel shafts in A, R, S, and X. In women's clubs, however, drivers are usually stocked in a 12 or 13 degree loft, lengths are an inch shorter than the corresponding men's model, and shafts are offered in only one flex.

The problem is that the vast majority of "average" women golfers need drivers with more loft than what is offered, shorter lengths for all the woods, a set makeup that eliminates the 3- and 4-iron completely from consideration, and a choice of at least two different shaft flexes, both of which should be more flexible than any men's shaft.

It is just as bad, if not worse, with "senior" golf clubs.

To begin with, when the golf industry says "senior," they are talking senior men only. Have you ever seen an ad for the Shazam 3000 Senior WOMEN'S model? Like, somehow, senior women don't play golf?

Second, most of the golf club companies do not really offer a specially designated "senior model" even for men. Other than the availability of an A-flex shaft, every other specification of the clubs offered to seniors is precisely the same as the regular men's clubs. That includes the absurd 45-inch driver, a set makeup that includes the 3- and 4-iron, and no driver loft higher than 12 degrees. All these things are woefully inappropriate for what the golf industry considers the "average senior man," I can assure you.

So, what's the difference between the designated "senior clubs" and the regular men's models? Basically, it's a logo on the head or shaft that says "senior," which has the dual function of (a) misidentifying the clubs as being somehow different, and (b) offending most men over the age of 60.

If we can say the "average senior man" has a swing speed no higher than 80–85 mph and at least some loss of body flexibility, then their needs are VERY different from the "flat-belly" players. The average senior needs more loft and a shorter length on the driver, shorter lengths on the fairway woods (which need to be offered at least up to a 9-wood), often a shaft more flexible than the typical A-flex, and no hint of a number on the irons lower than a 5 or even 6.

In most retail golf shops, even juniors have it better than the women and seniors because at least the kids' sets are offered in two "sizes," "age 5–9" and "age 10–13."

Since all clubs stocked in pro shops and off-course golf stores are made to standardized specifications, none of them will satisfy all the individual fitting factors that the many different men, women, senior, or junior golfers possess. If you want to address women's, senior, junior, (and yes) men's fitting needs properly, they need to be fitted individually. If that were really the case, a golf retail store would have no segmented "departments" and I would not be compelled to write this chapter.

If you are a woman, senior, or junior, the question then becomes: how SHOULD I buy my golf clubs? What should I look for, and what should I look OUT for? Let me answer that by taking each group in turn, beginning, of course, with ladies first!

How About a Break?

It pains me to say this, but, by and large, the women get a raw deal when it comes to golf equipment. Male golfers get to choose from several different head designs, driver lofts, and shaft flexes, in steel or graphite. Women get to choose from one head model, maybe two but usually only one driver loft, and one flex of one model of shaft in one length.

Recently, a good friend of mine who writes for one of the major golf magazines told me that in 2002, at two of the four largest golf equipment companies in the world, not more than 7 percent of their total club sales came from their women's club models, with the other 93 percent coming in their men's lines. Given the increase in women who have taken to the game in recent years, this is surprising.

Could it be that the women golfers recognize their offerings from the big golf companies are too limited for their needs? Could it be that the predominantly male sales staff of the golf retail stores doesn't offer enough assistance or may inadvertently intimidate the women who shop independently for golf clubs? Or, is it that the golfing husbands and boyfriends who do the club shopping for their partners end up buying "cheap" clubs from a mass merchant retailer or sporting goods store and that's why sales of the premium women's clubs are so low? I'm not sure, but I do believe some of each may account for this very low sales percentage in the premium models of women's golf clubs.

I will say I thought there was maybe a light in the tunnel in 2004 when a few of the larger club companies decided to revamp their women's club models and develop a few hybrid set offerings. One company went so far as to create a 6-club set with lofts spaced much farther apart, aimed at the very slow swing speed woman player. This 6-club set, by the way, was the closest thing I could find to an appropriate SENIOR woman's set of clubs.

Contrast this, however, with the women's versions put out by most of the major club companies. The impression you get in their advertising is that these are unique castings that are based on the design features found in the men's models, but are specifically designed for women. Sometimes this is true, but in many (if not most) cases, it simply is not so.

If you look at the design specification information for male and female clubs, you'll see that the typical set makeup is the same for both: the same driver, 3-, 5-, and 7-woods, and #3 through PW. What kind of difference is that? OK, there are some 9-woods in there too, but there are 9-woods available for men as well.

All too often, the women's heads are nothing more than men's heads created in colors believed to be more popular with women (i.e., mauve, taupe), with the word "Lady Shazam" (or whatever) engraved on it. They are made to be one inch shorter than the men's clubs but assembled with an L-flex shaft.

Then we have the shafts themselves. In Chapter 5 we discussed the problem of shaft flex at some length. We cited a study that showed that shaft flex is not standardized and, therefore, its letter code designations for flex are virtually meaningless.

Regarding women's shafts, we have to amend that conclusion. With the "L-flexes," the results of the study were both predictable and meaningful. Every one of the women's shafts tested was out of sequence compared to the other A, R, S, and X shaft flexes. They were ALL too stiff for a woman golfer with a 65 mph swing speed—especially when cut and installed to the final assembly length.

Given the importance of shaft stiffness in helping to get the ball up in the air and delivering a solid feeling of impact to the golfer, this means that most female golfers who shop only within the women's lines of clubs may be having their game hindered by one company's L-flex shaft being so much different from the next.

Recently, a few shaft companies have come out with what they call an "LL-Flex." Translated, the LL-flex means: "We-finally-figured-out-there-are-differences-in-women-golfers'-swing-speeds-just-like-there-are-with-men-so-we-decided-to-finally-do-what-we-do-for-men-and-offer-you-a-choice." I look forward to seeing the data that confirm the LL-flex as being what it is supposed to be. If it is, it'll be a breakthrough in at least admitting that different levels of strength and swing speed exist among women golfers just as they do with the men.

Finally, there are the grips, but here there is good news. Yes, there really is such a thing as a women's grip. Because the distaff hand is, generally, smaller than the male hand, the grip companies have all produced lighter, smaller-diameter grips for the women. But just because you are a woman, don't assume these grips are right for you. Remember the final test for a grip is how it feels in your hand. If you feel more comfortable with a larger "man's" grip, then by all means use it despite what any man might say—including me, as in the case of my triathlete wife who insists men's standard grips feel the best to her!

Fitting the Women in General

Remember my fitting philosophy with respect to gender and age? Perhaps I can paraphrase that by saying most women golfers are simply smaller men with slower swing speeds. Or, perhaps, most men golfers are just larger women with faster swing speeds? Whatever gets the point across that we are all golfers with a need for a wide variety of fitting options, so we can come up with a set that will complement each of our own, distinctive, individual swings.

As I mentioned above, there are a number of women who, from a fitting standpoint, are the same as many men golfers, possessing the same strength, swing speed, and swing mechanics. If you doubt it, I'll introduce you to some women golfers who will substantially adjust your attitude by about the third hole of any course you'd care to play.

But, because the vast majority of women golfers are not as strong, do not possess the same swing speed, and are not as athletically skilled as most men golfers, I want to talk specifically about the particular fitting requirements of the average woman golfer. For you women who are as strong and/or who possess the same or higher swing speed as many men, go back to Chapters 1 through 8 for your education on what club design and fitting requirements are best for you.

Specifically Fitting the Women

This section will assume that you, as a woman golfer, are not as physically strong or as athletically experienced as the average man. Either way, whether you are a male, female, young or old, the first step in finding the right club for you is to GET YOUR SWING SPEED MEASURED, because everything starts there.

If your driver or fairway wood swing speed is less than 70 mph, if your mid-iron swing speed is less than 55 mph, if you are 5 feet 6 inches or less in height, if you are not as strong as the average man, and you are not as athletically inclined as the average man, the following golf equipment fitting guidelines are specifically addressed to you.

The Set Makeup Is CRITICAL to Your Success

The most important swing factor in determining set makeup is your swing speed. The second most important factor is your swing ability and how easily you get the ball airborne with lofts of 27 degrees or less. (That is, how well do you get the following up in the air: 3-wood, 5-wood, 7-wood, 9-wood, 3-iron, 4-iron, or 5-iron?)

Knowing your swing speed is super important here because the higher the swing speed, the farther and higher the ball will fly with each club in your set. Knowing at what point you begin to have difficulty getting the ball up in the air is also very important because that too helps dictate the best set makeup for your game.

With a wood swing speed of 70 mph or under and an iron speed of 55 mph or less, your ability to hit the ball high in the air to make it carry as far as possible is reduced. You will definitely need a very carefully thought out recommendation for the best set you can buy.

But not to worry. Your good taste and wisdom in buying this book are about to, yet again, be rewarded; for I just happen to have some of those recommendations for you.

- First, if your swing speed is 70 mph or lower with the woods, don't even think about using a standard driver/#1 wood unless the loft is 15 degrees or higher. And, even then, that's only if you generally do not struggle with getting the ball up in the air. If you struggle with hitting a 5-wood off the ground, if your best shots fly no higher than the gutters on a one-story home, don't even think about a conventional 12 or 13 degree loft "ladies" driver head.
- If your swing speed is less than 70 mph and you do not get the ball well up with your swing, your "driver" should be a fairway wood of no less than 18 degrees loft. Take a look at the following table indicating what loft carries the ball what distance for slower swing speeds. About the only place you have a prayer of finding a driverhead with 14 degrees or more loft is from a professional custom clubmaker. Most of the big club companies do not make drivers for women with more than 13.5 degrees of loft (see table 9.1).
- If you can't find a driver head with that much loft, use a fairway wood with 16–18 degrees of loft as your tee shot club. That might be a 3-wood or a 5-wood, but because fairway wood

Table 9.1—The Effect of Launch Angle on Driver Distance

Swing Speed (mph)	Driver Loft (degrees)	Launch Angle	Carry Distance (yards)
60	11	12.1	106
	15	15.2	117
	19	18.1	122
70	11	12.1	145
	15	15.2	154
	19	18.1	156
80	9	10.5	174
	11	12.1	181
	13	13.7	185
90	9	10.5	206
	11	12.1	211
	13	13.7	213
100	8	9.6	231
	9	10.5	234
	10	12.1	236
110	7	8.8	254
	8	9.6	256
	9	10.5	257

Note: Table information based on a swing angle of attack of +2.5 degrees, which means hitting the ball on the upswing with the driver traveling upward at an angle of 2.5 degrees. The average golfer will have a slight upward angle of attack with the driver. For golfers who do not hit the ball on the upswing, the optimum driver loft for maximum distance will be a little higher loft than what is shown in the table.

Because the majority of women golfers do not generate a high swing speed, it is especially important for them to find a driver loft that will achieve an optimum launch angle and therefore result in maximum distance.

lofts vary between companies, you will want to verify the lofts before you buy.

- Your fairway wood makeup can be 3w, 5w, 7w, 9w if your swing speed with the woods is right around 70 mph or higher. At that speed, the distance difference you will get with each of these woods will justify their presence in your bag—that is, as long as the loft increment is 3 degrees and the length difference is one inch between the woods. If you have loft changes of 2 degrees and length spacing of one-half inch, forget it. You won't have enough distance difference between the fairway woods.

- If your wood swing speed is 60 mph or less, you won't need all those woods because the distance difference between them won't be great enough to justify buying them. Therefore, if the 3-wood is your driver, your fairway woods will be the 5-wood and 9-wood. I would also urge you to think about carrying an 11-wood. I'd normally say jump from the 9- to the 13-wood, but I can't. It's almost as impossible to find 13-woods these days as a winning lottery ticket. So if you are comfortable with fairway woods, use an 11-wood although the distance difference between it and a 9-wood won't be that great. This will allow you to start your iron set with no iron longer than a 6- or 7-iron.

- If your wood swing speed is 60 mph or less, do not buy, use, or carry a 3-, 4-, or 5-iron. Even if you have relatively little trouble getting the ball up in the air, shots hit with 7-, 9-, and 11-woods will fly higher and farther than shots hit with the ironhead of the same loft.

- If your 5-iron or middle-iron swing speed is closer to 50 mph, do not carry a 6-iron. Irons labeled as "lady lofts" rarely have more than 1 degree higher loft than the same numbered irons in men's set. Thus, thanks again to "shrinking loft disease," a women's 6-iron just does not have enough loft for a 50 mph iron swing. You simply won't get the ball up in the air. Your 9-wood and 11-wood will replace hitting shots that normally would be hit with a well-struck 3-, 4-, 5-, and 6-iron.

- You might consider "hybrid clubs" as a replacement for those long irons that are impossible to hit high enough to get good distance. Unfortunately, most of the hybrid clubs are neither short enough in length nor flexible enough in the shaft to be well suited for women with an iron swing speed of 60 mph and lower. Custom clubmakers can and will build hybrid clubs with the specifications you need.

- If you prefer hitting an iron to a high-lofted fairway wood, then be SURE the lofts of any potential 5- and 6- iron are not lower than 28 and 32 degrees, respectively.

- If you prefer the 5- and 6-irons over a 9-wood and 11-wood and those two irons do not have very much loft, then go to a professional clubmaker who can bend the lofts higher and get them into the proper incremental loft change from club to club. If you have no idea of your lofts (and don't care to know) that is even more reason to go to a competent clubmaker who can take care of this for you.

- Since you probably won't be carrying 14 total clubs with these overall set makeup recommendations, you have room to put more wedges in your bag. Because a 70 mph wood swing speed and 55 mph iron swing speed won't hit the ball that far, you MUST rely on your wedges to lower your score. DO take the time to work with a competent short game/wedge teacher to learn how to play all types of wedge shots close to and around the green. When you learn the proper techniques with the wedges, then you can make use of having multiple wedges in your bag. You should always be striving to "get the ball up and down" in the fewest numbers of shots.

- Take the time to fit your putter for the correct length, loft, lie, and weight. Many women of 5 feet 6 inches or under will not find the golf industry's "standard lady" putters fit them properly for length or lie angle. Because putting is THE critical element of scoring, and because 70 mph and 55 mph swing speeds won't allow you to hit many greens "in regulation," you must become the best putter you can be to keep lowering your score. Custom putter fitting is important for ALL golfers, but it is critical for golfers with slower swing speeds.

- If your swing speeds with the woods and irons are faster than 70 mph and 55 mph, respectively, you start to become a candidate for an A-flex shaft. But, as I have said, not all A-flex shafts are the same stiffness, so be sure to connect with a competent clubmaker or knowledgeable salesperson who can steer you to an A-flex shaft that is truly matched to your swing speed. However, whether you can use the lofts associated more with men's clubheads still depends chiefly on your ability to get the ball WELL up in the air. Thus for women golfers of higher-than-average swing speed and strength, the proper fitting requirements more often become a combination of men's and women's fitting parameters.

Since there are no "half men's and half women's" clubs sold as standard in the retail golf shops, where do you go for help? Most definitely, the nod goes again to the experienced professional clubmaker in your area. He or she can build your clubs from a variety of head, shaft, and grip options and can make all the required alterations of length, loft, swingweight, and grip size for the "in-between women's" game.

(On a personal note: if you happen to live in the San Francisco Bay area, give Shelley Gates at Marin Golf Company a call. With her 25 years of clubmaking experience, she is one of the best fitters of female golfers in the country.)

Iron Length and Lie Are Also Extremely Important

While the standard women's clubs made by the big club companies are one inch shorter in length than the men's clubs, these standard women's lengths will still be too long to allow most of you to swing the clubs with full control. In short, if the 45-inch length of the standard men's drivers is too long for 90 percent of all men, the 44-inch standard women's driver length will be too long for at least 90 percent of all women. The same thing is true with the irons. Women's irons that are always made one inch shorter than the men's will not be suitable for probably 90 percent of women golfers.

Here again, all women golfers should be measured for length just like any other golfer. Perform the wrist-to-floor measurement to get your initial length recommendations from a length-fitting chart. That length-fitting chart is NOT gender specific so it will place any man or woman golfer into the initial length guidelines best suited for their height plus arm length.

It is unlikely these length recommendations will be increased by very much based on a flatter swing plane or better ball-striking skills for women golfers with 70/55 swing speeds (i.e., 70 mph driver, 55 mph 5-iron). These swing speeds rarely if ever match well with lengths that are longer than the recommendation that comes from the golfer's wrist-to-floor measurement. On the contrary, there is a very strong possibility a woman with such swing speeds may actually be better off with a final length that is a little shorter than the length recommendations as indicated by wrist-to-floor measurement.

If you have that 70/55-swing speed and you are lower than many in strength and athletic ability, yes, do decrease the recommended lengths of your clubs by about an inch per club. Golf is not a game played very well with clubs that hit the ball off-center and have a low flight trajectory. Hence, to err on the side of shorter lengths for most women golfers is a far wiser way to go.

For women of 5 feet 6 inches or shorter height, when the length is fitted properly, it is almost a cinch that the lie angles of the standard made women's ironheads will not fit properly. Thus, it is very important for women golfers of this physical stature and with 70/55 swing speeds to be properly fitted for the lie angles of their irons, and if possible, fairway woods as well.

Sure, it could be said that the number of yards of off-line misdirection from someone with a 55 mph iron swing would not be that much. But that's not the point. No one feels good about aiming in one direction and seeing the ball take off in another, or seeing the toe end of the irons stick well up in the air when they address the ball.

The "L" Might Not Stand for Ladies

If we're talking "letters" in golf, we're talking about shafts. As with ALL golfers, the primary consideration in the shaft is its weight and whether it is a help or a hindrance in getting the ball up in the air. If the ball can't get up and fly, it can't go very far, and that is especially true with the lower swing speeds associated with most women golfers. Because there are far more women golfers who are less strong than the average man, the weight of the shaft becomes more important for the average woman than for the average man.

You might guess what I am about to say, but don't start hiding your wallet just yet. The vast majority of women golfers will be better served by having light graphite shafts in ALL their 13 woods and irons. Graphite equals lightweight, which equals a lighter total club weight, which equals more comfort and ease of swinging the clubs—not to mention a higher swing speed. Nowhere is this more important than in the irons.

Irons all weigh more than the woods in terms of total weight. Total weight is what you feel when you heft the club off the ground; and going with the lighter graphite shafts in ALL the clubs can really help women be all they can be as golfers. When I say "light graphite" I mean the shaftweight by itself is not more than 70 grams in the irons, and under 60 grams in the woods, if you can find them.

Why lighter shafts in the woods than in the irons? Although the woods are already going to be lighter in total weight than the irons, they are also going to be much longer in length. Longer length with even lighter total weight makes for the possibility of more distance where you need it most, and a much easier time at swinging 40 to 43 inches of club length.

Let's take a look next at the flex of the shaft. In Chapter 5, I mentioned that the only other significant performance function of the shaft is to contribute to how high you hit the ball for any given loft on the clubhead. Since most women have a swing speed that is lower, they are already at a disadvantage regarding shot height and distance; and, as I have been preaching, slow swing speed golfers MUST get the ball well up in the air so it can fly the farthest possible distance.

The loft on the clubhead is definitely the number one determinant in shot height. But shaft flex becomes even more important for the average woman golfer versus the average man for getting the ball up high enough to FLY, again because of the difference in swing speed between most women and most men.

Let's say we were to leave the shaft stiff for the woman and just keep increasing the loft on all her clubs as her only means of getting the ball higher. Fine, that'll get the ball up. But there will come a point when the ball starts to go "too much UP and not enough OUT." The ways we trick the golf gods for the slower-swinging golfer are to (a) use a driver with a lot more loft than what most men use, (b) use fairway woods and irons that have a little more loft than men use (like 2 to 3 degrees more), and (c) then use a LOT more flexible shaft to make it all work.

Why use such a highly flexible shaft? If the shaft can flex forward more before impact, it will contribute as much as 2 degrees more toward the optimal launch angle. That means the lofts on the fairway wood and irons won't have to be so insanely high, which is something that can be tough to find in golf clubheads today. And, if that happens, the average woman golfer will get more ball velocity from those lofts and further cheat the golf gods out of a few more yards of distance.

All the above sounds great, but I must warn you. It will ONLY happen if the shaft is made more flexible to match the woman's swing speed.

Generally, the L flex shafts that are installed in the premium club company women's models, as well as the L flex shafts made by the "name" shaft companies, are okay for women players with swing speeds of 65–75 mph in the woods and 55–60 mph in the irons. That's fine, but just as there are many women who swing faster than that, there exist plenty of women golfers who do not swing their woods and irons anywhere near that fast. It is for these slower-than-average swing speeds that there is a need for the LL-Flex shaft. Unfortunately, as of this writing that shaft does not exist in any of the standard made women's clubs you see in the pro shops or off-course golf stores.

Again, here is where the friendly professional clubmaker can come to the rescue and provide a real shot at beating those golf gods out of their precious yards. Independent custom clubmakers have access to hundreds (if not thousands) of shafts with which they can meet any golfer's shaft fitting requirements. Plus, they can install any shaft so that it can play more flexibly (or more stiff, if desired) simply by the way they cut and install the shaft in each head.

Just remember, more flexibility in the shaft is good for about 95 percent of all golfers. For golfers with slower swing speeds, such as most women and many senior men, it is more than good; it is mandatory!

Ladies, Move to the Head of the Class

Ladies, I would be remiss if I did not mention a few key points in the selection of the type of clubhead that, in all likelihood, would be best for your game. Because all club fitting recommendations originates in the golfer's swing, there are some important clubhead design features you will need to consider.

Before we start, however, I want to be sure we're clear on something. When I say "slower-than-average swing speeds," I'm talking about ALL golfers with slower-than-average swing speeds, not just the women. So, you men, listen up, because there are an awful lot of you with wood swing speeds of 70 mph and under, and iron speeds of 55 mph and below.

Driverhead Design

There is no scientific reason why a woman golfer in the 70/55 swing speed range cannot hit a large titanium driverhead, as long as the loft is high enough, and the length is correct for her. In other words, just because a driver may be 400 cc in size, the wind resistance to swinging this versus a smaller head is not enough to cause concern for any significant loss of distance. After all, you're pushing air with a 400 cc driverhead at the end of that stick—not a Chevy Suburban.

On the other hand, many women golfers simply do not like the look of a very large driverhead. When it comes to clubheads, golfer psychology is not something to tinker with—forcing a head into the hands of any golfer who is not comfortable with its size or appearance is a sure way to increase the number of poor swings.

So, ladies, if you do not like a big driver, don't buy one. As you might already know—size isn't everything. There is nothing inherent in clubhead size that will make one driver perform better or worse, given your swing speed and ability to get the ball up.

There is one other factor in driverhead selection for women in the

70/55-swing speed range or lower. A high COR on the driver face (Coefficient of Restitution—remember that from Chapter 2?) won't mean a thing at these swing speeds unless you KNOW the face is designed to fracture at a swing speed of 90 mph or higher. I say this for two reasons.

First, no golf company on the planet makes drivers with a superthin face that is designed only for slower swing speeds. Thus, even in the women's drivers made by the big companies, those faces will survive an impact with the ball from swings of up to 120 mph. So, if you have a swing speed of 70 mph or less, how much do you think you will flex the face inward to make full use of the high COR? That's right, nada. Increased ball velocity off a high COR face only happens when the golfer's swing speed is high enough to flex the face inward.

The other reason I know this is because I tried it once in my design life. Years ago I designed a line of high-COR woods for the Snake Eyes and the Lynx brands. Face thickness was scaled down for slower-swing-speed golfers to maximize how much a slower swing would flex the face of the driver inward, and thus generate a higher ball speed for that slower swing.

Because the heads would break if a golfer with a much higher swing speed used them, we put a big sticker on the face of the drivers to warn about this. It all worked very well and definitely increased distance for the slower-swing-speed golfers, but it didn't last long. Such a design multiplied the inventory requirements when you realized each face-swing-speed thickness also had to be offered in a variety of lofts. So, unfortunately, my bosses at the time shot my design down as being too much of a hassle to inventory! But I have to tell you; it DID work!

So my point is that if the proper driver loft for your swing speed only exists in a smaller steel driver, so be it—don't hold out for a high-COR titanium head because it won't make any difference in distance for these swing speeds.

Here is a good driver design feature for women golfers who both slice/fade the ball and need every bit of assistance in getting the ball up in the air. Why not consider an offset hosel?

Some, not many, but some drivers are designed with the hosel positioned a lot more in front of the face, instead of the reverse with the face more in front of the hosel (see Chapter 2). These "offset hosel" drivers are an excellent feature to consider because moving the hosel forward helps to move the center of gravity farther back in the head, which helps the shaft increase the height of the shot. It also helps give the golfer just that much more time before impact to rotate the face more closed, and thus help reduce that tendency to slice or fade the ball too much.

Fairway Woodhead Designs

Here again, loft rules the roost in fairway wood selection. If you have a 70/55 swing speed level and lower, having MORE loft than the men's fairway woods is critical, unless you have a swing that can really get the ball up no matter what. Most golfers with slower-than-average swing speeds do not.

The woman who has a 70/55 swing speed or lower but who CAN easily get the ball up in the air still should play with a 3-wood loft of no less than 16 degrees to help KEEP the ball in the air longer so it can fly farther. Women who do not get the ball up well into the air should not even have a 3-wood, unless they plan to use it ONLY off the tee with the ball sitting on a peg. Those women players who struggle with getting the ball up off the ground with their woods should start their fairway wood collection with no less than a 5-wood that has no less than 19 degrees of loft.

For women with a swing speed at or above the 70/55 range, there will be enough distance difference between fairway woods so that it might be okay to stuff the bag with 3-, 5-, 7-, and 9-woods. But don't go buying fairway woods that change in loft by only 2 degrees or change in length by only one-half inch or else you will not have enough distance between each individual club to justify their existence in the bag.

For women with swing speeds that are more in the 60 mph level (or slower) for woods, choosing every other fairway wood will be a much wider and more useful set makeup. Again, such slower swing speeds just don't, and won't, create enough of a difference in distance between woods of 3 degree loft separation to merit all the odd-numbered fairway woods being in the bag. For these slower-swing-speed women, every other odd-numbered fairway wood (i.e., 3, 7, 11) will work much better to provide real usable distance differences between the fairway woods.

Almost every golfer who has struggled with getting the ball up in the air from the ground fears a head with a taller face and a larger body. The reason is they know that shallow-face fairway woods are so much easier to hit high.

For slower-swing-speed players, it can literally be the difference between success and failure in trying to be as good as you can be with the fairway woods. Believe me, golfers with swing speeds in the 70/55 level or lower need easy-to-hit-high fairway woods as they need food.

Shallow-face fairway woods are defined by a face height of no taller than 33–34 mm, or between 1.25 and 1.375 inches if your ruler only has hash marks in the Imperial form of measurement. Shallower is even better for slow-swing-speed players, although in the world of golf equipment trends and fads, the industry has "been there, done that" so you might be hunting for something that doesn't exist any more except in the used club barrels.

How big a "footprint" the fairway wood makes when you look down at it on the ground is another important psychological design feature for women.

Most women who struggle a little with getting the ball up with the woods will probably not like the look of a larger fairway woodhead. Bigger fairway woodheads are in existence these days because many designers just think they look better in relation to the grapefruit-size drivers that have become popular. So this one I leave to you to determine. Just go to a golf store and place several different fairway wood models side-by-side on the ground, and see which shape and size you like.

Another thing, although we are talking head design here: don't make the length differences less than one inch between each odd-numbered fairway wood. This will make for a better distance contrast between each club.

Iron Recommendations

For a golfer with a slower swing speed who needs every yard possible, this is a no-brainer. Cavity-back, cavity-back, cavity-back, and wider, wider, wider sole, and get one that is nicely curved around the lower front edge of the face. A little offset on the hosel can help a bit with the height of the shot, but here too there are some golfers, women included, who just don't like the look of the hosel sitting out there way in front of the face.

Try to avoid the larger ironhead shapes, not so much because of the height of the heads, but because larger ironheads mean a longer sole length from heel to toe. More sole length can be a little tougher for the slower-swing-speed player to "dig" through the ground and take a divot because there is more turf resistance there. Wider sole, and I mean wider from the face to back, is OK as long as there is some curvature to reduce the amount of sole that is actually in contact with the ground on a given shot. What you don't want is a flat sole from face to back. So how do you identify this?

Ladies, I will teach you how to hold an iron to look at its sole radius like a pro. When you get this down, I guarantee, if you do this in front of a salesman at any golf store, one of two things will happen. Either the salesman will know what you are doing and will know immediately that you are a "player," or the salesman will have no idea what you are doing, which will tell YOU something about HIS knowledge of golf clubs.

Pick up the iron and turn it so the grip points down at the floor with the shaft straight up and down. Hold the club with your dominant hand on the shaft about 4 inches down from the hosel, and hold it high enough up so the sole is even with your eye level and the toe end of the head points directly away from you. Tilt the clubhead a little away from you so you are looking right across the surface of the sole from heel to toe. Look to see whether there is some curvature from the face to back. If you want, you can use your other hand to hold a small ruler across the sole from face to back as well to see the curvature in relation to the straight edge of the ruler.

Practice this at home a few times before you do it in the golf store, and I'll guarantee you, the salesman will be eating out of your hand!

So let's summarize. Ironhead design: not too large or long-bladed, big deep cavity back, wider sole with some curvature across the sole from face to back, bottom edge of the face not sharp-edged but rounded so it won't "dig" into the ground as much, and perhaps a little offset on the hosel if you don't mind looking at that.

Oh, another thing. No 3-iron, 4-iron, and only a 5-iron if you feel very comfortable in getting the ball up in the air. Otherwise, your irons should start with a 6.

Wedge Designs for Women Players

To be sure, wedges are important for all golfers, but even more so if the golfer has a slower swing speed, as do many women golfers. Slower swing speed means less distance off the tee and with your approach shots. Because you are giving away so much distance, you need to "get 'em on the greens" with your short game. And that's where the wedges come in.

There are four types of wedges you need to be concerned with: the pitching wedge, the gap wedge, the sand wedge, and the lob wedge. The most important factor in the wedges will be their lofts, followed by their sole angle (i.e., the amount of "bounce" that is designed into the sole) (see fig. 9.1).

The Pitching Wedge (PW): The choice of loft for the pitching wedge starts with a look at the lofts of your numbered irons. If you have a 70/55 swing speed or lower (and you've been reading this book), you should have a set of irons with about 2 to 3 degrees more loft than what you'd find on an equivalent men's club. Okay, now pull out your 9-iron. Your pitching wedge needs to be at least four degrees higher in loft than your 9-iron. Don't know what that is? There are two solutions. One, see whether you can look up the loft of your model on the Web site of the company who made the clubs. Or, two, find a competent local clubmaker to measure it. (And by the way, I will tell you how to find a competent clubmaker later, in the Appendix section of the book.)

The Gap Wedge (GW): If you have a 70/55 swing speed or lower, there really does not need to be a "gap wedge" as long as the space between the loft of the PW and the loft of the SW is not 7 degrees or more. If the loft difference between your PW and SW is 6 degrees or less AND your swing speed with the irons is not more than 55 mph, you really won't have a serious distance "gap" between those two wedges. Well, I should say you won't have a serious distance gap there as long as you are comfortable making full swings with your PW. If you don't like swinging the PW full, then by all means look for a "gap wedge" with a loft halfway between the loft of your PW and SW.

The Sand Wedge (SW): The ideal loft for your "sandy" should be no less than 56 degrees, with a higher loft being even better. This is because slower-swing-speed golfers don't normally hit the ball as high. I say normally. If you do hit the SW high enough to allow the ball to arc nicely up

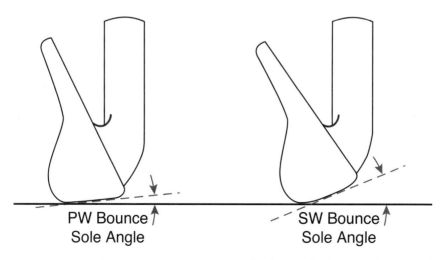

PW Bounce ↑
Sole Angle

SW Bounce ↑
Sole Angle

Figure 9.1. It is also important for women to be fit into the best combination of wedges to improve their chances of scoring well around the green.

and land softly down on the green, then 56 degrees for your sand wedge is fine. Otherwise, go with a sand wedge of 58 degrees. And if you do, then almost certainly you will have a loft gap between your PW and SW that will necessitate using a "gap wedge." The sand puts up more resistance to a slower swing speed, and it all adds up to say that a 57–58 degree loft SW is better for the average woman golfer.

The Lob Wedge (LW): Higher loft wedges such as a lob wedge of 60 degrees, which is normally only used from grass, can also be a solid addition to the average woman's bag.

The key to the success of your sand wedge will be to have a LOWER degree of bounce on the sole angle. You see, if you have a slower-than-average swing speed, it will mean the SW can't dig as deep into the sand under the ball. If you add a lot of bounce to the clubhead design, then you will probably have a lot of trouble getting the ball up high and out of the sand.

In addition, it is a fact that any player who consistently struggles with getting the ball out of the sand will find a wider-sole SW to be easier to use. Just be sure if you do head to a wider-sole SW that the bounce sole angle is not more than 6–7 degrees. Wider soles magnify the effect of whatever bounce is on the sole; that's why lower bounce with wider sole is a must for slower-swing-speed golfers.

What it boils down to is this. Considering the average normal sole width SW is made with 12 to 15 degrees of bounce, choosing a SW for the average woman golfer with 8–10 degrees of bounce can help. The same thing is true for the bounce sole angle on the PW and LW too. Slower swing speeds just do not need more bounce on the sole angle. Thus, a PW bounce of not more than 4 degrees and a LW with not more than 6 degrees bounce can help with improving the percentage of well-hit, high-flying wedge shots for the average woman golfer.

Chapter 10—SENIORS, JUNIORS, AND THE DISABLED

Senior Golfers: Who ARE These People?

Talking about "senior golfers" is very difficult without defining precisely to whom we are referring, and that's where the difficulty lies. Let me try it this way. Senior golfers, for this discussion, are any golfers who have reached a point in their golfing lives where they notice a loss of distance or loss of playing skills that they are able to attribute to age. Note that this does not necessarily refer to a birth date or the color of anyone's hair, but rather to a time in each golfer's life when he or she begins to lose swing speed and the backswing gets a little shorter from a loss of body flexibility. That could be at age 75 or age 45. It depends on the person.

The golf industry tends to use the term "senior golfer" pretty much in a male connotation. Obviously, there are women golfers who become senior golfers, but at present the golf industry does not create specific club models for women who notice a loss of swing speed and flexibility.

For senior women golfers, your equipment recommendations lie within the women golfer sections of the previous chapter. In Chapter 9 I labeled the average woman golfer as having a 65–70 mph wood swing speed and 55–60 mph iron swing speed. But I also talked about ladies with swing speeds *under* the 70/55 swing speed level. Usually, that's a senior woman golfer. Read my recommendations in that chapter as being intended also for the senior women players.

Now, don't be upset, ladies. I am not trying to get rid of you while I talk secret stuff to "the guys." In fact, I am about to send the men back to Chapter 9 with you.

Do you remember what I said in the very first paragraph of Chapter 9: "There is no such thing as gender or age when it comes to fitting golfers." This chapter will be a perfect example of that.

As I have said so often in this book, the correct selection of golf clubs requires an analysis of the golfer's swing speed, strength, swing tempo, and athletic ability. Let's be honest, as a senior male golfer your swing speed may be at the lower end of a young, athletic woman player. That being the case, my equipment recommendations for you can also be found in Chapter 9. Remember, golfers are golfers, devoid of gender and age. The only reason I put all that information in a chapter aimed at "Women Golfers" is because most golfers are trained to think about their equipment in terms of gender and age. Everything I offered in the previous chapter for helping women golfers is really aimed at ANY golfer with a swing speed of 70 mph or less with the woods and 55 mph or less with the irons.

And since we're on the topic, I think perhaps it's time for a little heart-to-heart talk with you senior men. I will not mince words here. What I am about to say can be confirmed by any professional clubmaker who's been in business for more than six months. By FAR the number one thing that gets in the way of a senior golfer playing with the best equipment for his game is plain and simple EGO.

I am 53 years old now, but I feel just as I did when I used to play tournament golf and compete with other low-handicap juniors, then college players, and after that, fellow PGA club professionals. But my swing speed is 7 mph slower than it was back then, and my backswing is not parallel to the ground anymore. So sign me up. I am most definitely a "senior golfer" within the definition I just gave. But I am also a career golf club designer and I like to think that has had some effect on my personal approach to getting the most from what I presently bring to the tee. Thus with NO trepidation I switched from S- to R-flex shafts in my irons four years ago, and this year I switched to an R-flex shaft in my woods. I play with a 43.5-inch driver length although my wrist-to-floor measurement plus the factors of my swing plane and athletic ability says 44 inches to 44.5 inches. The loft of my driver is now 12.5 degrees where it was 9.5 three years ago.[1] I now carry a 5- and 7-wood where that used to be a 3- and 5-wood. My irons do not include a number lower than 4, and the 4- and 5-iron now happen to be hybrid long iron replacement clubs. Thus my "real irons," all of which DO have a cavity in the back, start with the 6-iron, where before I was carrying real irons from #3 to

---

[1] I live at 6,500 feet elevation. Three years ago I lived at 1,000 feet elevation. The science of aerodynamic flight says that at high altitude you need more driver loft than you do at low altitudes because the lower air density way up here makes the ball fly lower for the same loft. Were I still at 1,000 feet elevation, my 9.5 loft would be changed to 11 degrees because of my drop in swing speed with the driver, combined with my level angle of attack into the ball.

the wedges. Because my "touch" and "finesse" with my hands is not what it was, I now have a 58 degree SW and a 61 degree LW that I now hit with more of a square setup instead of the wristy, flippy hands that worked so well years ago.

Now here's my point. I am PROUD to carry this set makeup, and I don't give a hoot if some other golfer, who still has the letter "S" on the shafts of all his clubs, wants to snicker at it. Even if the snickering comes from my 52-year-old triathlete wife who has R-flex shafts and a 44-inch driver!

To be honest, I am the one who feels bad when I see other senior golfers with stiff shafts and a single-digit number for the loft engraved on the sole of their 45-inch driver. I know how, in all likelihood, that is going to translate into on-course performance.

Get the point? If you are interested in playing the best golf you can play, then the game is all about common sense and playing as "smart" as you can play. I mean, if there is anything that a senior golfer should know, it is the old saying: It's not "HOW," but "HOW MANY."

Let's get back to talking about the clubs YOU need to play your best.

Tricking Father Time

So you've lost some swing speed and you're not in the same shape you used to be. It's certainly not a club with an elite membership. You can't hit it to the same 150 marker on the 6th hole anymore, you're having to grab a lower-numbered iron for the second shot, and from that I bet you are probably trying to swing harder as you fight with golf course denial.

There is no question that things like committing to a regular flexibility workout at the gym and signing up for a weekly yoga class will help. But I also know that since I don't do that myself ('yet' is the word I need to add here), I know that neither do most other senior golfers. So here's the common sense of using the science of golf club performance to trick Father Time and make you look forward to your next round.

Your New Senior Driver

If your swing speed is still over 75 mph, don't worry, I'm not going to insist you retire the #1. But I will retire your CURRENT #1 with a new driver that has the following: more loft, shorter length, and a lighter graphite shaft that is also more flexible.

Depending on whether your loss of swing speed and flexibility has started to magnify or introduce an accuracy problem with it (which is rare, but can happen), the new #1 might have a different face angle to address that decrease in accuracy. If you are developing a slice, I might add an offset hosel or a more closed face angle. If accuracy and slicing are not a problem, then the face angle will be square and the face will still sit in front of the hosel on the woodhead (meaning no offset driver).

Next, I'll make sure the grip is the most comfortable you have ever wrapped your hands around and the swingweight/MOI of the whole driver will be rematched to your current strength and swing tempo.

If, and I mean IF, you have a smooth swing tempo and a little flatter swing plane, and you have been playing a long time and know how to control your swing timing and rhythm, then I would make your driver a little longer than what your wrist-to-floor measurement would indicate in hopes of stealing back a few yards.

Longer, did I say? I who have been preaching how heinous the big club companies are for making all those 45-inch and 45.5-inch drivers am now saying LONGER in length? Yes, I am. But ONLY if you meet the prerequisites of smooth tempo, the ability to control the driver now reasonably well, and a little flatter swing plane that I just spelled out with a capital IF.

And you know what? If your driver swing speed has moved down to 90 mph or less and your old driver has 10 degrees or less loft on the face, I will bet you dollars to doughnuts that this new driver with more loft will allow you to not just gain back the yards you have lost, but will hit the ball FARTHER than you did before Father Time started to pick on you!

Surely you have not forgotten the point I made about higher driver loft and more distance in Chapter 1. There's a chart there that shows the relationship of swing speed, swing angle of attack, and driver loft to distance. Here it is again (see table 10.1). Read it; it's important. If you truly want to get some or all that distance back and your current driver loft is lower than what the chart says it should be, swallow your pride and head out to your local clubmaker for a fitting.

Now, if you really are bothered by going to a double-digit loft and a "lower" flex letter on the shaft, here's what you can do. It's an old clubmaker's trick.

Press a little half-inch-long strip of lead tape over the loft number on the sole. It'll stay there forever, and no one will know what driver loft you are using. Then take a razor blade and just lightly scrape the flex letter off the shaft. It's only a silk-screened paint or part of a decal, and it

Table 10.1—The Effect of Launch Angle on Driver Distance

Swing Speed (mph)	Driver Loft (degrees)	Launch Angle	Carry Distance (yards)
60	11	12.1	106
	15	15.2	117
	19	18.1	122
70	11	12.1	145
	15	15.2	154
	19	18.1	156
80	9	10.5	174
	11	12.1	181
	13	13.7	185
90	9	10.5	206
	11	12.1	211
	13	13.7	213
100	8	9.6	231
	9	10.5	234
	10	12.1	236
110	7	8.8	254
	8	9.6	256
	9	10.5	257

Note: Table information based on a swing angle of attack of +2.5 degrees, which means hitting the ball on the upswing with the driver traveling upward at an angle of 2.5 degrees. The average golfer will have a slight upward angle of attack with the driver. For golfers who do not hit the ball on the upswing, the optimum driver loft for maximum distance will be a little higher loft than what is shown in the table.

Like women golfers, most senior golfers do not generate a high swing speed. It is therefore equally important for them to find a driver loft that will achieve an optimum launch angle that will result in maximum distance.

will come off with no damage to the shaft. Now, no one knows your new driver specifications and you can tell your buddies with the sharp needle whatever you want to tell them about its fitting specifications. (Hey, come on, it's cheaper than a Botox injection!)

Actually once they see you back up to the 150 marker or at least farther down the fairway than you have been, they too will probably want a driver like yours. Then you can either fess up with a Cheshire cat grin on your face, or, if your relationship is really competitive with them, tell them it's a new X-flex shaft with a head that has 9 degrees of loft. Then start snickering when they rush off to buy one!

Your New Fairway Woods

More often than not, a decrease in swing speed brings with it a decrease in the height of your shots. Less swing speed always means lower ball velocity and less backspin, both of which contribute heavily to how high you hit the ball. So if you have noticed a drop in the height of your fairway woods as you began to detect your swing speed going a little south, then again, loft can help.

But you're going to have to know the lofts on your current fairway woods to be able to know where you need to go with the loft on the new ones. Chances are if bought your current fairway woods within the last 3–4 years, your 3-wood is in 14 degree territory. And that's the one we really want to address to start.

If your swing speed has decreased to the point where reaching the par-4s is dicey, believe me when I tell you that a 14 degree 3-wood is not doing you any favors. That is, unless your course has those tan-colored fairways I mentioned once before, and there are no hazards in front of any green. Moving to at least a 16 degree 3-wood will help the 3-wood almost like the way more loft helped with your driver. Remember, when you are struggling to reach the par-4s and 5s, your 3-wood has to be your club for most distance off the turf. Getting the ball UP to FLY when you start losing swing speed and shot height requires more loft on your driver AND 3-wood.

After the 3-wood, you start talking set makeup, and that all depends on your long iron play. Would I be too presumptuous if I assumed that the last time you hit a high, solid 3-iron (or 4-iron?) was when we were all reading about President Clinton and the infamous blue dress? Before that, you say? Like back when Jimmy admitted occasionally having "lust in his heart?"

Well, okay, the "when" is not as important as the "what." I want you to chuck the 3- and 4-iron, add on a 7-wood and maybe even a 9-wood. Do you want extra loft on them? Nope, because physics says that more loft on the woods results only in a better launch angle and more distance in the #1 and, with slower swing speeds, in the #3. It does not occur in the other fairway woods, unfortunately.

So once you nail down that new 3-wood loft at 16 degrees, then just be sure the spacing goes in increments of not less than 3 degrees from 5 to 7 to 9, if that last one makes the new lineup. And one inch between those new fairway woods for their lengths too, so each fairway wood has its own unique distance.

Shaftwise, what's good for the goose is also good for the gander. So when you moved into the right shaft with more flexibility in the driver, do this for the fairways too. Yes, graphite and yes, light graphite, like "65 grams or under" light.

Your New Irons

I forgot to tell you a little good news that went along with more fairway woods and fewer irons. If you still carry and walk or you have a long walk from the car to the cart, your load is now lightened because fairway woods weigh less in total weight than the equivalent long irons. In other words, you're packing fewer pounds by dumping the long irons and adding higher-lofted woods with this new set makeup!

There is a little confusion in the golf industry surrounding the matter of using higher-numbered fairway woods or going the route of the hybrids to replace your long irons. You probably forgot this one from Chapter 3 when I was talking about the hybrids.

Any hybrid clubs that are longer in length and lower in loft than your existing long irons will not be "same-distance" replacements. Remember the procedure if you are shopping hybrids.

First, take your long irons to the golf club store or the clubmaker's cottage and have them measure their length and loft. Then, be sure the new hybrids are THE SAME for both fitting specifications. If they are, you're home free with hybrids that will match the distance of your long irons. If they aren't and can't be found in the golf store, it's time to find a local clubmaker who can find and build such hybrids with the same length and loft as the long irons you are dumping to fit your needs.

Retiring your long irons might be a "one at a time" project, or an "all in one fell swoop" proposition. That depends on your current swing speed and swing mechanics.

- If you are a senior (according to my definition) whose driver swing speed has dropped from 90 mph to 85, AND you still have the delayed release of the wrist-cock, AND you keep your head well behind the ball at impact; OK, maybe you can just retire the #2 iron and use that 5-wood or a real 2-iron hybrid in its place.
- But if your present driver swing speed is under 90 mph and you can't hit the #3 and #4-iron high and solid 8 times out of 10, put 'em both out to pasture and put 7- and 9-woods (or real

distance-matched hybrids) in their place. And, while you're at it, let the #5-iron join them if you can't hit your current #5 solid and high 7 times out of 10 either.

- Most 5-irons today are 25, 26, or maybe 27 degrees in loft. For a 5-iron swing speed of under 70 mph, today's "shrunken loft" 5-irons are tough to hit solid and get up high enough to merit their retention—not when there are 11-wood and true 5-iron hybrid alternatives. There is no question they are worth checking out to see whether you can achieve greater height and the same distance as your current 5-iron with a higher percentage of on-center contact.

- When the 5-iron swing speed drops under 60 mph for the senior, you would be playing smarter golf with no "real" iron longer than a 7-iron in the bag. You'll either learn to "feather" your 9- or 11-wood to cover that 6-iron distance, or you can hunt for a real 6-iron hybrid, rare though it will be. That will likely come only from your local professional clubmaker and his drawer full of clubhead catalogs.

As to style and design of the irons that will be left in the bag, need I say more than the words, "deep cavity back"?

- If you are not much of a divot taker now, which means you are chiefly sweeping the irons off the grass, then add a wider sole with not more than 2–3 degrees of bounce on the sole angle for each ironhead.

- If you are still tearing up a little sod with the irons, then just be sure that you have a little bounce on the sole angle and that the bottom edge of the face (the leading edge) is well rounded from the face, over and under to the front of the sole. This will help reduce the incidence of the dreaded "fat shot."

Graphite in the iron shafts is always an option for seniors because chances are most of you were still playing steel when you started to notice that first real drop in swing speed. As I mentioned often, the change from steel to light graphite in the irons will decrease the total weight a lot. That alone can sometimes restore the first senior drop in swing speed. But as the 5-iron swing speed begins to decrease down to the low 60 mph level or under, graphite in the irons becomes almost a necessity for being able to retain distance.

- If you have never had a problem with height on your irons, if you are going to chuck the 3-, 4-, and 5-iron, then you can consider going to a less-lofted iron set for the #6 through the PW. Your local clubmaker can also do this in the form of a bend of the loft angle on each of your current irons. For most seniors with the ability to get decent height on the irons, accommodating less loft on the 6-iron down to the PW will definitely bring back a little lost distance. But don't get too carried away with this, if you're going to decrease iron lofts to get some distance back, the 6-iron should not start with less than 29 degrees. The club-to club loft increment should still not be less than 3.5 degrees, and for sure you will need to add on a gap wedge because going lower in loft on the #6 through pitching wedge will increase the loft spread between the PW and SW.

It is also a must that you get more flexible iron shafts. While a move into a full flex less won't really increase the height of your iron shots much if any, it will restore a more solid feeling of impact in the center of the face, which is very important for your ball-striking feedback. All too often when golfers begin to notice their current flex feels more stiff than it used to, they begin to swing harder with the clubs, which, as we all know, ends up trashing your swing tempo and timing.

Your New Wedges

At this stage of your game, if you don't have a gap wedge in your bag, you now have something new to put on the birthday, Christmas, anniversary, or Father's Day list. As I told the women, you'll want to take a good hard look at your sand and lob wedge play and think about whether you're still able to hit high wedge shots when you need them, both from the sand and the turf close to the greens. If you are, fine, stay within the realm of normal SW and LW specifications for loft and sole bounce angle.

If not, then increasing loft on the SW to 58 as a minimum will help. For the sole angle requirements, if your 5-iron swing speed is still in the >60 mph area, your choice of the bounce will be based on your current habits from sand. Digging too far behind the ball, digging in too deep under the ball (i.e., leaving the ball in the sand too often) will mean a move to a wider-sole SW as first consideration, or to a normal-sole-width SW with more bounce as the second thought.

What's the difference? If you only rarely or occasionally get the ball up out of the sand on the green the "first time," go with a wide-sole SW. If you occasionally leave the ball in the sand, you can opt for a normal sole width but with bounce up to 15–16 degrees—if the thought of such a wide-sole wedge is not satisfying to your brain.

Your New Putter

A loss of swing speed or backswing length should have nothing to do with your putting. Sometimes the "touch" for the putter begins to wane with age, sometimes not. If your putting has somehow started to suffer as well, first thing, get yourself to a good clubmaker who can be sure to set your putter lie angle and length where it really needs to be for your setup and stroke. You probably have never been fitted for these things in the putter, so that alone will probably do wonders for your game.

The other thing you might look into is a heavier head on the putter. Sometimes if the loss of touch with the putter is age-related, a much heavier putter head, in the area of 360 grams, can settle things down a little with the hands and bring back a smoother stroke. In addition, adding weight to the end of your putter grip to both increase its total weight and increase the weight you feel in your hands has also been shown recently to offer a chance for a more settled and controlled stroke with the short stick.

A Final Word to the Senior Golfer

There are some seniors who are as fit and active (if not more so) than when they were 25 years old and can slam a 250-yard drive without thinking twice. If you fall into that "hale and hearty" category, congratulations. The advice I would give you would not be any different from the advice I would give a 30-year-old. There is nothing senior-ish about your game, and all the standard recommendations made throughout this book would apply.

For the rest of you (us!) I can only say, play to your strengths. You will not outhit those young flat-bellies, but you can "out-straight" them off the tee, out-think them on the approach, and positively eat their lunch around and on the greens. You'd be amazed at how satisfying (not to mention profitable) that can be.

Clubs for Your Blooming Tiger or Annika

Earl Woods, Tiger's father, has probably spawned more fantasies in the minds of young fathers than the last 100 issues of *Playboy* magazine. Beats there the heart of a father that didn't quicken when he saw Tiger hugging his dad after winning his first Masters in 1997? Yet, despite all that, there is one thing that Earl has consistently said that seems to get lost in the hoopla: "I always made sure that Tiger had clubs that fit."

Let me put it another way. If you want to make dead certain that your little Tiger or Annika will develop a swing as lame as yours, all you have to do is cut down a set of your clubs and give them to them. They will be too heavy, too stiff, the wrong loft, the wrong lie, and probably the wrong length. Other than that, they will be just what the kid needs to develop a great swing.

Should you perhaps cut one down just to find out if he or she will enjoy taking cuts at a golf ball? Sure, that makes sense, although you might first try to hunt for a single junior club these days for $5 to $10 at a used sports equipment store. As soon as you hear them ask for another bucket and complain about leaving the range too soon, that's the time to get them some proper junior clubs.

Now, keep in mind that there are junior clubs and there are "junior clubs" on the market today. If your junior is just beginning the game, is under the age of 12, and of "normal height" for his or her age, the junior sets in golf shops are likely to be a decent starting point. Since 2000, there are a couple of companies who have made a real niche for themselves in offering good-quality premade junior sets. Lofts are friendly, shafts are more flexible, weights are a little lighter, and grips are smaller. They offer the sets in premade categories of "age 5–8" and "age 9–12" with the substantial difference being their lengths, judged on the basis of average heights for kids in these two age groups.

The only drawbacks to the premade junior sets may be their price and the possibility that your junior happens to be outside the national average for height for his or her age from which the standard lengths of these sets are created. Thus, we come back to your local professional clubmaker who can custom build junior sets as well.

Custom built clubs for my kid when I don't have custom clubs for me yet, you say?

Hold on. It's been my experience that the vast majority of clubmakers do not charge prices for their junior clubs that come even close to the prices you would pay for the premade premium-branded junior sets found in retail golf shops. They understand the parents' point of view in forking over hundreds of dollars for clubs their kid will grow out of.

They also understand that length is super important to allowing your kid to develop decent swing fundamentals and getting to a point of consistently hitting the ball well up in the air. They have very good charts in their catalogs to guide them to the right lengths for your kids, no matter if they are over, under, or in the middle of those "growth charts."

Kids instinctively know that ground balls are not a good thing in any sport. Getting them to the point of consistently keeping the ball in the air will definitely be enhanced by the proper fit for your junior golfer.

You have to resist the temptation to buy clubs that are too long with the expectation that they will "grow into them." They might well do that, but if they are too long, you are forcing them to hit with something that may very likely cause a bad change in the swing, just to handle the longer length, that becomes tough to unlearn.

If that means you need to get them a new set every year or two, get over it. As long as your kid is really into the game, it's a better deal than those tap-dancing lessons you sprang for, not to mention the $125 glow-in-the-dark basketball shoes they just had to have (this month anyway). You're giving your kid a gift that will literally keep giving for the rest of his or her life, long after you're gone. That's no small thing. Besides, it's a small price to pay for watching your son walk up the 18th fairway at Augusta with a 12-stroke lead, or your daughter take that dive into the pond at the Dinah Shore, right?

Golfers with Disabilities

My clubmaking friend Tom Grundner has a lot of experience in working with golfers with disabilities, so I will talk about this from the experiences he has had.

His introduction to physically challenged golfers came about mostly by accident. He had recently opened his first custom club and repair shop at what he tells me is the "legendary" Decile's Driving Range in Cleveland, Ohio. He was tinkering away late one afternoon when he saw a blind person being led up to the desk to buy some range balls. A few minutes later, another blind person came in, then two more, then another and another. He learned that the Cleveland Sight Center's golf program was having a practice day at the range. Never having seen anything like this before in his golfing life, Tom went out to the tee line to watch.

What he saw were golfers—REAL golfers. They were blind, yes; but they were out there with their golf outfits on, with their caps, their golf gloves and their clubs—feeling the sun on their faces, smelling the newly cut grass and smiling with delight at the world being painted by their senses. Each one had a "coach" who pointed him or her in the right direction and described what happened to the ball after he or she hit it. Some of the shots were bad, many were amazingly good, but each one of those people was as much a golfer as you, me, or Tiger Woods.

My own initial experience with clubmaking for a disabled golfer concerned a golfer many of you may be familiar with.

In the early 1990s I was contacted by Dennis Walters, he of the amazing traveling trick shot show that he puts on all over the country. Dennis and his sidekick Benji Hogan, the touring pro from the Miami dog pound, put on a show that is just as amazing for its shot making as it is for its inspiration on what a person can do with sheer will and commitment.

In the early 1970s Dennis was a budding tour pro, sharpening up his game for the upcoming Tour School, where he hoped to win his tour card to play the PGA Tour. Unfortunately, a tragic accident with a golf cart severed his spinal cord and left Dennis paralyzed from the waist down. But being a golfer to the core, Dennis could not give up the game, and with an amazing spirit assisted by a specially made golf cart with a swivel seat, he created the Dennis Walters Golf Show.

Dennis contacted me for help in creating some of the crazy golf clubs he uses in his trick shot show, as well as to custom build his "play set" with which he can and does break 80! It was one of the most interesting and satisfying times I have ever had in my clubmaking life, not so much because of the challenge of the fitting, but because of being able to get to know Dennis himself.

It has only been in recent years that the golfing establishment has taken the disabled golfer seriously, and that was due largely to an act of Congress. In 1990 Congress passed a sweeping piece of legislation known as the Americans with Disabilities Act. Besides prohibiting discrimination in areas such as housing and employment, it forced the elimination of physical barriers in public places, thus allowing disabled people access to most of the same buildings and recreation sites that the nondisabled take for granted. Among the first to comply with these new regulations were governmentally owned facilities, including the thousands of municipal golf courses around the country. Suddenly, golf was available to everyone, and the disabled started showing up.

There are about 50 million people in the United States with disabilities, and that doesn't count the millions more who have temporary limitations due to an accident or illness. We know that about 12 percent of the general public plays golf, and it is not unreasonable to think that, given the opportunity, about the same percentage of the disabled would also be interested in the game, if given half a chance.

The first problem is how to accommodate the equipment and educational needs of the disabled. The Professional Clubmakers Society (PCS) recently formed a Task Force on Fitting the Physically Challenged Golfer to teach clubmakers how to work with this new population and produced a booklet of case studies called the "Forgotten Foursome." Professional clubmaker Alex Pali is a friend of mine, and he is to be given a huge pat on the back for his dedication and commitment in starting this movement within clubmaking. I strongly recommend that you visit the Professional Clubmakers' Society Web site (www.proclubmakers.org) and purchase a copy of this book.

Numerous organizations have been formed for disabled golfers (see the Appendix). Even the USGA has formed a group to amend the Rules of Golf to make the game more equitable for golfers with disabilities.

The second problem is to get the word out to the disabled about these resources and to get them interested in the game. I suspect, however, that it will take little encouragement to get them out on the links, especially those who were avid golfers before their disability.

Equipment for the Disabled

The equipment needs of this new population are as divergent as the disabilities themselves. These can range from blindness and paralysis to minor movement and grip restrictions due to arthritis. Even chronic pain in the shoulders arms or hands can inhibit a person from playing.

Unfortunately, the nature of the game does not help in that regard. The game calls for hitting a hard ball with a hard clubhead, and that always involves shock and vibration. It requires making full turns that reverse themselves at the top of the backswing. And it involves covering over 6,000 yards of territory during a typical round.

However, there is a great deal that can be done to make the game accessible to golfers with almost any level of disability. The key to it is in selecting or creating equipment that maximizes comfort and ease of use. And because this is not a domain of any of the golf companies with their equipment offerings, it is an area of golf equipment strictly handled by the professional local clubmaker who has expanded his or her skills to learn the points of their craft to help such players. For example:

People with joint and tendon injuries can benefit greatly from the new lighter-weight graphite shafts. Shock levels can be greatly reduced by using graphite shafts or by using steel shafts with vibration-dampening systems built in like the True Temper Sensicore shafts. You can also use conventional shafts fitted with shock-relief inserts as fitted by your local clubmaker.

Grips can be built up, or special training grips installed, for people who have trouble holding their clubs while they swing. Arthritis will do that to you. You can also get special golf gloves with leather loops that will hold the club to your hand when your grip can't.

Almost everyone will experience decreased flexibility and strength as they get older, and this will translate into a loss of distance. The usual instant fix for distance loss is to increase club length. The problem, as we have seen in other chapters, is that the longer the club, the harder it is to control. This is especially true of drivers and especially true for persons with disabilities.

But there IS another trick left in the bag. Don't increase the length of the woods; increase the length of the mid-to-short irons. By slightly increasing the length of, say, the 5- or 6-iron through the wedges, you get increased distance on the SECOND shot without running the risk of total insanity off the tee.

There are other things that can be done.

Golfers who have lost flexibility can often benefit from having a light total weight but high-swingweight clubs. This helps them to better feel where the club is located in space as they start their swing. Furthermore, they are likely to benefit from a more flexible shaft.

Even the lack of mobility has been overcome. First, almost all public and most private courses are now barrier-free. The person who is wheelchair-bound or who uses a cane or walker now has access to the course. There are even specially designed golf carts with seats that tilt out and swivel to allow a "turn through the ball" just like the one that the Yamaha Cart Company pioneered in the 1970s for Dennis Walters to use, so even the paralyzed golfer can still play.

As more and more of this kind of equipment is available, the greater the numbers of disabled golfers who will be showing up on our courses. They are ready to play. The question is, are you ready for them?

Playing Golf with the Disabled

Technically, this section does not belong in this book. I mean, this is a book about golf clubs, and this section will not contain the word "club" or "shaft" or "grip" even once. Nevertheless, the word needs to be gotten out somehow, so why not here?

Someday, somewhere, you might be paired with a disabled golfer; and, frankly, you may not know what to say or do. So, presented below are some guidelines for you to follow. They apply on the golf course, and they apply in life.

Let's start by looking at the language we use.

There are three terms that people tend to use interchangeably but are not interchangeable. They are impairment, disability, and handicap.

An *impairment* is a deviation from normal function that may be permanent or temporary. Things such as hearing, sight, cognition, or mobility can all be impaired to one degree or another.

A *disability* is a condition resulting from an impairment that substantially limits any major life activities.

A *handicap* is something that happens TO a person with a disability. A person in a wheelchair, for example, is disabled. He or she becomes handicapped when the only way to get into a building is via stairs.

Ten Do's and Don'ts

First, people with disabilities are often portrayed in one of two extremes: either as courageous, inspirational human beings or as objects of pity and in need of special attention. They are neither. People with disabilities are (a) people, who (b) happen to have disabilities. Period. Nothing more. Nothing less.

Second, forget using the kind of trendy terminology you heard at a wine and cheese party—terms like "challenged," "handi-capable," "differently abled," or "physically challenged." These are mostly invented and used by people who have no disabilities themselves and are viewed as condescending by many disabled people. Most people with disabilities prefer to be called just that: people with disabilities.

Third, remember that a person with a disability is a person first and a disabled person second. Don't refer to a person by his or her disease or disability. The golfer next to you is not "a cripple" or "an epileptic"; he or she is a golfer who uses a wheelchair, or a person with a disability.

Fourth, talk about the disability if it comes up naturally, but don't pry. Some people have no problem talking about it, others do, and for others, the mood can shift from day to day. Let them take the lead here.

Fifth, conversely, mention a person's disability only if it is relevant to an issue. If it's not relevant, don't mention it. The only exception to this is if you need to know something for the safety of the person with the disability or others.

Sixth, do not assume that a person who has one disability also has others. A person in a wheelchair does not necessarily have a mental defect, and a person who is blind is not necessarily deaf.

Seventh, feel free to offer assistance to a person who is disabled, but wait until your offer is accepted before you do anything. Allow the person to react to your offer and indicate the kind of help that is needed, if it is needed at all.

Eighth, don't make assumptions about what a person can and cannot do; you'll probably be wrong. And, for Pete's sake, don't *insist* on helping.

Ninth, speak directly to the individual in a normal tone of voice and not through an accompanying friend or companion. If you have difficulty understanding people with speech impairments, just explain that you didn't understand and would like them to repeat what was said.

Finally, the most important point of all. If you are not sure what to do or say in any given situation, ASK! Allow the person with the disability to assist YOU. Trust me; they have a lot of practice at it.

JUNIORS DO GROW UP

When does a "junior" become simply a "short adult" for purposes of club fitting? There are no age, height, or weight standards for that. You just have to watch for the development of adult strength and coordination characteristics. That can occur at almost any age and at almost any size.

The point is, there will come a time with your budding Tiger or Annika when they need to make the move from "junior clubs" to regular clubs that are fitted and built as if to a shorter adult. Generally speaking, the key is in their height, strength, and athletic ability with a golf club. Kids who develop adequate strength and a reasonably good golf swing may be able to make the move into shorter adult clubs when they reach a height of 5 feet tall.

SENIORS ALSO GROW UP

The toughest thing for a senior golfer to do is to check his machismo at the door when he goes in for a club fitting.

The body might be 65 years old, but the brain is EXACTLY the same one that used to crack those 290-yard drives, not to mention hit those massive home runs and score those lightning touchdowns.

Keep the brain. Don't ever let those memories of past victory die, but realize your body has turned over several times since then, and, therefore, the tools you use must change as well. Forget lamenting about the "way it was" and focus your energies on using your experience to play "smart golf." Or as I mentioned before, it's not "HOW," but "HOW MANY." Do that well, and you have something completely different to smile about every time you play as you trick both Father Time and the Golf Gods all on the same day!

CHAPTER 11—SOME ADVANCED STUFF —FITTING YOUR EQUIPMENT TO YOUR SWING

Your Golf Swing and What It Has to Do with Fitting

In writing a book like this, it's hard to know when enough is enough regarding the technical side of seeking and finding the perfect set of golf clubs. For some, a general discussion of loft, lie, flex, and a few other topics is about all they want. Others, however, want to know everything there is to know and then some. This chapter is a perfect example of that dilemma.

Because the golf swing is ultimately the basis for all fitting decisions, in this chapter I want to provide you with visual depictions of different golf swing movements and positions, along with an analysis of what specific club-fitting recommendations are indicated by each. If you are a student of your own swing, you might see in these pages some of your movements, and you will thus know more about what fitting recommendations are best for you, and why.

If, however, you find your eyes glazing over at this level of detail, feel free to move onto the next chapter. This information is not necessarily vital for every golfer; plus, it's all stuff that your professional clubmaker (after reading this far, you ARE going to get one, are you not?) should already know.

But don't flip those pages just yet. Maybe read along with me a while. You might find this stuff is more interesting than you think.

Here's the problem we're dealing with.

The fitting decisions for grip size and club length, for example, can be made from taking easy measurements of your hand size and the distance from your wrist to the floor. But the fitting decisions for shaft flex, loft, face angle, lie angle, total weight, and swingweight have to be determined, in whole or in part, from observing your individual swing movements. Just as the flight of every shot can be explained by what led up to clubhead contact with the ball, so too your fitting decisions have to be referenced to your golf swing.

Before I got totally hooked on the club design and fitting side of the game, I began my career in 1972 as a PGA teaching professional. While unlocking and translating the secrets of physics and how they apply to the performance of golf clubs reigns supreme in my work, I have always remained interested in the mechanics of the swing. The deeper I got into club-fitting research, the more I realized that the golf swing held the key to virtually all fitting recommendations. It dawned on me that, if you know the swing as it relates to fitting golf clubs, you will know what golf club factors will maximize the person's ability to play and enjoy the game.

During the time I was fortunate enough to work with Payne Stewart, I also had the opportunity to work closely with Chuck Cook. Chuck was Payne's swing coach, coached three other U.S. Open champions, and is also recognized as one of the top ten teachers by virtually every golf publication that makes such rankings. During the time I designed Payne's clubs, I was also able to learn a lot more about the golf swing from Chuck. Chuck was interested in picking my brain about club design, and I wanted to do the same with him to expand my knowledge of the swing. The result was a wonderfully enjoyable time in my career, one that made me even more aware of the links between specific movements in the swing and certain club-fitting requirements.

Let me make a comparison here. Recommending changes in golf clubs is not unlike going to a physician when you don't feel your best. When you visit your doctor, he first listens as you describe your symptoms (poor shotmaking results). He might take your temperature, blood pressure, heart rate, etc. (taking fitting measurements). From that, the doctor might prescribe medications (fitting recommendations) that will get you back on your feet (hit the ball better) in no time.

Sometimes, however, the doctor can't quite determine the diagnosis from the basic tests and observations performed in his office, and you might have to undergo more intensive diagnostics such as blood tests, an MRI, etc. This is somewhat like the clubmaker, who not only obtains basic fitting measurements, but will also study your actual swing looking for specific movements that verify or change his initial "diagnosis."

Since we're about to talk golf swing and fitting, it's important to set the stage with a comment about what I call golf's version of "which came first, the chicken or the egg."

Do you fit golfers for how they swing and play NOW, or do you fit golfers for how they will swing and play in the future once they take lessons, practice, and improve?

I can't tell you how often I have been asked that question, almost always by beginning clubmakers. The answer is very simple and becomes very clear once you have worked in club-fitting for more than a couple of years.

If you are presently working on your game with a competent teacher and you are seeing a real change in your swing and ball-striking ability, and you honestly believe you have the time and commitment to keep working on it, then hold off heading for a club-fitting until you feel you have achieved most of the swing changes you have been working to develop. Otherwise, in ANY other case, get fitted for clubs on the basis of how you play NOW.

What are the things to watch for to know if your present set is not right for your swing and you need to be refitted?

- Your consistent average swing speed has increased or decreased by more than 5 mph.
- Your swing path has changed from outside in to inside out or vice versa; or, you have noted your shot direction is *consistently* different in terms of direction and amount of curve by 10 yards or more.
- Your divots with the irons are deeper on one side than the other.
- Your incidence of off-center hits in play and on the range has increased (or decreased) by 2–3 shots out of 10.
- Your clubs feel too heavy or too light and/or you can't really feel the presence of the clubhead during the swing.
- Your shafts feel too flexible or too stiff and you sense this is a source of either distance/direction problems, or begins to affect your confidence in hitting the ball.
- Your present shots with the driver or woods display a consistent curving shape in either direction.
- You believe you should be hitting the ball farther than you do, and you can't figure out why you don't.
- You feel you need to hit the ball higher or lower to be able to be more consistent with your shotmaking.
- You hit the ball off-center with the driver or woods more than one-third of the time.

The Swing as It Relates to Accuracy in Fitting

I thought about teaching you the whole interaction of the swing path with the face angle of the clubhead relative to the swing path, but that becomes WAY too complicated. So instead, let's make this easy and take more of a "cause, effect, and cure" approach to this. In the end, I suspect you don't want to know "why" as much as you want to know whether a club change can help and how much. I am going to address this first with regard to specific ball flight patterns. The idea is that if you read a description that applies to YOU, you'll know what to do about it.

The Dreaded Slice: I call a slice any curve of the ball to the right (left for you golfers who stand on the "other" side of the ball) that finishes in the rough, the next fairway, or sailing through someone's window off the property of the golf course. A fade is a shot that curves to the right but usually stays in the short grass. They are both caused by a combination of your swing path and how you deliver the clubface to impact.

If the ball slides across the face from the heel to the toe at impact, it will slice. The more open the face is, the more the ball will develop sidespin, and the more it will slice. I don't need to draw you a picture of this type of swing because this is an area of fitting that does not have to be approached in a "cause, effect, and cure" manner. "Cause and cure" will do.

A change in the face angle of the head from what you currently have to an angle that is more closed can help get rid of a fade and reduce a slice. Add an offset hosel to the head design and you will definitely get a reduction of the slice.

The bad news is that if your slice is in the area of 40 painfully curving yards or more, those clubhead changes will reduce it, but not as much as you would like. Golfers who slice the ball more than 40 yards need to work with a swing teacher to reprogram their swing path and/or face angle delivery. (In other words: A really bad swing will overcome really good engineering, every time.) The good news is that once you get that curve down to 30 yards or less, then an offset/closed face angle head will kick in and do its job to make your days on the links a lot more fun.

What I am really saying here is that all golfers need to know when fitting changes in their clubs will do the job and when they won't. A slice that curves 30–35 yards sideways can be reduced by a more closed face angle in combination with an offset hosel design. A slice of over 40 yards can't because no one on the planet makes woodheads with THAT much of a closed face angle. That's where lessons come in.

If the slice extends to your irons, first go to your local clubmaker's shop and get dynamically fitted (i.e., hitting balls off a mat or board with lie adjustments made in accordance with the point of impact on the sole). If that doesn't make the slice respond to the point where you can play with it then, again, you're headed to the lesson tee for a reprogramming of your swing path and/or face angle delivery.

The Duck Hook: You slicers who dream about learning to hook the ball are about to find a reason to be thankful you slice it. Virtually no golf club company, whether the ones whose clubs are stocked in the pro shop or the ones who supply the serious custom clubmakers, makes woods with more than a one degree open face angle. In short, from an equipment change standpoint, if you're a hooker, you're stuck. See what I mean about being thankful your problem is a slice and not a hook?

A duck hook, and by that I mean a shot that curves to the left (left-handers, you know the drill on this) more than 30–35 yards, will only be able to be addressed by lessons. Now, if the golfer wants to turn that hook into a straight or slightly fading shot (a draw), you can do that with a head that has a slightly more open face angle. Fortunately, *slightly* more open-face-angle woods CAN be found at the local clubmaker's shop.

If you draw the ball with the irons more than you would like, again, get yourself to the clubmaker's cottage for a dynamic lie fitting. Chances are good a nagging draw with the irons will straighten itself out once your irons are properly fitted for lie angle.

The Awkward Pull and Push: Fades, slices, draws, and hooks are all shots that curve in flight. Pulls and pushes simply go to the left or right in a straight line with no curve on the ball. The swing path most often causes pulls and pushes. Either you "swing across your body" (what teachers call the "outside to inside" swing path) or you "swing out too much" (which your teaching pro calls an "inside to outside" swing path).

There is also a chance that a slight to medium pull or push is being caused by your irons, again, not being fitted properly to your size, setup and swing. So if you see your shots being pulled or pushed slightly off line, and you don't think it's caused by swinging across your body or swinging out too much, head over to a clubmaker's shop for a dynamic lie fitting. If you get fitted for the proper lie on your irons and you still pull or push the ball, then start thinking about the total weight and/or swingweight of your clubs as possibly being too heavy (push) or too light (pull).

If your pull or push is substantial, and by that I mean you aim at the green and the ball goes left or right 20 yards or more, well, that too can indicate it's lesson time. An ill-fitting lie angle will not be responsible for a push or pull that goes that far left or right of your target, although a swingweight or total weight that is way too light for your swing tempo and strength might.

Dynamic Lie Angle Fitting: I know. We've been there/done that on this subject. But just so you won't have to page back through the book:

dynamic lie fitting is fitting the lie angle of the irons by noting the point of impact on the sole while hitting from a special mat or board. If the consistent point of impact with the ground is out toward the heel or toe side of the sole, the ironhead must be bent in a loft and lie machine to the correct lie angle.

The point I am trying to make here is that the golf swing controls every lie-fitting decision, and dynamic lie fitting is the ONLY way the effect of your swing on your lie angle can be determined. While it is noble to think that you can be properly fitted for lie angle using a static wrist-to-floor or height measurement (as many on-line fitting methods attempt to do), in no way will that method be as accurate as a true dynamic lie fitting.

The reason is because of a very interesting thing that happens as a result of the action of the swing. Believe it or not, in every full swing you make the shaft actually bows downward in a slight curve. This bowing of the shaft is called "shaft droop" and happens simply because almost all the weight of the clubhead sticks out in front of the shaft. The amount the shaft droops is different for every club in the bag because each club is made to a different length. That means as the clubs get shorter they droop less on the downswing. Thus, the reason lie has to be fitted dynamically for each iron is because the droop of the shaft is different in each club.

Dynamic lie fitting is intended to make each club arrive at impact so that the CENTER of the sole becomes the point of contact with the ground instead of the heel or toe. So dynamic lie fitting is the only form of lie fitting that can account for the natural amount of droop that will happen in the shaft of every club.

The Swing as It Relates to Distance and Fitting

It's as predictable as dawn. If a golfer is around when I fire up our hitting robot for a test session, immediately after seeing the robot crank one out there 275 just as easy as pie, their comment is always the same. "Can you figure out a way to implant one of those things in my body?" Show me the golfer who isn't jealous as hell of the people who can bust it out there 20 or more yards farther than they can and I'll show you a golfer who isn't really a "golfer."

EVERYONE wants to hit it farther than they do. Heck, even Tiger wants to hit it farther than the 10 to 12 guys on tour who now put him in the position of being "away" on that second shot into the green. That's the only reason he is experimenting with switching from the 43.5-inch steel shaft driver he played for the first 5 years of his career to a 45-inch graphite shaft driver. (With which he can only hit 50 percent of the fairways!)

When it comes to distance, the swing IS the determinant of how far you can hit the ball. Virtually every time a clubmaker conducts a fitting session for a golfer, the primary request from the golfer is, "Can you build me a driver I can hit farther than the one I have now?" I like my clubmaking buddy Tom Grundner's response every time he fields that request. "Yes, or I can build you a driver that will hit the ball as far as you are able. Take your choice."

This leads me to the "good news" and the "bad news" about buying clubs to hit the ball farther. The good news is that 90 percent of all golfers today DO have 10 more yards begging to be unleashed with a properly fitted driver. The bad news is that once the correct length, loft, total weight, and swingweight/MOI of that driver is found, built, and delivered, that's as far as you will ever be able to hit the ball. (Well, okay, unless you embark on a physical training and flexibility-enhancing program with your personal trainer and you stick to it.) The reason comes again from the textbooks of physics.

Distance is a product of swing speed, which is then *optimized* by (NOT created by) the golfer's proper selection of loft, length, shaft, and the club's swingweight/MOI. In other words, those who are bigger, stronger, and more athletically inclined, and who groove the proper swing fundamentals, will always swing the club faster and get more distance than those who are not and do not. (Provided they are also fitted with the right specifications in their clubs, of course.)

So exactly what are the fitting specifications necessary to get you more distance? Well, you might be able to get more distance if . . .

- Your driver swing speed is less than 90 mph and your current driver has a loft angle of 11 degrees or less.
- Your current driver, fairway woods, and irons have steel shafts.
- Your current graphite shafts weigh over 85 grams. (Great, you say, now how the heck do I know that? OK, here's how. You find a reasonably accurate scale at home or in the office. If your grips are standard size, and your graphite driver weighs over 11.75 ounces (or your graphite 5-iron over 14 ounces), you have "room" to go with a much lighter graphite shaft—as in 55–60 grams light—and lower your total weight enough to pick up a little more swing speed.)

- Your current driver is 45 inches in length and two or more of the following apply: (a) your wrist-to-floor measurement is 37 inches or less; (b) you have an upright swing plane; (c) you have a faster-than-average swing tempo; (d) you are of average to below average athletic ability; (e) you unhinge the wrist-cock before your arms reach waist-high on the downswing; or (f) you are not considered a "good" ball-striker.
- Your angle of attack is level to the ground or downward to the ball, your swing speed is 100 mph or less, and the loft of your current driver is 11 degrees or less. (I will teach you how to estimate your swing speed AND your angle of attack in Chapter 12.)
- Your 3-wood loft is lower than 15 degrees and you do not hit the ball very high with any of your clubs.
- You are physically strong, you have a faster than average swing tempo, and the swingweight of your clubs is lower than D1 (men's clubs) or C6 (women's clubs).
- You have a handicap of 6 or higher and you are still using a conventional #2, 3-iron instead of using well-fitted hybrid long iron replacement clubs. Add a 4-iron to that list if your handicap is 12 or higher, and add a 5-iron to it if your handicap is 18 or higher. (OK, I know that some of you defy that rule. If you do hit these implements well, at least give me the benefit of the doubt and try a real long iron hybrid just for kicks some day.)
- Your swing speed has just begun to head south (or is already there) and you're still using the same clubs with the same shafts you had when your swing speed was higher.

The Swing as It Relates to the Height of Your Shots

It's easy to tell a golfer to "change loft angles," "use shafts that change trajectory," or "get clubheads with a different center of gravity," as the remedies for altering the height of your shots. Yes, those fitting changes can increase or decrease how high or low you want to hit the ball, but not for all golfers. Why? Because some golfers possess swing characteristics that just won't allow these fitting changes to do their job. Again, why? Because of that club-fitting credo I laid on you earlier in this chapter: "A really bad swing will overcome really good engineering, every time."

It is very common to see two different golfers of the same swing speed hit the ball totally different heights with a club that has the same loft, same clubhead center of gravity, and the same shaft. The reason is that the two golfers have totally different swings.

The "low-ball-hitting" golfer will usually keep the hands even with or a little in front of the clubhead, which keeps the shot from flying too high when impact occurs with the ball. This is another way to describe that the low-ball hitter has a more "downward angle of attack," or in plain terms, hits more down on the ball. Also, the low-ball hitter might have evolved the habit of putting the ball farther back in their stance, which does the same thing.

The "high-ball-hitting" golfer does the opposite in his swing. He usually allows the wrists to break forward as the clubhead approaches the ball. This causes the clubhead to get in front of the hands, which in turn increases the loft on the head when impact occurs. Also, many high-ball hitters have slipped into a habit of the ball being more forward in their stances, which does the same thing in terms of causing the clubhead loft to be higher at the moment of ball impact.

Take a look at these two pictures (see fig. 11.1) and note the differ-

Figure 11.1. The position of the hands at the time of impact is a key specification affecting trajectory and shot height.

ence in where the clubhead is in relation to the golfer's hands. I think it's pretty easy to figure out which one is more likely to hit the ball low and which one hits the ball high. If you have a decent video camera, shoot your swing and when you play back the footage, stop the action just before or at impact with the ball and compare your position to that of the two contrasting swings in figure 11.1.

If your impact position is close to the position on the right in figure 11.1, you'll know that changing your shot trajectory by altering the trajectory fitting factors of loft, shaft, or clubhead center of gravity will not be easy. If your impact position is "in between" these two photos, then yes, changes in the clubhead CG, loft, and shaft design may very well be successful. Of course, the first thing to look at when you want to change shot trajectory is your ball position. Even the pros find that they slip into a more forward or more rear ball position from time to time. That has to be corrected for them to get their shot height back to where they are most comfortable.

The Swing as It Relates to Shaft Fitting

Now I can show you some pretty (and not so pretty) photos of different golf swing characteristics to illustrate how the swing has a definite bearing on the flex and flex profile design of your shafts. But let's first get an important part of shaft selection out of the way, namely, knowing the best weight of the shafts for your swing and your game. That we don't need pictures for, so I'll tell you what to look for in your swing and your physical makeup to come up with the right shaft weight.

Shaft Weight Selection for Distance: The first reason to go with a lighter graphite shaft in your clubs is distance. If more distance is a number one priority in your game, you have to go with the lightest shafts you can control; and, by control, I mean your ability to maintain consistent swing tempo and rhythm in the swing. You might recall that earlier I talked about how the swingweight of your clubs HAS to be matched with the weight of the shaft, and those matched to your swing tempo and physical strength. Get the total weight and swingweight too light, you lose control of the club by getting too quick with the swing. Choose a heavy shaft with too high a swingweight, and the clubs feel cumbersome and laborious to swing.

Just remember, it is definitely possible to be strong with a relatively fast tempo and still use very light shafts for a low total weight in the club(s). You just have to push the swingweight up higher to prevent the clubs from feeling too light and losing control.

Here are the guidelines when using very light shafts:

- A man with smooth tempo, swingweight no lower than D0.
- A woman with smooth tempo, swingweight no lower than C4.
- A man with a moderately quick tempo, no lower than D2
- A woman with a moderately quick tempo, no lower than C6
- A man with fast swing and fighting the tendency to really hammer down on the ball too quick, D4 or higher
- A woman with fast swing and fighting the tendency to really hammer down on the ball too quick, C8 or higher

If you have any of these tempo and rhythm tendencies and are physically very strong to boot, add 2 more swingweight points to each one. Physically weaker than average compared to other golfers of the same age and gender, drop that swingweight by 2 points. A "point" in swingweight language is the change of one number in the swingweight reading, such as D2 to D1, is a one-point decrease in the swingweight.

And, finally, please realize that these are only general tendencies. A competent clubfitter is always going to be the best judge of the best swingweight or club MOI for your swing and physical characteristics.

Shaft Weight Selection for Comfort: The second reason to go with the lightest shafts you can (afford!!) is comfort and ease of play.

Candidates for this category are: (a) any golfer who has lost a full club or more in distance from a decrease in swing speed due to age or injury; (b) any golfers who notice that a full bucket of balls (35 balls+) starts to tire them out; or (c) any golfer who just senses the club has begun to require more effort to get around to the ball, or who starts noticing more shots "hang" out to the right side of their target (left side, of course, for you southpaws).

What about moving to heavier shafts? What type of golfers would be the best candidates for those? Logic dictates, first, that it will be golfers who are already satisfied with their distance, since heavier shafts make for clubs with a higher total weight, and you know what that means to swing speed. But the primary reason a golfer should opt for a heavier shaft weight is comfort and sense of control with the club during the swing, although here, the comfort preference is for clubs with a heavier total weight feel. There are a number of golfers who are physically stronger and athletically inclined who simply feel they are more comfortable and have more control over their swing tempo and timing with a heavier club.

However, you will see many of these golfers choose graphite in their woods and steel in their iron shafts. That's because even stronger, more athletic players want as much distance as they can muster off the tee. That, in turn, means graphite in the driver and most likely in the fairway woods as well. Only if this strong athletic golfer does not like the feel of graphite for whatever reason—perhaps because even with a high swingweight the clubs still feel too light—then the use of a heavy shaft becomes a personal decision that is totally based on comfort and feel.

Whether you should use a heavy steel or heavy graphite shaft (yes, there are 120 gram graphite shafts), that too becomes an individual feel decision. It is most often made because of the difference in impact feel between the two shaft material types—a more "crisp, sharp" feel with steel vs. a more dampened, softer feel with graphite.

I remember when I designed PGA Tour player Scott Verplank's clubs. He opted for a 120 gram graphite shaft in the irons because he wanted the heavier total weight for his swing timing and control, but wanted graphite to be able to dampen the effect of impact vibration on his surgically repaired elbows.

Shaft Flex and Flex Profile Fitting and the Golf Swing

If there were one area in clubfitting that really depends on the characteristics of the swing as the key elements for selection, it would most definitely be the shaft flex and the distribution of stiffness over the length of the shaft (called the shaft flex profile).

You know the shaft flex as the letter code that indicates the overall general flex of the shaft—L, A, R, S, or X. The "shaft flex profile" is whether the shaft is made to be stiffer, about average, or more flexible in the grip end, the center, or the tip end of the shaft, all within the confines of the shaft's letter flex design. The overall flex in conjunction with the shaft flex profile is all about helping to control the height of the shot, and determines the bending feel the golfer may notice from the shaft.

The first swing element to consult for shaft flex selection is the golfer's swing speed (see fig. 11.2). Earlier in the book when I was talking about shafts, I explained how most of the shaft companies offer a swing speed rating system for each flex of their different shaft designs. I also explained that not all shafts of the same letter flex are made with the same stiffness. Therefore, in the face of that confusion, the only way to match swing speed to the selection of flex is to have a chart of the 2000+ shafts, each ranked individually by its initial swing speed requirement.

Fat chance, eh? Even if there were one complete list of all shafts, I guarantee you would not want to scan through it!

I did offer a general swing speed vs. shaft flex chart back in Chapter 4 which was intended to offer a guideline for flex selection among the stock shafts used by the big golf companies in their standard clubs. Each of the branded shaft companies (i.e., Aldila, UST, True Temper, Royal Precision, Grafalloy, etc.) offer swing speed vs. shaft flex information for each of their different shaft designs, all found on their Web sites. If you are considering a premium shaft made by a brand-name shaft company, it is definitely worth the effort to surf through the shaft company's Web site to dig up information on the swing speed rating for each shaft model's flex. You also have the option to visit your local professional clubmaker, who will have all this swing speed–to–flex information on hand, provided by the various shaft supply companies.

Figure 11.2. Shaft flex fitting must start with an accurate measurement of the golfer's swing speed.

Remember, shafts for woods key off a driver/3-wood swing speed, while the shafts for irons all are metered from an analysis of the golfer's swing speed with a 5-iron. So don't use a wood swing speed to hunt for an iron shaft flex or vice versa. For most golfers, the driver swing speed will be some 20–25 mph faster than their 5-iron swing speed. You can see what a mistake it might be to get things switched around!

Shaft flex selection has to begin with a measurement of the golfer's driver and 5-iron swing speeds. Then the driver and 5-iron swing speeds can be compared to the swing speed rating for the shafts being considered. But just like the wrist-to-floor measurement has to be compared with other swing characteristics before the golfer's proper club length can be determined, so it is that other factors must be considered along with the swing speed before the final flex recommendation can be made.

True Temper Sports, the largest maker of steel shafts in the golf industry today, has a saying they use in their shaft flex fitting, "It's not how *fast* you swing the club; it's how you swing the club fast." At first, that might sound like "doublespeak," but what they mean is this. It is definitely possible to have two golfers with the same swing speed who BEND the shaft in different amounts during the swing. The idea behind this fitting phrase is this. Given two golfers with the same swing speed, the golfer that bends the shaft more in his or her swing probably needs a slightly stiffer shaft than the golfer who doesn't.

Now let's put YOUR swing and its characteristics into the flex fitting picture, or to be more precise, the characteristics of your downswing.

Backswing to Downswing Transition and Flex Fitting: The way your swing changes direction from the end of the backswing to the beginning of the downswing is called the "transition." Some golfers have a smooth transition, with a distinct pause between the end of their backswing and beginning of their downswing. Some golfers are moderately quick in the transition, while others are very quick, as if they start pouring on the coal before they even finish their backswing.

The more forceful or quick you are, the more you will bend the shaft at the start of the downswing. If you are a golfer who starts the downswing very quickly or with an immediate acceleration of the club, you might need a slightly stiffer flex than what your swing speed might indicate. On the other hand, if your transition is smooth to only a little fast, and your acceleration of the club has a more gradual buildup, you would be better off staying with the rating of the shaft flex that matches exactly to your actual swing speed. Let me give you an example in table 11.1.

Wrist-Cock Release and Shaft Flex Fitting: Whether you unhinge

Table 11.1—Backswing to Downswing Transition vs. Shaft Swing Speed Selection

Swing Speed (mph)	If Your Backswing to Downswing Transition Is	Choose a Shaft with a Swing Speed Rating of (mph)
50	Quick & very forceful	50–60
	Slightly quick, forceful	Under 50
	Smooth with pause	Under 50
55	Quick & very forceful	55–65
	Slightly quick, forceful	50–60
	Smooth with pause	Under 50
60	Quick & very forceful	60–70
	Slightly quick, forceful	55–65
	Smooth with pause	50–60
65	Quick & very forceful	65–75
	Slightly quick, forceful	60–70
	Smooth with pause	55–65
70	Quick & very forceful	70–80
	Slightly quick, forceful	65–75
	Smooth with pause	60–70
75	Quick & very forceful	75–85
	Slightly quick, forceful	70–80
	Smooth with pause	65–75
80	Quick & very forceful	80–90
	Slightly quick, forceful	75–85
	Smooth with pause	70–80
85	Quick & very forceful	85–95
	Slightly quick, forceful	80–90
	Smooth with pause	75–85
90	Quick & very forceful	90–100
	Slightly quick, forceful	85–95
	Smooth with pause	80–90
95	Quick & very forceful	95–105
	Slightly quick, forceful	90–100
	Smooth with pause	85–95
100	Quick & very forceful	100–110
	Slightly quick, forceful	95–105
	Smooth with pause	90–100
105	Quick & very forceful	105–115
	Slightly quick, forceful	100–110
	Smooth with pause	95–105
110	Quick & very forceful	110–120
	Slightly quick, forceful	105–115
	Smooth with pause	100–110

11.3

11.4

Figures 11.3 and 11.4. Late release *(top)* and early release *(bottom)* of the wrist-cock hinge on the downswing. A key element in shaft fitting is how late in the downswing the golfer releases his wrist-cock. The earlier the release, the more flexible (and more tip-flexible) the shaft should be.

the wrist-cock early, halfway, or late on the downswing also has a bearing on your selection of shaft flex.

If you can hold the release of the wrist-cock until your arms are at or below the level of your waist (see fig. 11.3), you are said to have a "late release." This type of swing will apply more bending force on the entire shaft as well as specifically the lower (tip section) portion. You will be able to see visible differences in shot height if you were to try shafts designed to hit the ball higher or lower.

Depending on your desire for shot height, you would be able to choose either a high, mid, or low flight design shaft and be able to experience the differences in trajectory. However, if you have no preference for shot height, your late release would make you more of a candidate for shafts designed with a stiffer tip section in the flex profile of the shaft.

The earlier you unhinge the wrist-cock on the downswing, the less effect high, mid, or low flight design shafts will have on your trajectory and shot height. If you release the wrist-cock early in the downswing, well before the arms reach a point of being level with the waist (see fig. 11.4), you will typically be better fitted with shafts that have a more flexible profile. This is because by the time the club reaches the bottom of the downswing, you have already "spent" the bending force that can come from the release of the wrist-cock. Golfers who do not release the wrist-cock as early or as late as illustrated in the photos are most often better off with shafts that have a medium-stiff tip section or flexible tip section design. These "mid-downswing release" players will only see slight trajectory differences between high, mid, or low flight shaft designs.

Stance and Setup Position vs. Fitting

How often have you read of a tour pro that ended his slump by simply making a change in his stance or ball position? Swing coaches are adamant about this point.

Until the golfer gains the ability to achieve the SAME stance, posture, and ball position every time they address the ball with the same club, he or she will never be able to achieve their highest level of swing consistency. It's simple. If you don't stand exactly the same way each time, there is no way the swing can duplicate each of its positions in the backswing and downswing. Working hard to get the same stance and setup will also ensure that your custom fitted clubs will work the way they are designed and deliver more consistency in ball flight and performance.

CHAPTER 12—TEN THINGS YOU CAN DO FOR YOUR EQUIPMENT FOR UNDER $25

It's Time to Take Possession

There was a time when, to be a good golfer, you had to be part player and part clubmaker. Heads were prone to breakage, wooden shafts could be practically destroyed by a good soaking on a rainy day, and the closest club repairman might be miles away (on horseback!). You either took care of your clubs and learned to be a do-it-yourself club repairman, or you gave up the game.

The modern golf club is a completely different animal. Made from the latest high-tech materials, it has a projected lifespan well into the next Ice Age. That does NOT mean, however, that you can just leave your clubs sitting in the trunk or garage, do nothing to them, and expect them to perform to their full design capability. Besides, that's just not the way to treat an investment that costs as much as some clubs do today.

There are a number of things you can and should do to make your equipment as effective as it can be. Given what you paid for those little beauties and what you have invested in the game, don't you think a few minutes of your time and a few bucks in materials are worth it? There are also some things that after reading this book, you will want to measure or estimate as part of your own search for the perfect golf club.

This chapter will present 10 projects, mostly using basic household items and materials, which will keep your clubs in tip-top shape and help you learn more about what golf clubfitting specifications are correct for you. None of them are difficult, none will cost you more than about $25, and each one is guaranteed to either save you money or save you strokes.

The 10 projects are:

1. How to properly clean and polish your clubs.
2. How to revitalize your grips.
3. How to find the sweet spot on your driver and putter.
4. How to calculate the right length for your clubs.
5. How to estimate your swing speed.
6. How to determine the angle of attack of your swing.
7. How to identify the most stable roll and flight of a golf ball.
8. How to find the correct swingweight for your clubs.
9. How to repaint the engravings on your clubhead.
10. How to straighten a bent steel shaft.

So, go to it. Everything you need to know is right here. And have fun!

PROJECT 1: How to Properly Clean and Polish Your Clubs

Importance:
Have you ever closely watched a PGA or LPGA caddie at work? You are no doubt aware of the obvious things they do such as giving the pro yardages, helping to read putts, replacing divots and such. But have you ever watched what the caddy does whenever he or she is handed a club? He cleans it before putting it back in the bag. Automatically. EVERY time.

Why?
Part of it is psychological. Hitting every shot with a club that is clean and shiny gives a golfer—any golfer—an added degree of confidence. It's as if the club were saying: "Yup, here I am, 100 percent ready to go, boss. Now, let's do something great with that ball."

But there is a larger reason. A club that is NOT clean may not perform the way it is supposed to. If the clubface is dirty, or if the grooves are filled with junk, the friction between the clubface and the ball cannot control the ball the way it is supposed to.

There is also a third reason. You made a significant investment in that set of yours, why not take care of it and keep the clubs looking good?

Even a casual golfer needs to give his clubs a thorough cleaning every few months and ALL Northern golfers need to do this before putting their clubs away for the winter. As with most things, there are a few "tricks of the trade" to be learned.

Here's how it's done.

Time Required:
   20 minutes to a half hour for a full set

Materials Needed:
   - Soft-bristle scrub brush
   - Bucket or tub
   - A soft cloth rag or towel
   - Dishwashing or automotive soap
   - Automotive body or chrome polish
   - Can of acetone or nail polish remover (optional)
   - Fine grade steel wool, or a fine Scotch-Brite pad (optional)
   - A can of WD-40 (optional)

Procedures:
   1. Add soap suds to a bucket or tub of warm water. You can use almost any all-purpose cleaner, or dishwashing or automotive soap. Put the clubheads in and let them soak for a few minutes. (Do not do this with "wooden" woods, that is, if they are a shade of brown in color and there's a separate piece of a different color in the middle of the face!! Instead, just dampen a cloth and clean them.)
   2. Using a soft-bristle scrub brush, clean the heads, shaft, and grips thoroughly. Give extra attention to scrubbing the groove lines on the clubhead faces and to scrubbing the grips vigorously.

      Make sure you get ALL the dirt out from the grooves of the clubhead, and don't forget to scrub the grips good and hard. You'd be amazed at how many grips just need a good cleaning to restore their tackiness and feel.
   3. Dry the clubs with a soft cloth or towel. While you are doing this, inspect your shafts. Check your graphite shafts for cracks or any separation of a layer of the graphite material. Check your steel shafts for pitting or corrosion, and then sight down their length to see whether the shafts are still straight.
   4. If a graphite shaft is cracked, you will need to take it to a custom clubmaker to see if it is just a surface blemish (and can be ignored) or if the shaft needs to be replaced. If you

find a rust spot anywhere on the club, clean it up with a Brillo pad or steel wool and WD-40. If the steel shaft is bent, see Project 10 in this chapter for straightening instructions.

5. Inspect each clubhead. If you still have marks left on the clubheads (e.g., from range mats, ground strikes, tee paint, etc.), they can usually be removed with a bit of acetone. Just wet the corner of a rag with the solvent and rub the marks off. In a pinch, you can use nail polish remover instead of acetone. (I'll leave it to you for a creative explanation of what HER nail polish remover is doing in your shop.)

6. If you have marks on the top paint edge of the woods from (horrors) a shot in which you skyed the ball, you may be able to rub them out a little. If you are a cigar smoker, dip your finger in water, then dip your wet finger tip in cigar ash and rub firmly over the sky mark. The ash works as a rubbing compound to remove any of the marks that are surface marks. If the sky mark left scratches in the paint surface, we can't do much here, but at least the ash rubbing should get rid of the ball marks.

Bonus Tip:

If you use either acetone or nail polish remover to clean up your club, be sure you don't rub the acetone on the graphite shaft, the woodhead paint, or the paint filling in the head's engravings too hard. It won't damage the shaft, but sometimes it will dull the gloss of the paint or remove the paint from the engravings on the head.

7. Finally, you can restore some of the luster of the metal finish on your clubheads. For any of the metal surfaces of your woods and irons that are a mirror/chrome (i.e., very shiny) finish, polish those surfaces of the heads (and steel shafts too!) with a good-quality automotive body or chrome polish. Look at it this way: If it works on the metal of your car, it will work on the metal of your clubs. Just don't get the stuff on your grips; it's hard to get off.

If the sole and face of your woods, as well as the surface of your irons were originally a brushed or satin polish finish, you can use a fine steel wool pad (000 or 0000 grade) or a fine Scotch-Brite pad to buff them back to a brighter satin finish. Just keep your eye on the direction of the "brushed finish" and rub with the pad in the same direction for best appearance.

8. Another nice touch that really makes your clubs look new again is to reshine the plastic ferrules with acetone. Fold a paper towel twice and wet it with acetone. Quickly spin the ferrule once around through the acetone section of the towel in one motion and you'll see the shine come instantly back to the plastic ferrule. The trick to this is to keep the ferrule moving against the acetone as you spin it once around.

9. Wipe down your clubs with a soft cloth and put them back in the bag.

10. If you will be storing your clubs for a while, wipe all the metal surfaces with a light coat of WD-40. This will protect them during the coldest of cold, damp winters in the garage.

Obtaining the Materials:

- All the basic items can be found around the house or easily obtained from almost any supermarket or hardware store. These include: a soft-bristle scrub brush, bucket or tub, a soft cloth rag or towel, general purpose or dishwashing soap, and a fine steel wool pad or fine grit Scotch-Brite pad.
- Automotive body or chrome polish (and/or automotive soap): any automotive store, and most hardware stores.
- Can of acetone: Any builders' supply store (look in the paint section) or most hardware stores.
- Can of WD-40: Any builders' supply or hardware store. Even many drugstores will carry this.

PROJECT 2: How to Revitalize Your Grips

Importance:

If there is any part of the golf club that is most often overlooked by the average golfer, it is the grip. We initially select grips as an after-thought; we rarely, if ever, clean them; and we will wear them down until they look like something the cat would refuse to drag in. Yet few things about the club are more important.

The grip is nothing less than the component that joins two amaz-ingly complex machines: the golf club and you. The grip allows you to control the club without excessively tightening your hands. When you tighten your hands, you tighten your forearm muscles. When you tighten your forearm muscles, you develop "alligator arms," and your swing becomes short and cramped as opposed to long and fluid. You can buy all the $500 drivers you want, but if the grip is wrong, or worn out, or has simply lost its tacky characteristics, you've wasted your money.

Golf grips do wear out, that's a fact, and when they do, they need to be replaced. But in my experience, many grips I've replaced really weren't that worn. They had simply lost their tackiness and feel. That, however, can be corrected in a few minutes with very little effort.

Here's how it's done.

Time Required:
20 minutes to a half hour for a set

Materials Needed:
- Scrub brush
- Dishwashing or automotive soap
- Bucket or tub
- A cloth rag or towel
- Automotive tire cleaner
- 150 grit sandpaper (optional)
- A damp rag or sponge

Procedures:
1. Start by washing the grips with soapy water and a scrub brush. Be sure to thoroughly scrub the grooves that might be molded into the grip surface (see Project 1).
2. Next, clean the grips with a good-quality automotive tire cleaner such as Westley's Bleche-Wite or a similar product. (Figure it out. Car tires are made of rubber; grips are made of rubber, ergo . . .) Follow the product instructions. Spray the tire cleaner on the grips, let it set for a few minutes, and wipe off with a damp sponge or cloth.
3. In most cases, just doing the previous two cleaning steps will remove enough sweat, grime, and oils from the grips to make them like new. If, however, you want some additional tackiness, use a piece of 150 grit sandpaper and sand the entire surface of your rubber or cord style grips. (Nope, you can't do this on Winn or Winn-style wrap grips.) Once you finish, you'll restore a completely fresh surface of rubber by having sanded off the grips.

Bonus Tip:
NEVER apply Armor-All (or similar product) to your grips. It will make your grip look great, that's true; but swinging the club will be like hanging onto a greased pig.

Obtaining the Materials:
- All the basic items can be found around the house or easily obtained from almost any supermarket or hardware store. These include: scrub brush, bucket or tub, sponge, and an old rag or towel.
- Automotive tire cleaner (e.g., Westley's Bleche-Wite or similar product): any automotive store, most hardware stores.

PROJECT 3: How to Find the Sweet Spot on Your Driver or Putter

Importance:
The "sweet spot" is a term that's misused continually by almost everyone in the golf industry. You frequently see ads about how this club or that has a "larger" or "increased" sweet spot. Technically that can't happen because the actual sweet spot (officially known as the Center of Gravity) is a point that's about the size of the sharp end of a pin. It can't get "larger." It can't get "smaller." It just . . . is.

If you hit the exact center of the golf ball on the surface of the clubface directly in front of this tiny spot, the clubhead will recoil straight back, and the ball will fly straight and true. Any deviation from this perfect contact, and the head will start to twist and the ball will begin to slide across the face, imparting sidespin to the ball, making it curve.

The problem is that the sweet spot on any given golf club is usually not directly in line with where the little mark on the top of the head indicates. Or sometimes there isn't an alignment mark on the top of the woodheads. *To hit the ball solidly, you need to know where that sweet spot is located.* Fortunately, finding it is quite simple.

Here's how it's done.

Time Required:
Five minutes

Materials Needed:
- The golf club(s) you want to test
- A golf ball
- Marker pen (optional)

Procedures:
1. Hold the club (be it driver, putter, or whatever) by the grip with the fingers of your left hand with the clubface facing you.
2. Hold a golf ball between the thumb and first finger of your right hand and strike the clubface with the ball hard enough to drive the clubhead backward. If the clubhead moves straight back, you are hitting on the sweet spot. If it wants to twist in one direction or another, you are missing the sweet spot. Keep pinging until you find it.
3. Once you've located it, you have the choice of marking that location with a marker pen or just remembering where it is! In all likelihood, the mark will be off center—probably to the inside of the centerline mark of the clubhead.
4. You now get to struggle with the same dilemma that the original club designer had. You can permanently mark the top of your club with the location of the actual sweet spot (but with a line that looks off-kilter); or you can leave it as is, in which case the head will look great but the original mark will be totally deceptive. It's your call.

Obtaining the Materials:
- Golf club and ball should, by definition, already be owned by the golfer.
- Marking pen can be obtained at any office supply or drug-store.

PROJECT 4: How to Calculate the Right Length for Your Clubs

Importance:
If I ever wanted to commit vocational suicide, I swear the fastest way to do it would be to get out of the golf business, open up a shoe store, and run it the way golf retail stores are run. I would stock 100 different styles of shoes, but they all would be the same size. They will all be ordered to be the national average for men's and women's shoe size. Any customer who happened to fit that statistical average, they'd be in luck. If not . . . I'd tell them to shut up and buy the shoes anyway.

Sound crazy? It is. But that is EXACTLY what happens to most people who buy their clubs, pre-made, off the rack.

One of the most important things you can do for yourself as a golfer—at ANY level—is to make sure that your clubs actually fit you. I will take you through the process of at least getting into the ballpark of one of THE most important fitting specifications—the correct length for every one of your clubs.

When you are done, you can decide if the lengths of your present clubs fit you, or whether they need to be cut down, or made longer, or whether you need a completely new set. The important thing is that, from now on, when you go into a golf store, you won't need to guess at what is approximately the right length for your clubs.

Here's how it's done.

Time Required:
>   Five minutes

Materials Needed:
>   • A yardstick or tape measure
>   • Pencil and piece of paper
>   • The wrist-to-floor length fitting chart in this book

Procedures:
>   1. In front of a full length mirror wearing flat sole shoes, stand comfortably erect, shoulders perfectly level, arms hanging relaxed at your sides, and your feet about 12 inches apart. Best to do this on a tile or cement floor instead of lush carpet.
>   2. Using a tape measure or 48-inch yardstick, measure the distance from the major crease at the base of your RIGHT hand to the floor (assuming you are a right-handed golfer). (If you are left-handed, measure from the wrist crease on your LEFT wrist.) Compare the number on the ruler to the chart shown below (NOTE: Men and women use the same chart) to determine how long your driver and your 5-iron should be. Write down those figures in their respective locations below.

So, for example: Suppose you are a right-handed male and the measured distance from your right wrist bone to the floor is 36.5 inches. You would look this number up in the men's table and see that your driver should be 44 inches and the 5-iron should be 38.25 inches long.

To calculate the exact length of each club, you need only to figure a one-inch decrease per wood using the driver and a half-inch difference up and down from the 5-iron, respectively, as the starting point.

Table 12.1—Driver and 5-Iron Length Recommendations Based on Wrist-to-Floor Measurement of the Golfer (in inches)

Wrist-to-Floor	Driver Length	5-Iron Length
27 to 29	42	36.5
29 to 32	42.5	37
32 to 34	43	37.5
34 to 36	43.5	38
36 to 37	44	38.25
37 to 38	44.25	38.5
38 to 39	44.5	38.75
39 to 40	44.75	39
40 to 41	45	39.25
41 to 42	45.5	39.5
over 42	46 and up	39.75 and up

Note: An accurate measurement of your wrist-to-floor distance is the best starting point for club length. Your final length, however, may be different based on your swing plane, swing path, swing tempo, and general athletic ability.

For example: If your driver is supposed to be 44 inches, your 3-wood would be 43 inches, your 5-wood 42 inches, your 7-wood 41 inches, and so forth. Fill in YOUR numbers for the woods in the next chart.

For the irons, the numbers go up and down from the 5-iron. So, let's say our club length fitting guide says your 5-iron should be 38 inches. Write that number in. Now go up from there a half-inch at a time: 4-iron —38.5, 3-iron—39, and so on. Then go down from there a half inch at a time: 6-iron—37.5, 7-iron—37, 8-iron—36.5, until you get to the 9-iron. At that point, for now anyway, make all your PW and gap wedge the same length as the 9-iron, then your SW and lob wedge each one-half inch shorter than the 9-iron, PW, and gap wedge.

Bonus Tip:

Once you've calculated this table, don't leave home without it, especially if you are going to the golf store.

Obtaining the Materials:

A yardstick (or tape measure), pencil, piece of paper are all commonly found in most homes.

Club Length Calculator—Men and Women	
WOODS	IRONS
1-Wood _____	1-Iron Noooooo!
3-Wood _____	2-Iron Noooooo!
5-Wood _____	3-Iron Maybe
7-Wood _____	4-Iron Possible
9-Wood _____	5-Iron _____
	6-Iron _____
	7-Iron _____
	8-Iron _____
	9-Iron _____
	PW _____
	GW _____
	SW _____
	LW _____

PROJECT 5: How to Estimate Your Swing Speed

Importance:

The key datum for knowing which shaft flex you should be using is swing speed. There are other things that need to be factored in to make the final flex selection as I mentioned in Chapter 11, but swing speed is the starting point.

The best way to get your swing speed is by purchasing or borrowing a "swing speed meter." These are small electronic devices that give you a digital readout of your swing speed for any given club. They cost about $100 or so, but most teaching pros or clubmakers will have one. If you whisper some sweet nothings into the teaching pro's ear (or the equivalent: promise the clubmaker you'll bring donuts next time), he might let you borrow it.

Failing that, however, you can get a good estimate of your swing speed with the following procedures.

Here's how it's done.

Time Required:
Two minutes

Materials Needed:
- The charts in this book
- A dash of honesty

Procedures:
1. To find your swing speed with irons, all you have to do is (honestly) answer one question: What club would you use if you had to CARRY the ball 150 yards?

   Please bear in mind that you have to be both honest and sensible in your answer. We're not talking about which club you WISH you could use, nor are we talking about your making a "career shot" with it. Rather, under normal circumstances, what club would you honestly grab?

   Then, look up your answer on the following chart. And remember, these figures are based on 1,000 feet in elevation at 70 degrees Fahrenheit temperature.

Estimated Swing Speed with Irons

Club Needed to Carry 150 Yards	Estimated Swing Speed (mph)
7-wood	55–60
4-iron	60–65
5-iron	65–70
6-iron	70–75
7-iron	75–80
8-iron	80–85
9-iron	85–90

2. To find your swing speed with woods, ask yourself (honestly) how far do you hit your 3-wood ON THE FLY off a tee, and then compare the number to the chart below.

Estimated Swing Speed with Woods

3-Wood Carry Distance (yards)	Estimated Swing Speed (mph)
Less than 85	50–55
85–100	55–60
100–120	60–65
120–140	65–70
140–160	70–75
160–175	75–80
175–190	80–85
190–205	85–90
205–217	90–95
218–230	95–100
230–237	100–105
238–245	105–110
245–252	110–115
252–260	115–120

Obtaining the Materials:
All necessary materials are provided in this book.

PROJECT 6: How to Determine Your Launch Angle and Your Swing Angle of Attack for the Driver

Importance:
Being able to know exactly what loft angle in the driver will maximize your carry distance can be determined ONLY if you know the angle of attack of your swing. The angle of attack is the term used to describe whether your clubhead travels on a downward, level, or upward path when it contacts the ball.

Golfers with a downward level of attack need more loft to maximize their distance than golfers with an upward angle of attack. Thus, it is not possible to offer a sweeping generalized statement that all golfers with a 90 mph driver swing speed need to use a driver loft of 12 degrees to maximize their carry distance. A 90 mph golfer with an upward angle of attack might be optimized with a 10 degree loft, while a 90 mph golfer with a downward angle of attack may require 15 degrees of driver loft to achieve his perfect launch angle for maximum distance.

Normally, angle of attack has to be determined with a launch monitor. With such an electronic analytical tool it is easy for a trained clubfitter to read the launch angle, compare that to the loft of the clubhead used in the test, and know the golfer's angle of attack. But thanks to good old American ingenuity, if you have access to a hitting net, I can tell you how to figure out what your angle of attack is. And from that, you can work with the information in Chapter 1 and 2 and be able to know what driver loft will bring you more distance off the tee.

Time Required:
15 minutes

Materials Needed:
- Hitting net, or access to a hitting net and hitting mat with 2-inch rubber tee
- Masking tape
- Baby powder or impact stickers
- Sheet of newspaper
- Driver of 11 degree loft angle
- Yardstick or tape measure
- Charts in this section

Procedures:
1. Get your swing warmed up by hitting a number of balls into the hitting net. Start with the short irons and gradually work your way up through the set until you are warmed up enough to be able to hit shots with a driver.
2. It is important to use a driver whose loft angle is known. To make this exercise a LOT easier for you (in other words, so I won't have to toss a math formula at you to solve!!), use a driver with 11 degrees loft. Frequently, drivers will have their loft angle number engraved or placed as a decal somewhere on the head. However, that is no guarantee that is the real loft of the head due to manufacturing tolerances as well as

the quality of the foundry making the head. But usually, for premium-brand driver heads (and for all MY heads!!) the loft will be within one degree and usually one-half degree of the stated loft, which will be close enough. The main goal of this test is to discover if you have an upward, level, or downward angle of attack, and a one degree error won't mean that much. So start by using a driver for which you know the loft angle is 11 degrees from the loft number seen on the head.

3. In this test, you can only count hits that come off the very center of the face. There are two options you can use to determine which hits are dead center—in other words, where the impact loft is the same as the stated loft of the driver. Impact labels are specially made labels you can stick to the face of any clubhead. The force of the ball contacting the face will leave an imprint of the ball at the exact position on the face it was hit.

   If you do not have impact labels (many retail golf stores have them, by the way), you can substitute baby powder. In that case, put a light coat of baby powder on the face and gently spread it around with your finger. You won't coat the whole face evenly, but you will be able to get enough on the face to be able to see where you hit the ball. Remember, you can only count shots hit from the very center of the driver face.

4. Tape a sheet of unfolded newspaper to the surface of the hitting net. You can use little strips of masking tape on the corners of the newspaper sheet to keep it in place. Position the sheet of newspaper so that the bottom edge of the paper is exactly 21 inches from the floor.

5. Position the hitting mat so the rubber tee is exactly 9 feet back from the surface of the sheet of newspaper. The rubber tee needs to be 2 inches tall for these measurements to be accurate within one degree.

6. Now . . . have at it! Hit shots with the driver until you make contact with one right in the center of the face. Hopefully, this won't take more than a handful of shots so you can identify which hole in the newspaper resulted from that on-center shot! Note the location of that hole.

7. Now, measure the distance from the floor to the center of

the hole in the newspaper made by your on-center shot. Measure this as accurately as you can to the nearest one-eighth inch on the yardstick or tape measure. Compare that measurement to the chart that follows to find your launch angle and angle of attack for that shot. Obviously, it is best to do this for four or five on-center shots and take an average of the readings to determine your average launch. Your angle of attack measurement will typically be the same regardless of what driver you use, providing the drivers are within an inch to 2 inches in length.

Launch Angle and Angle of Attack for an 11 Degree Loft Driver

Distance from Floor to Center of Hole (inches)	Launch Angle (degrees)	Angle of Attack (degrees)
21	8	Downward –2.5
22-1/8	9	Downward –1.6
23-1/4	10	Downward –0.8
24-3/8	11	Level 0
25-1/2	12	Upward +0.8
26-5/8	13	Upward +1.6
27-3/4	14	Upward +2.3
28-7/8	15	Upward +3.1
30	16	Upward +3.8

Bonus Tip:

If you use a driver with a loft other than 11 degrees for this test, you can subtract or add the difference in loft from the entries in this chart to determine your rough launch angle and angle of attack.

Obtaining the Materials:
- Hitting net: If you do not have your own hitting net or the use of a friend's you might try your local golf retail store. Other than that, well, you now either have an excuse to buy one or add it to your family's gift list!
- Masking tape: Actually, any tape will do to attach the sheet of newspaper to the hitting surface of the net.
- Baby powder or impact stickers: Impact stickers are usually available from various retail golf catalogs, retail stores, or

retail golf internet suppliers. There are separate size impact labels for woods and irons based on the typical shape of the wood vs. iron face. Baby powder, well that's a lot easier to come up with from your bathroom cabinet.

- Sheet of newspaper: You probably have a pile that gets larger every day.
- Driver of 11 degree loft angle: If your own driver is not 11 degrees, borrow one. Adding or subtracting to the entries in the chart will not be as accurate, but it will be close enough to let you know where you stand for launch angle and angle of attack relative to the loft of the head used in the test.
- Yardstick or tape measure: Since the measurements on the chart are all below 36 inches, you will likely have a 36-inch yardstick around the house you can use.

PROJECT 7: How to Identify the Most Stable Roll and Flight of a Golf Ball

Importance:

I'll never forget the first time I saw this demonstration. I was visiting a friend's research lab, and he had just bought a new robot putting machine. He fired up his robot putter and invited me to watch a demonstration.

He took several golf balls with a big lump of modeling clay stuck on their sides and put them into the robot putter. As expected, the out-of-balance golf balls went all over the place—everywhere but in the hole.

He then took me over to his workbench, opened up a sleeve of brand-new balls, and did the balancing procedure I am about to show you.

Back over to the robot putter.

Every time he put a ball into the putter with the balance mark to the outside, the ball missed the hole, often by as much as three to six inches. Every time he lined up the balance mark so it was straight up, the ball rolled end over end into the hole. With a little practice, I could make those balls wander almost anywhere I wanted, depending on where I pointed the balance mark.

That sold me on golf ball balancing. The pros do it; now you can do it, too. For about $2.50 worth of material, you can make a ball balancing test kit that will last for years.

Here's how it's done.

Time Required:
 10 minutes

Materials Needed:
- Resealable plastic bowl
- One cup of Epsom salts
- Marker pen
- Dry rag or paper towel
- A quantity of golf balls

Procedures:
 1. Pour one cup of Epsom salts into a resealable container.
 2. Slowly add two cups of warm water. Stir while adding the warm water to dissolve the Epsom salts.
 3. Place a golf ball into the solution, spinning it slightly to make sure the ball is covered with water.
 4. Wait for the ball to right itself and stabilize.
 5. Select a dimple that is at the very top of the ball and poke it with a marker pen so that a small identifying mark is made. Feel free to retest the ball. If the ball is already perfectly balanced from the factory, that dot will not come up again. If, however, it does keep coming up, then . . .
 6. Pull the ball out of the water and mark the dimple more completely.

You have now located the center of the light side of the golf ball. The heavy side is submerged on the opposite side.

After use, be sure the top of the kit is securely closed. As long as you keep the water from evaporating, you can use this kit for years.

Bonus Tip:
 USING THE BALANCED BALL: Using the balanced ball is simple but amazingly effective. Anytime you putt, or anytime you place the ball on the tee, place it with the marked dot straight up. (This is 100 percent legal, by the way.) Thus, when you hit it, the heavy and light sides will spin in a more stable axis, as opposed to the wild, non-gyroscopic, slice- or hook-magnifying ride it might otherwise have gotten.

Obtaining the Materials:

- Resealable plastic bowl: almost any supermarket or "dollar store"
- One cup of Epsom salts: almost any drugstore
- Sharpie pen: almost any drug store or office supply store
- Dry rag or paper towel: common household item
- A quantity of golf balls: temporarily possessed by all golfers.

PROJECT 8: How to Find the Correct Swingweight for Your Clubs

Importance:

The golf club is essentially a balance beam. At one end of the shaft is the clubhead, which has a certain amount of weight to it. At the other end is the grip, which also has a certain amount of weight. In between, the shaft itself has weight. When you pick up a club and waggle it, the head has a certain feeling of "heft" or heaviness to it. Without heading back to those complicated definitions, that feeling is called swingweight.

If the swingweight is right, the golfer will perfectly sense the presence and location of the clubhead from the setup, through the backswing and on down to contact with the ball. If it's too light, the player will tend to swing too fast (almost never a good thing). If it's too heavy, the swing will be "cumbersome and laborious." Either way, if the swingweight is wrong you will have an erratic swing that will result in erratic shots.

The swingweight should be pretty much uniform across the clubs (woods or irons), at least up through the 9-iron. Then, if you choose, the PW can be up to 2 points heavier than the 9-iron, the SW at least 6 points higher, and the LW maybe 4 points higher than the nine. An allowable deviation from this in a well-made set would be about one swingweight point from high to low in the set, as in a spread from D0 to D1.

All that is great, but how do you know which swingweight is right for you? There is a way of finding that out.

Here's how it's done.

Time Required:

About 45 minutes

Materials Needed:

- An old 3-wood and/or a 7-iron
- A package of impact stickers or baby powder

- Some one-quarter-inch lead tape (or some loose change and a bit of masking tape)
- A bucket of balls at a driving range

Procedures:

1. Get an old 3-wood or 7-iron (or both) that is the right length and grip size for you. You can use just one or the other, depending on whether you want to find the swingweight for just your woods, or just your irons. This will be your test club.

   Ideally, you want the test club to be on the light side—swingweightingly speaking—maybe around a C8 or so for men and about a C3 for women who are of average women's strength and athletic ability. Many clubmakers can also provide you with such test clubs.

   Take the club and materials outlined above to a driving range and hit some balls to get loosened up.

2. When you are ready, place an impact sticker on the face of the club and hit five balls. Baby powder sprinkled and rubbed on the face will also work to mark the point of impact. Note where the five shots contact the face of the club. Take the sticker off, mark it as "ZERO," and keep it for later reference. This is your starting point.

3. Now, add two swingweight points to the club head. Remember that will be a change in this test club from C8 to D0, or C3 to C5 for the women's club. You can do this by adding two four-inch strips of one-half-inch-wide lead tape, or by adding two dimes with some masking tape.

4. Apply another impact sticker to the face (or powder it up again) and hit five more balls. Again, note where the contact points are located. Take the sticker off, note on it how much weight you added, and keep it.

5. Add two more swingweight points and test it again with five shots on a new impact sticker. You should see the predominant contact point moving around. Keep adding and subtracting weight until your contact point is more or less consistently in the center of the clubface.

6. When you have the contact points making a pattern close to the center of the face, take the club to your clubmaker and have him or her determine its exact letter/number swing-

weight on his scale. That's the number to which the rest of your clubs should be set.

Bonus Tip:
For purposes of playing around with the weights, note that:

Four inches of half-inch lead tape = 1 swingweight
A dime = 1 swingweight
A nickel = 2.5 swingweights
A quarter = 3 swingweights

Obtaining the Materials:
- An old 3-wood and/or a 7-iron: if you do not have any old clubs lying around the house, go to a used equipment store such as "Play It Again Sports." You should be able to pick up a stray club for about $10.
- Baby powder or impact stickers: impact stickers are usually available from various retail golf catalogs, retail golf stores, or retail golf internet suppliers. There are separate size impact labels for woods and irons based on the typical shape of the wood vs. iron face. Baby powder, you already know the drill on that one from the launch angle and angle of attack test.
- One-half-inch-wide lead tape (or some loose change): any well-stocked pro shop or golf store. You're on your own for the loose change.
- A bucket of balls at a driving range.
- A bit of masking tape: common household item.

PROJECT 9: How to Repaint the Engravings on Your Clubhead

Importance:
You probably paid extra to get those clubs from the big club company in your bag. That's fine, although you now know that the best set you can ever hope to own will be custom fitted and built to your individual size, strength, and swing characteristics.

The problem is that, over time, the paint starts to disappear from those proud engravings in the clubhead. The PING looks like "ING," you can't read half the numbers on your irons, and the nicely painted score lines on the faces of your favorite clubs are a faded memory.

Stress not. Repainting those engravings is FAR easier than you think.

Here's how it's done.

Time Required:
20 minutes, plus overnight drying time

Materials Needed:
- Model airplane paint (enamel) in appropriate colors
- A small artist's paint brush
- Smooth surface paper towels (Note: We don't want all the little surface bumps on the towel the TV ads say picks up a full bucket of water. Look at your paper dinner napkins for a paper towel with a smooth surface)
- A small can of mineral spirits

Procedures:
1. The first step is to thoroughly clean the heads with particular attention to the painted engraved areas such as numbers, clubface score lines, manufacturer's name, etc. Use a tooth-pick, sharp pointed tee peg, or whatever you need to make sure ALL the dirt is out of these grooves.
2. Next, take some of the model airplane paint in whatever color is appropriate, and brush it into the engraving, making sure it is well worked into all the engraving grooves. It's okay to have it smeared all over the surface around the engraving.
3. Let the clubhead set for a few minutes, then DAMPEN (not soak) the smooth area of the paper towel or napkin with mineral spirits and quickly swipe it straight across the surface of the head over the engraving. Don't dig down into the engraving, just wipe ACROSS the surface of the head over the engraving. This will remove the smeared paint from the surface but leave the paint that has been deposited into the engraved word or number intact.
4. Repeat steps 1–3 for each engraving and using each color you wish to restore. Then let the clubs sit overnight before you play them. This will allow the paint to cure and will make your heads look as if you just bought them.

Bonus Tip:
I recommend getting the "pen" type of paint applicator as opposed to the bottle and brush type. They are neater and easier to control. The

less smeared paint you have to wipe off, the more paint stays down in
the engraving groove.

Obtaining the Materials:
- Model airplane paint in whatever colors you wish: available at any toy or hobby store
- Small artist's brush from the same toy or hobby store
- Smooth surface paper towels or napkins: common household item
- A small can of mineral spirits: available at almost any building supply or hardware store (look in the paint section).

PROJECT 10: How to Straighten a Bent Steel Shaft

Importance:
Yeah, right. You didn't throw it. Your playing partner / caddie / boss / wife (choose one) ran over it with a golf cart / stepped on it / threw it at you / bent it over their knee (choose two). In any event, your shaft looks more like an implement Robin Hood would use to ward off the Sheriff of Nottingham, and it is completely unusable.

Visions of a repair bill are dancing in your head. The club will have to be taken in and reshafted. It will probably take weeks, and a small fortune, before you get it back.

Actually that might not be so. Depending on where the bend is located and how severe it is, you might be able to fix it yourself . . . with a roll of paper towels.

Here's how it's done.

Time Required:
About 2 minutes

Materials Needed:
- A roll of paper toweling
- A table

Procedures:
1. Locate the bend point. If the bend is so severe as to cause the shaft to crimp, then all is lost. You will need to take the club in to a qualified repairman to be reshafted. If the bend point is down very low, near the top of the hosel, the follow-

ing technique might or might not work because the shaft is real tough to bend close to the head. But if the bend is further up from the head to the center area of the shaft, it's worth a shot.

This trick is so simple I am almost embarrassed to tell you, but it is done just this way by professional repairmen all the time.

2. Place a fairly full roll of paper toweling on the edge of a table. Locate the midpoint of the bend and place it over the edge of the table on top of the paper toweling—one hand will be gripping the shaft above and one below the area of the bend.

3. Then . . . bend the bloody thing back to where it should be! (What could be more obvious?) It might take a few tries until it's completely straight, but you'll get there. No reshafting. No repair bills. Just a little common sense.

Obtaining the Materials:

- A roll of paper toweling: common household item.

CHAPTER 13—Adventures in Clubmaking

There are many places in this book where I make reference to my work with this or that professional player. Usually, I am making a point concerning the differences between their clubs and the ones YOU have access to at the local golf emporium. If these professionals, with their skills, need proper clubfitting, how much more would it benefit you, at YOUR level? The pros are good enough that they CAN play with clubs that have features which are not precisely matched to their games. You and I and almost every other golfer do not have that athletic skill level, so custom fitting will simply work better for us.

I will have to admit, though, the times I've spent designing and building clubs for those pros have been among the most enjoyable and memorable in my life. They are experiences that people frequently ask me about, so I thought maybe some of those stories might be a good way to end this book. Just don't forget the underlying lesson about fitting.

For example . . .

In Chapter 8 I told you about making a set of clubs for Payne Stewart. That anecdote was 100 percent true, but now let me tell you the rest of the story.

An Introduction to the "Vintage" Payne Stewart

In late 1998 the company for which I was working bought the assets of Lynx Golf Company and took over all rights to the Lynx brand. The decision was made for me to create a new line of Lynx designs that would be sold exclusively by the company through their chain of retail stores. To help better promote and breathe new life into the brand, we decided we needed to sign a tour player of some prominence to endorse the brand and play the new Lynx clubs.

One Saturday in early 1999 when I was practicing on the range at Austin CC, Tom Kite, who was a longtime member at ACC, came out to hit some balls. Tom and I were pretty good friends, having gotten to know each other from the mid-1990s when I had the opportunity to design the Harvey Penick line of clubheads, shafts, and grips, and later when I had helped Tom a couple of times with his own clubs.

I knew that Tom had signed a new deal with Titleist after his Hogan contract had expired, so he was locked up and was not approachable. I told him about the Lynx opportunity and asked his advice as to whom he thought might be a good player for us. He said he thought Payne Stewart was through with his contract with Top-Flite and had not made any decisions on a future deal.

To make a long story short, the calls were made, an offer presented and negotiated, and in March, the company's marketing VP and I flew to the TPC at Sawgrass to meet with Payne and his agent to finalize the deal. I also wanted to start the dialog with Payne to get an idea about what he was looking for in the new clubs I would design for him.

Designing a new set of clubs for a tour player can be a trying experience because it's tough to get the time you need to work with them. If they do not choose to make themselves readily available, the designer is forced to "read their minds" to know what they want.

Payne told me that he came to Austin fairly often to work with Chuck Cook on his swing. Chuck, one of the world's best teachers and well known for the tour players who come to him for help, was headquartered at the time at Barton Creek Country Club's Lakeside course, located 30 minutes west of Austin in the middle of the Hill Country. Payne told me that he could "double us up" when he came to Austin and work with Chuck in the mornings and then come into town to work with me on the new clubs in the afternoons.

Right after our meeting at the TPC, Payne came to Austin for a session with Chuck. He gave me a call, and I told him I would come out to Lakeside to meet with him, watch him hit some shots, and start going through my "40 questions" routine to start the design process.

As will be the case with aspiring junior golfers, my son Kyle, who was 14 at the time, caught wind of this and begged me to take him with me. I agreed but said the usual "dad" thing in advising him to only speak if Payne addressed him first.

When we arrived at the Barton Creek Lakeside course, the assistant pro gave us a cart and told us to catch up with Payne on the back side, as he was playing with Chuck. We caught them on the 11th hole and followed along as I watched Payne's club selection for various shots and asked him certain questions about his perception of clubs and what he wanted to see in the clubs' appearance, performance, and feel.

As this was just an informal round, other groups were on the course, and by the 16th hole, Payne and Chuck had caught up to the group in front and had to wait on the tee. The 16th at Barton Creek Lakeside is a short par-3, but has trouble everywhere from bunkers, to water, to a cliff on the left side. Whiling away the time before he could hit, Payne decided to narrow his focus on my son Kyle, who was standing next to me at the back of the tee box.

"Hey," Payne called to Kyle. Startled and not sure if Payne's address was aimed at him, Kyle somewhat froze. I gave him a light elbow and nodded with a look that offered a clue that he might want to respond.

"HEY," the address came a little louder from Payne this time, with Kyle now having no doubt he was the target.

Payne walked over in Kyle's vicinity, and asked, "Can you *play?*" with the accent clearly on the final word.

I think wanting to make sure his response was not perceived as meek, Kyle popped right back at Payne with a tone of defiance in his words, "YEAH, I can PLAY!"

With that, Payne took the short iron he was holding in his hands, never changed the stern look on his face, tossed the club right at Kyle, threw a ball on the ground, and countered, "Well, let's see if you CAN play."

As a dad, my first thought was to the effect of, "Whoops, Kyle got himself in this one now and there's no one with a shovel to dig him out but himself." My second thought was something to the effect that I was glad I was not the one on the spot!

Probably feeling too much pressure to ask for a tee peg, Kyle nudged the ball to the edge of a divot, and made a pretty smooth swing considering the circumstances and with no warm-up. We all followed the trajectory of the shot and watched it check up, about 10 feet right of the hole. The wave of relief on Kyle's face would have been obvious even to a nongolfer!!

Payne walked up to Kyle. Feigning roughness, he grabbed the iron away from Kyle and uttered, "OK, OK, so you can PLAY; but you didn't have to show me up!!" Finally breaking into a big smile, Payne put an arm around Kyle and shook him to let him know he was "OK"!

As I learned over the rest of that year, that was just a classic example of "vintage Payne," having fun and realizing what 20 seconds of his attention could mean to someone. To this day, my son never tires of telling that story, although I think the last time I heard him relate it to someone, the story had improved to the point where his iron shot lipped the hole!!

Another Dose of Payne

Later in 1999, when my work on Payne Stewart's new set had progressed to the point where I had prototypes for him to test hit, Payne's trips to my workshop consisted mostly of range time. More specifically, they were ball-striking sessions in which he'd hit and I'd listen to translate his observations into the details that would help move the clubs into their final form.

The morning of one such visit, one of the teaching professionals attached to the Harvey Penick Golf Academy stopped me in the hallway to inquire if today was the day that Payne was scheduled to stop in for a hit-testing session with the new clubs. Scott Cory was known around the company as a superb teacher, a super nice guy, and an extremely good player who frequently played well enough to cash some decent checks in Central Texas PGA sectional tournaments. Actually, he was so nice that he almost bordered on being a bit meek at times.

That's what made Scott's comment so unusual. "Tom, when Payne gets here, I want you to tell him that anytime, anywhere, he and I, $100 a hole." Well you could have knocked me over with a feather when I heard this coming out of Scott's mouth! But, a fraction of a second later, Scott cracked up and I could instantly tell that someone else had put him up to this little exchange. So, I laughed and we both went about our business.

Later in the day when Payne was hitting balls with the new clubs, I noticed that Scott was teaching a lesson about 30 yards down from us. I stopped Payne to relate that encounter I had with Scott in the morning. Payne snickered, looked at me, and winked as he headed off down toward Scott and his pupil.

Saying nothing, Payne parked himself right behind Scott and his student and began to glare at Scott. Although Payne was just in shorts and a T-shirt, there was no mistaking who he was. Both stopped and turned toward Payne, who continued to glare at Scott. With that, Payne stuck his right hand in his pocket and shot a demand at Scott.

"WHIP IT OUT!" Payne said to Scott. Scott, clearly intimidated, stood there speechless as Payne pulled his money clip from his pocket and repeated the comment even more loudly.

"WHIP IT OUT! A hundred a hole! Anytime! Anywhere!"

Fortunately, Payne erased that growl from his face and replaced it with a big toothy smile from ear to ear so Scott could see that he had just been "had!" Payne walked up to Scott, introduced himself, shook hands and then put his arm around Scott to make sure it had all been perceived as a good ribbing. But that was Payne, and Scott I am sure will never forget the "challenge" he got from one of the best players in the world!

Tricking Payne's Irons

Designing the new forged carbon steel ironheads for Payne Stewart eventually boiled down to the point of my having to make little grinding changes to the heads so that they all had the "look" he desired when he set the clubs behind the ball. Performance was good, flight trajectory was what he wanted, the feel of impact was just right, but he had gotten to the point in the project where there were a few little elements of the "look" of the heads that he was not completely comfortable with and wanted addressed.

One of these was the fact that Payne decided that he wanted to keep that little bit of offset I had designed on the irons to help in the trajectory of the shots, but he did not want to "see" that offset when he set the clubs down behind the ball. Now that one had me scratching my head.

How the heck do I keep the hosel a little in front of the leading edge but not have him see it? This was a situation I had not encountered before in my previous experience of custom grinding heads for a player. Offset is offset. It is there, or it isn't. Despite my explanations of this to Payne, that was what he wanted, and as he left my workshop that day to head back home to Orlando, he smiled, patted me on the back and said, "You'll figure it out!"

For about a week, I stewed. I was trying to think of everything I knew about the relationship of the hosel to the leading edge of the irons. I mean, everything else was perfect on the heads, but how the heck was I going to leave the offset intact but not make it show up to him when he looked down on the heads in the playing position?

One day I was sitting at my workbench with one of Payne's irons in my hands and decided to try to go back to basics to think this out again. The words were only audible inside my head as I thought about the primary definition of an offset hosel design. "Offset is measured from the forward wall of the hosel back to the leading edge." And then, POW, the light went on and it hit me. If offset is measured from the front of the hosel wall to the leading edge, then who says the whole hosel has to be the same outside diameter all the way down the hosel to the leading edge of the blade?

Virtually all irons in the game have been made so that the diameter of the outside of the hosel is the same from the top of the hosel down to where the hosel blends with the blade of the ironhead. This has been done because it is just easier to manufacture them that way, and easier for the foundries to polish and produce. So, with that, I left the top of the hosel with the same diameter it presently had to keep the distance from that point of the hosel to the leading edge intact for the offset Payne wanted. But I began to taper the outside diameter of the hosel down toward the blade. This had the effect of reducing the curve at the bottom of the hosel into the leading edge, which in turn allowed the eyes to think they were seeing less offset than was really there.

When I finished this tapering adjustment to the outer shape of the hosel on the first ironhead, I stuck a shaft in it and put it on the floor into its playing position. And *voila*, there it was—less offset to the eyes, but the same offset as measured in a specification-measuring gauge! Carefully I finished each head and could not wait for Payne's next trip to show the heads to him. And sure enough, when that day came and Payne took a look at each head, he looked at me with his patented narrow glance and said, "You made a whole new set of heads, didn't you?" To which I responded, "Nope, same heads, just a little trick I figured out after banging my head against this brick wall of offset for about a week."

In measurement with calipers, the change of the hosel was very slight, but to the eyes, it was the difference between pass and fail for the heads. Payne took the clubs out to the range, hit balls with each club, and in what was music to my ears, he pronounced the job as done.

Two weeks later, Payne "officially" put the clubs into play in the 1999 Dunhill Cup at St. Andrews, Scotland. While the event has changed to a pro-am competition today, back then the Dunhill Cup was still a 3-man team competition by country. Right after his return to the states, Payne came by again to drop the clubs off because he wanted the lie angles "final tweaked" on a few of the heads. He said that he would be back to pick them up just before the season-ending Tour Championship event for the Top 30 money winners at Champions CC in Houston.

He never got back to pick up the clubs.

From time to time, I think about that year in which I was so fortunate, not just to have designed the last set that Payne played in competition, but to have had the opportunity to get to know him and become a friend.

Bruce Lietzke: Golfer or Fisherman?

I have to believe that every club designer who creates new clubs for a tour pro would wish that he or she would be as easy to please as Bruce Lietzke. One Bruce can easily make up for the other pros that fuss over the smallest little detail on their clubs!

Back in the 1990s, Bruce was enjoying a life of "semiretirement" as a PGA Tour player. When his kids both reached school age, Bruce decided to reel back on the number of tournaments he played so he could truly be a "home father" and enjoy helping his kids in whatever activity they pursued. While a normal tour pro plays an annual schedule of 25+ tournaments, Bruce was quite content to "show up" for no more than 10 tournaments at this point in his career and divide the balance of his time between his kids, fishing, and his love of tinkering with old cars.

When I was asked to build a new set of clubs for Bruce, he made it clear right from the start that he had no interest in my designing a brand-new model for him from scratch. In fact, I could not quite believe my ears when he told me, "Just build me a set of cavity-back irons where the heads aren't too big and don't have much offset and I'll be fine. Standard length with Dynamic Gold S-300s and we'll put the grips on when I get there."

Whaaat? No sole grind? No special tipping on the shafts? I was flabbergasted because I had never encountered a pro like this. I was sure that when he got there to test out the clubs, there would be any number of things wrong and I would be back in the workshop to adjust and alter.

Bruce's brother Brian happened to work at the same company as I did at the time, which of course was the big reason the company had been able to negotiate an endorsement contract with Bruce. Brian was a teaching professional at the company's driving range and for the 10 tournaments a year that Bruce played on tour, Brian was his caddy. So I went to Brian to bounce some ideas off him for Bruce's head model, figuring that Brian knew exactly what Bruce liked and disliked. With Brian's help, I selected a nonoffset cavity-back iron model that I had designed for the company's product line the year before and proceeded to finish the assembly with the Dynamic Gold S300 steel shafts.

The day Bruce arrived to hit the clubs and meet everyone around the company, the first hour was filled with the usual "handshakes and hi's." Brother Brian knew that Bruce wouldn't head down to my workshop to do the grips, so he picked Bruce's grip of choice and told me to install them a "smidgen oversize."

A smidgen oversize? In the world of precise dimensions, how helpful is THAT? So, I installed the grips to a +1/64-inch oversize and set them aside to dry. Fortunately, the owners of the company had lunch with Bruce so the grips had plenty of time to set up before he would hit the clubs.

After lunch we all met on the driving range behind the company's offices. Normally, I prefer to work one-on-one with a player with no one else around so I can watch and ask questions, so neither one of us loses focus on the job at hand. But as I headed out to the range with the clubs under my arm, I could see that a solo session was not the order of the day. Company officials, the company photographer, shoot, you name 'em, and they were out there with Bruce.

So I walk up, Bruce says hi, and I hand him the clubs. Brother Brian steps in and gets them all lined up in number order leaning against a bag holder on the range. Brand-new Titleists were in a bucket on the grass, all ready to be hit by Bruce with the new clubs.

Bruce grabs the 9-iron. No warm-up swings, but instead of the Titleists, Bruce rakes over about 10 balls left over from a bucket of range balls close by. "No sense making someone sort these good balls out from the range balls when you pick the range tonight," he says as he sets up to the first shot. Three shots later he changes to the 7-iron, three shots after that comes the 5-iron and three more balls later he moves to the 3-iron. After 12 total shots he turns to me and says, "Tom, these'll be fine." And that was it! Everyone there was flabbergasted except for brother Brian, who finally broke the silence by saying, "That's Bruce."

But the most amazing thing I saw that day wasn't Bruce Lietzke the golfer, it was Bruce the fisherman. The company wanted to get as many photos taken as possible to use in future promotions, and the time spent with the photographer was at least 10 times as long as it took Bruce to decide on his new clubs. One of the shots they staged was with Bruce holding a casting rod, since it was well known how much he loved to fish. During that session, Bruce started casting with the rod and pretty much nailing any target you might point out! You see that little pile of balls out there, 30 yards out, a little to the left? POW, he nails it first time with the rod and says to everyone, "Wish I was that good with my sand wedge!"

Bruce Lietzke is a club designer's dream and one heckuva nice guy. He most definitely has the game in the proper priority in his life!

The Pleasure of "Tutoring" Arnold Palmer

As a junior golfer I got hooked on the game during what has been called the "Palmer Era," when the battles between Arnold and Jack seemed to set up golf's equivalent of the Hatfields versus the McCoys. I was a Palmer fan all the way and can still remember his famous 4th round "charges" that contributed to the boom in golf in the 1960s.

While the furor of the C.O.R. (Coefficient of Restitution) controversy is pretty much behind us now (see Chapter 2), you may recall just a few years ago when the debate pulled "the King" into the melee and threatened to soil his reputation.

At the time, Arnold Palmer had just signed a new contract to be a spokesman for Callaway Golf Company and endorse their products. About the same time, Callaway Golf decided to produce both conforming and nonconforming versions of their ERC titanium driver and let the public make their own decision whether they would follow the edict of the USGA or play with a nonconforming driver.

Palmer became embroiled in the controversy when he spoke publicly in favor of Callaway's offering of both versions of the ERC driver. As a result, tons of mail poured into "the King's" office in Latrobe, PA, much of it not very complimentary to Palmer's public stance.

Because Arnold is also a major shareholder and chairman of the board of the Golf Channel, he chose the opportunity of his annual January interview on golf's cable television network to try to clear the air and clarify his position in response to the negative mail he had received. He realized, however, that his background on this subject was not as deep as he desired, so he put the word out to his friends and associates in the golf business that he needed a "tutor" on the technical points of spring face drivers.

I will never forget the day when the phone at my desk rang, and the receptionist said, "There's a man named Arnold Palmer calling for you. Do you wish to speak with him?"

Of course, my first response was to the effect of "Yeah right, which one of my buddies is trying to jerk my chain today?" So, I got ready to sling the practical joke back in his face, as I responded, "Sure, send him through."

I had just the perfect stinging retort right on the tip of my tongue when I heard "the voice" on the other end of the line. Believe me, anyone who has been a big fan of "the King" could never mistake it. Almost stuttering as I both reacted in shock and made sure I swallowed the zinger on the tip of my tongue, I don't think I sounded very intelligent in my opening salutation to Mr. Palmer!

As polite as he could be, he explained the situation he was in, how hurt he felt because of the negative letters he had received from golfers who disagreed with his stance, and how he wanted to be as prepared as possible on the technical aspects of C.O.R. when he did his upcoming interview on the Golf Channel. He asked whether I had some time to help bring him "up to speed" over the next two weeks. I think my response was something to the effect of asking whether the Pope was Catholic or if bears did their thing in the woods!

I was naturally curious as to how he had chosen to call me, because I had never had the opportunity to meet or be around him in any of my projects. He indicated that he had asked several people in the golf industry from the editor of *Golf Digest*, to the industry reporter for the Golf Channel, to people he had known in the golf equipment side of the business for years, and all had given him my name. Well, at that point, he could have called at 3 A.M. and I would have walked through my bedroom wall to help if I could!

Over the course of the next two weeks Mr. Palmer and I spoke on the telephone four different times as I would give him a little more information to digest about the real effect of C.O.R. on distance, how it worked to increase distance slightly, and how much more distance could be achieved with a nonconforming higher C.O.R. driver over one that was right at the USGA's limit (which by the way is only 3.75 yards for a golfer with a 100 mph swing speed!).

I have to say the most pleasing of the calls came when I was at home. This being the week between Christmas and New Year's, my parents were visiting for the holidays, and if there was a bigger Palmer fan than me, it was my father. So knowing the exact time that Arnold was to call, I arranged for my dad to be closest to the phone, and put the word out to the rest of the family to ignore the rings so my father would have to answer the call. I still laugh when I recall the look on my father's face when he walked into the living room with the phone to tell me that Arnold Palmer was calling for me!

While he didn't get everything perfectly correct in his "State of the Game" interview with Peter Kessler that year, Mr. Palmer did very well. While time passed and with it, muted the negativity that had pushed its way into his life over the controversy, I have to say that the later "pay" I received for my services was what really made it worthwhile.

After the interview, Arnold called to ask how he could pay me back for all my help. I asked him whether he would mind writing a letter to one of my best friends who was sadly facing the end that ALS, or Lou Gehrig's disease, so unfairly brings. Peter Farricker became the equipment editor for *Golf Digest* magazine in the early 1990s. We became close friends from my involvement as a member of the magazine's Technical Advisory Panel, so when Peter had revealed his tragic fate to me the previous year, I was heartbroken.

I knew that Peter himself was also a big Palmer fan, so when I told Arnold about his situation, he wrote Peter a personal letter in longhand that had both of us in tears when Peter called to tell me he had received it.

Am I a big Palmer fan? It's the same answer about the Pope and bears in the woods, I can assure you.

Solving the Verplank Problem

Hailed as the heir apparent to the Golden Bear when he won the Western Open in 1986 as a collegian from Oklahoma State, Scott Verplank soon fell victim to a chronic elbow problem. That injury eventually pushed him to dead last on the PGA Tour's year-end statistics in 1992 for driving distance, driving accuracy, and 36-hole cuts made.

Fortunately, Scott found the right medical help and, after a series of operations on both elbows between 1994 and 1997, he was on the mend and getting back to the level of play that the golf world expected of him.

I had done Scott's first set in the mid-'90s, a set of forged muscleback blades that I had hand ground to change a number of sole radiuses and front-toe shape desires that he had. I was convinced that I would have to live with a constant stream of "re-dos" on Scott's clubs to make sure everything was to his liking. The nice term to describe such players was "discriminating," but I will say that I don't think that many players can feel the differences in clubs that Scott can.

In 1999 I completed work on a new set of forged blades. The prior year I had designed a set of forged cavity-back irons, so with the new blades it was possible to create a "mix-and-match" set utilizing the cavity back forgings in the long irons and blade model irons in the middle and short irons.

Scott was definitely all for a mix-and-match set for 1999 so he could stay with the blades in the lower two-thirds of his set but move to cavity backs for a little more forgiveness with the long iron shots. Because the two sets had not been designed simultaneously, side by side, and were originally intended to be two separate models, I had to do a lot of custom grinding to match the look of the cavity and the blade for Scott's discriminating eye. Ever since his elbow surgeries Scott had elected to play UST Tour Weight graphite shafts in his irons, feeling that the vibration-dampening capability of the graphite would keep undue stress off his elbows.

In prior sets that I had made for Scott I had pretty much gotten used to the fact that no matter what, there would be two or three of the irons that he would send back, saying they "felt different" in terms of the bending feel of the shafts. When I encountered this in the very first sets I had done I just chalked it up to his extremely fine sense of feel for the bending action of the shaft while hitting shots, and I would replace shafts in the "odd" clubs until he gave us the OK.

But this time, as I headed into the installation of the shafts in his new set, I decided to take a little different approach with the matching of the Tour weight graphite shafts to be used in his set. As part of my ongoing quest to dig deeper into the world of shaft analysis in my R&D work, some months before I had begun to take stiffness measurements over the entire length of the shaft as a way to better distinguish bending profile differences from one shaft to the other. At the time, we called this "zone frequency testing," and it was proving to open up many doors to explain how and why players detected differences in shafts that had previously been thought to have the same flex.

To start the shaft installation for Scott's new irons, I asked UST to send 100 of the same Tour Weight X flex iron shafts that Scott preferred. I took measurements of the stiffness of each shaft first at the grip end, but then included a separate stiffness measurement taken at the tip end. My goal was to find nine shafts that had the same stiffness measurement at each end. From the 100 shafts I was able to find 10 that matched well enough over their entire length to use in the set.

Finishing the clubs in early May of that year, I made plans to travel to the Master Card Colonial Invitational in Fort Worth to work with Scott during practice round days to "get him into his new set." After he had warmed up on the practice range, Scott asked me to hand him, in order, the 9-, 7-, 5-, and then the 3-iron, while he hit five or six shots with each new club. After finishing the group of odd-numbered irons he repeated the exercise with the PW and the 8-, 6-, 4- and 2-irons. Nine different irons times five or six shots each takes a little while, and during all this time I chose not to say anything about what I had done in the matching of his shafts.

Finally, after Scott was done, he stopped, and while holding the 2-iron at arm's length in front of him, he spoke. "Well, I don't know what you did with these shafts, but I am not going to give you any of these clubs back to tweak. These are in the bag come Thursday morning."

Talk about a big "PHEW" coming out of my mouth. I explained to him what I had done with the shafts, and because it made sense to him, he did not question any part of the procedure. It was then that I knew that I had been on the right track in terms of using the shafts' entire bending profile to be able to identify and eliminate little differences in bending for more precise shaft fitting.

Rock and Roll and the Crocodile Hunter

After his range session with the new clubs, Scott wanted to head out and play a practice round to get some experience with the new sticks on the course. Perhaps Scott's closest friend on tour is Bob Tway. They both played college golf at Oklahoma State University, they live in the same housing area near the Oak Tree CC in Edmond, Oklahoma, and they play a lot of practice rounds together when they are both out on tour.

This particular day I had taken my son Kyle to Ft. Worth with me because I thought, with his interest in the game, he would get a kick out of hanging around while I did my design thing with Scott. During practice rounds at most tour stops the rules are a lot more relaxed than during the actual tournament, so Kyle and I could walk with Scott and Bob inside the ropes and stay close to watch Scott's shot shape with the new clubs.

During the round, Scott was all business because he was going to put the new clubs in play at the Colonial tournament that week, so he really was interested in seeing exactly what the clubs would do. Tway, on the other hand, was just out for the exercise and, from the start of the round, struck up a conversation with Kyle. Thus, on each hole I was walking with Scott, and Kyle was always close to Bob. It really pleased me as a dad to see how well Bob and Kyle seemed to get along, as I assumed Bob was asking Kyle all about his game and sharing some sage words of advice for the budding junior golfer in my family.

The 8th hole at Colonial CC is a medium-length par-3 that runs along the edge of the Trinity River, which forms the northern boundary of the course. Cutting across the hole about 50 yards from the tee is a little creek that drains into the river under a bridge that allows the golfers to cross over the creek. As we headed off the 8th tee, Scott and I were in the lead with Bob and Kyle walking behind. About halfway to the green, Scott and I turned to see that Bob and Kyle had both stopped to look over the bridge and down into the creek. All of a sudden we could see them both just howling and pointing, and I could not mistake my son's loud belly laugh.

So I headed back to see what was up. When I got there, the two were pointing at a really large snake and talking all about the fact that both of them had seen a snake of similar size the night before on the "Crocodile Hunter" TV show! You know, the show with the absolutely crazy Australian guy who has no fear in handling monstrous poisonous snakes and other animals that the rest of us would never want within a mile of us!

Kyle and Bob had both seen the snake in the creek below and found that they both shared a common interest in the Crocodile Hunter's pursuit of life-threatening animals. So for the rest of the round the two were going back and forth reminiscing about past episodes of the show.

"Hey Bob, did you see the one where he was sticking his arm inside that rattlesnake pit, feeling around for a tail to pull one out?"

"Yeah, I saw that. I was freaking out when I saw him shove his arm into that hole! But did you see the one when he was in India hunting King Cobras? Man, that one must a been 5 feet long that he was messing with that time!"

Scott just looked at me and rolled his eyes as he turned and headed onto the green. I think he wanted to demonstrate a little friendship, so at the end of the round Scott called Kyle over. Scott pulled a ball from his pocket to give to Kyle as a "souvenir."

As you know, all the pros use some form of unique marking on their golf balls so that in the event of hunting for an errant shot, there is no question whether a ball they find is theirs or not. In Scott's case, he would write his initials on each ball in big letters with a Sharpie pen. When Scott handed over one of his balls, Kyle noticed the big letters "SRV" written on the ball, and in a voice of excitement uttered back to Scott, "S R V—hey, you got the same initials as Stevie Ray Vaughn!"

I thought Tway would bust a gut when he howled as he heard that one, while Scott just stood there and didn't quite know what to say! Oh, and the clubs were fine and Scott had another Top 10 finish that week.

Gentle Ben

There cannot possibly be a player on the PGA Tour . . . no, let me expand that . . . in the HISTORY of the PGA Tour who is or was more polite than Ben Crenshaw. I mean, really, if you get to spend a fair amount of time around Ben, you almost find yourself wishing that he would say something controversial just so you could feel that he was a "regular guy!"

Later on it dawned on me why Ben was that way. Since he was a teenager, he had been under the tutelage of Harvey Penick. If Ben was the most polite man on tour, then Harvey was the most polite man in all of golf.

I was given the task of fitting Ben into a new set of Lynx brand golf clubs in what could not possibly have been a worse time to do it. It was 1999 and Ben was the captain of the U.S. Ryder Cup team. Given the huge responsibility and the massive "to-do" list of a Ryder Cup captain, the only thing that made it possible was the fact that Ben and I both lived in Austin, Texas.

The other thing that was a challenge was the fact that Ben had all but quit playing golf himself when he took over as Ryder Cup team captain. Of course, there was the occasional round for relaxation, but competition wise, Ben was "on the bench." Because of this, he was not at all sure what he wanted in his golf clubs.

In his heart, Ben was a traditionalist and wanted to play with a forged muscleback design. In his head, however, he knew that he should probably use a cavity back because of the rust that was building up on his swing. He also knew that in 2000 he would turn 50 and be eligible for the Senior Tour, where he planned to play a full schedule.

Talk about a fitting dilemma. Do I fit the clubs for how Ben is playing now, or how he will play once he starts working on his game for the Senior Tour?

This was also the year (1999) that I was designing Payne Stewart's new clubs. On one trip to my workshop Ben took a look at the irons I was creating for Payne. "Man, these are gorgeous," he said. "Can you make an extra set for me to try?" I told him he could hit any of the irons I was making for Payne, since any scratches or wear he might put on the irons could easily be removed. So Ben took a few of the clubs with him and said he'd get back to me. About three days later Ben came back with the irons, a decision to go with a cavity back set, and a comment about how bad his swing was at the time!

Over the next two months I learned the routine with Ben was always the same. He stopped in my workshop, raved about the clubs I had for him, and then headed off on his own to hit them. Two or three days later he would come back with the clubs and a list of things he wanted changed on the next set.

After doing this three times with both irons and woods, I started to think about something that Mario Cesario, a fellow designer and good friend, had shared with me about doing a driver for Tom Watson. After the 16th driver Watson brought back with a list of things to change, Mario gave Watson the very first driver he had created for him, but told him this was a brand-new model. He was sure he would like it. Sure enough, Watson did like it and that became his driver, although Mario had not changed one thing on it from the first time Watson had rejected it!

All kidding aside, each pro is a little different in their perception of the clubs that they play. Some are infinitely picky, some moderately so, and some are like Bruce Lietzke, who just go out and play! My work with Ben Crenshaw was extremely enjoyable because we both shared a real passion for the history of the game. I am sure that a big part of Ben's indecision with his clubs was based in large part on the fact that he had so much else going on in his head with the Ryder Cup at Brookline coming up that year. And, as it turned out, that competition is the last one the Americans won (at least up to the time of this writing), so whatever he had in his head that year did work!

Designing for Harvey Penick

In January of 1994 I had the opportunity to meet with Harvey Penick and his son Tinsley, who at the time was the head professional at Austin CC. The purpose of the meeting was to identify specific design features that would be incorporated in the new line of Harvey Penick clubs that I had been asked to design by asking Harvey what various models of clubs he had liked over the course of his career.

I felt this was the best way to approach the task at hand, because I have always been an avid equipment historian and a collector of golf clubs. Therefore, I was confident of my knowledge and awareness of clubs made and sold during Mr. Penick's career. In fact, I felt that I would likely be familiar with the characteristics of almost any club model Harvey might recall. To prepare for the meeting I did as much research as possible on Mr. Penick, including reading his *Little Red Book* (for the third time), which had been published in 1993 and made the world realize who Harvey was.

As I walked up to the meeting on the back patio of the Austin CC clubhouse, I think I looked a bit like a John Steinbeck emigrant, carrying his belongings in his arms! I had old golf books and boxes of old clubs from my collection; anything I thought I might need to be prepared to talk clubs with Harvey. As this was my first meeting with the great teacher, he was polite and just looked at my armload without saying anything.

During the meeting I asked questions about his opinion of different club models over the years, and what clubs he would recommend to his members and pupils. I could tell in the beginning of our discussions that Harvey assumed, since I was some 50 years his junior, that I would not know much about the equipment that was popular when he was the head professional at Austin CC. But I started to get a kick out of the fact that most of the time this or that model was brought up in the conversation, I managed to find that model, or an example like it, in my boxes and present it with a response of, "You mean like this one?" After a few of these, I could see that Harvey was becoming pleased that I could "speak his language," so to speak, about the clubs with which he was most familiar in his career.

The crowning moment of this first meeting came when Harvey started talking about having personally known J. Victor East, a well-known golf professional who had consulted in equipment design for Wilson Golf Company in the 1930s and '40s. East's landmark book, *Better Golf in 5 Minutes*, is a classic among golf book collectors both for its teaching and early clubfitting advice. When I pulled my copy of the book out of another box, Harvey's face literally illuminated and he almost jumped out of his chair saying, "OK, young man, if you know East's philosophies, then we're going to get along just fine." The moment arrived when I knew I had been accepted!

Over the course of the next several months, as the work on each Harvey Penick clubhead design progressed from concept to model to drawings and on into tooling, Mr. Penick would regularly spend an hour with each class of students in his teaching academy. Because he had not been involved in the development of a new clubhead in his past, Harvey had no idea how many months were required to bring a design to completion.

Each time he came through the doors and into the area where my desk was located, I could hear him say to his attendant, "Now make sure I get over to Tom's desk so I can see whether he has my new clubs." And each time through the spring and early summer of 1994, I had to disappoint him with the same explanation of how these things take time and that I would be sure that he would be the first to see any of the finished models when they were ready.

Finally, in the early summer, finished samples of the first Harvey

Penick clubhead models arrived from the foundry. But wouldn't it be typical luck that the very week they arrived was the same week NBC television had scheduled filming of *the Little Red Book Video* with Harvey, Tom Kite, and Ben Crenshaw at Austin CC. I called Tinsley at the pro shop to let him know the first models were in, and to ask what day the following week would be best for me to stop by and show them to his father. Tinsley said, "Tom, as much as my dad has been chomping at the bit to see what you're doing, you better get out here right now. I can guarantee you that if any of the film crew frowns at the interruption, my dad will tell 'em who's the boss!"

As I drove out to the club, all I could think about was how "not happy" the film crew would be to have to suffer through an interruption, especially a crew from a big-time network like NBC. So I was more than a little apprehensive, compounded by the fact I knew Tom and Ben were also there and were likely to kibitz the new designs as well. Parking in the lot right next to the range, with all the people around, it was obvious this was not exactly a small video production crew. Walking up, I could see Mr. Penick sitting in a golf cart, dressed in a white shirt and red necktie, wearing his trademark cap, and talking with his son Tinsley. Tinsley saw me coming, motioned me over with just the right segue, "Tom is here with something to show you."

I have to say that the next 30 minutes stands as one of the proudest moments of my life. When I handed the first iron model sample to Harvey, his eyes literally lit up and he received it in his hands as if it were the crown jewels. Right in the middle of a "take" in the filming, Harvey called out, "TOM! BEN! Come here, I've got something to show you!" With that, Kite and Crenshaw immediately broke ranks from the film crew and jogged over to Harvey's cart.

The next several minutes were a wonderful back-and-forth discussion about this or that aspect of each head design that I had brought to show Mr. Penick. I felt as if I had died and gone to heaven because the smile that Harvey sent my way was the best pay I could ever have hoped to receive, and the smiles that both Tom and Ben offered were frosting on the cake. It was their silent way of thanking me for bringing pleasure to the man they loved and respected so much.

The Greatest Putter Harvey Penick Ever Knew

During the time we were offering the Harvey Penick line of heads, shafts, and grips to the market of custom clubmakers, there were numerous times when the company would ask Mr. Penick to come by for a photo or video filming session. One such time, Harvey came to the company to be photographed for a more formal portrait that would be used in an upcoming catalog of his designs.

As always, when his attendant wheeled him through the doors into the open office area where my desk was located, I could hear him say he wanted to ". . . stop by Tom's desk." My having dragged so many old books and clubs to my first meeting with him in the planning of the designs had really opened up our relationship. It seemed as if almost every trip to the company he brought something else from his own collection to show me.

This time I could see he was carrying a putter, and a rather odd-looking one at that. Well, at least it was odd compared to popular putter models of our current era. The putter head was wooden and was formed in a mallet shape with a brass soleplate covering the entire sole. In the middle of the striking face was installed a red fiber face insert with screws, and a thin "pencil" style steel shaft was installed in the head, with string whipping around the tapered shape neck. It was obviously a putter of the 1930s, but one that I had not seen in my experience of club collecting.

When Harvey's attendant brought his wheelchair to a stop next to my desk, I asked him, "Mr. Penick, what's that putter you have there?"

By this time, I knew that Harvey liked to banter a little with me, so it didn't surprise me when he smiled and said, "You mean you have never seen a Winter-Dobson putter?" I had to be honest, and I told him that he had me with this one. I asked who the Winter-Dobson Company was, after which he explained,

"Winter-Dobson was a company out of Dallas back when I was playing a lot of tournaments. Bud Winter was the salesman and Lou Dobson was the clubmaker. Winter used to drive all week making sales, and then Dobson would build the clubs. But Dobson enjoyed his liquor so there were a lot of times their deliveries were a little late! This one here was the pick of the litter that Dobson made for me to use, and it was my favorite putter. I used it in competition. Of course, I made sure he was stone sober when he made it for me!"

You have to understand that Harvey was such a polite man, the contrast when he would tell a little of what he considered to be an "off-color" story was at least half of the humor! Still chuckling from his story, I got up to wheel Harvey back to the photo studio for his sitting. While taking him back to his sitting, with Harvey still holding his putter, I could not help think about all the great professional players, men and women, that Harvey had taught in his career. So I asked him, "Harvey, who was the best putter you have ever seen or taught in your career?"

With a little turn of his head, gripping his old putter and moving it with just a hint of a waggle, Harvey replied in a voice that was completely matter-of-fact, "Tom, you're pushing him right now."

TV Time with Harvey

Not long after the Harvey Penick line of custom clubmaking components was released, the decision was made to shoot a television commercial that would include a promotion of the Penick club line. One segment of the commercial was to show an interaction between me, as the designer of the line, and Harvey himself, as if we were going over the models and discussing the various aspects of the designs.

While I can't say either Harvey or I had what you would call a lot of television filming experience, both of us knew how much time would be spent just sitting around and waiting for the film crew to finish their "futzing around" before the next take. As Harvey was 90 years old at the time, such delays in which we had to sit in place were especially uncomfortable for him.

Sitting under the hot lights made it even less of an enjoyable situation because both of us would start sweating. The makeup lady from the film crew would keep an eye on us and at the first sign of "glistening skin," she would come over, "dab us off," and apply fresh powder to keep our skin from shining too much for the cameras.

After about three or four of these wipedowns I began to notice that each time she came over to dab Harvey, he would put his arm on her shoulder and smile at her. By this time in our relationship, Harvey and I had gotten to the point we were both quite comfortable around each other. So, after the lady finished working on Harvey, I leaned over to joke with him.

"So you like the ladies, eh, Harvey?" I joked with a smile aimed right at him. Harvey broke into a grin, leaned over to me and whispered back, "Tom, when you get to my age, you have the right to smile at the ladies." We both cracked up at that one as it definitely helped break the monotony of the filming delay!

Appendix—FOR MORE INFORMATION

Introduction

If you've been a golfer for any length of time, you know the key to the game is constant *learning*. From the moment you pick up your first club to the last shot you ever hit, you will be in a state of constant learning. It is a process that never ends, because the game can never be truly, 100 percent, mastered. Paradoxically, that's part of its beauty.

The central message of this book is that this learning process also has to include your equipment. Knowing the relationships between loft, lie, and flex is every bit as important as grip, stance, and tempo. I hope this book has at least given you a start down that road.

But where do you go from here?

In this Appendix I have tried to pull together some resources in a kind of handy-dandy, easy-to-access form. I cannot promise that this will be an exhaustive listing, but I'll do my best to point you toward at least the largest ones.

The problem with doing a listing such as this, however, is that often the information is outdated before the ink is dry. Web sites change, content changes, and suddenly the listing is useless.

To help avoid that, I have set up a Web site in which all these listings (and more) will be maintained. More than that, it will have monthly articles to further your quest toward "golf club literacy," an area where you can ask questions concerning golf equipment, a nationwide list of clubmakers, and other goodies you'll not want to miss. You can access it at:

www.GolfClubLiteracy.com

For purposes of this book, however, let's begin at the beginning.

Finding a Clubmaker

I don't know how often in this book I said: "Get thee to a professional clubmaker." That is, trust me, sound advice, but how do you FIND such a clubmaker and, even if found, how do you know whether he or she is any good?

I can definitely help you with that because I have spent my entire career in the custom clubmaking side of the golf industry. Sure, I've had opportunities to work for some of the largest golf club companies in the world, but I chose not to because I just could not get that mantra out of my head: *"The best set of golf clubs any golfer will ever buy will be a set that is custom fitted by a competent clubmaker using quality designed clubheads, shafts, and grips."*

During my career, I have taught nearly 200 clubmaking schools and over 2,500 different clubmakers. I developed the first clubmaker accreditation testing programs to verify the skills of clubmakers, and I have written five other books plus a handful of videotapes that served as instructional materials for teaching clubmakers the skills of the craft. In short, I have seen tons of clubmakers in my life and I know there are differences in what they offer and how they do their work.

First, I need to tell you that there are clubmakers who are experts in clubfitting, and then there are clubmakers who are assemblers of golf clubs. There is a huge gap between the simple workbench skills needed to build a set of clubs and the knowledge necessary to fit a golfer with the *right* golf clubs.

The technique for properly attaching the clubhead and grip to the shaft can be taught in three hours and perfected in a day of practice. How to fit a golfer with the right specifications of the clubhead, shaft, grip, and assembly is something that takes years to master. In fact, to be honest, those of us with decades of experience in fitting are STILL learning. So you need to find a clubmaker who is a skilled clubfitter. We call these people professional clubmakers (see fig A.1).

Your professional clubmaker may operate from a rent-paying shop, or might work from home. Don't be scared or suspicious if a recommendation for a skilled clubmaker results in your driving to a residential neighborhood. Such is the nature of a "cottage industry" business. As proof that I am not blowing smoke is the fact that the Professional Clubmakers' Society 2004 Clubmaker of the Year, Jerry Hoefling, operates his 20-year-old business from his home workshop in Saginaw, Michigan.

The only difference between a professional clubmaker who pays

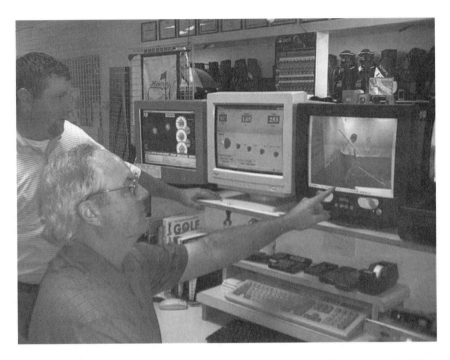

Figure A.1. Veteran clubmaker Dana Upshaw from Dana Golf in Warner-Robbins, Georgia. Dana is a multiple winner of the PCS Clubmaker of the Year award and is considered one of the best clubfitters and clubmakers in the country.

rent for a shop location or works from a home studio is the size of the business they wish to develop. Retail-location professional clubmakers wish to derive all their income from clubmaking while home workshop clubmakers have simply chosen to ply their craft as an avocation. I know of many expert clubmakers who work in both retail and home shop locations as well as some not-so-skilled clubmakers who work from those same locales.

So how DO you find a clubmaker that knows what he or she is doing? Let me answer that with a question. If you move to a new city or town, how do you find a good doctor, attorney, accountant, or any other service professional? You ask people you know and whose opinion you trust. The same thing holds true with a professional clubmaker.

If you see a golfer with a set of custom made clubs in the bag, ask who built the clubs, and whether the fitting experience was worthwhile and enjoyable. The vast majority of business a professional clubmaker gets is from word-of-mouth advertising. So take the time to ask around and if you get a positive recommendation, you're on your way to the best set you have ever played.

Next, there are clubmakers who strive for excellence by submitting their knowledge and skills to clubmaker accreditation testing. There are two associations of clubmakers in the world today that offer clubmaker accreditation testing.

The Professional Clubmakers' Society is the only independent professional association in custom clubmaking. The PCS stands as probably the leading organization in the field because, as an independent organization, their motives are strictly to promote the craft of PROFESSIONAL custom clubmaking worldwide. Clubmakers who have successfully completed the requirements of PCS accreditation stand as true professionals in the craft. Thus, if you have a clubmaker in your area who has achieved the status of "PCS Class A," you will definitely be in good hands in your search for the perfect golf club.

The other large organization of clubmakers is called the Golf Clubmakers' Association and is operated by a large seller of clubmaking components. It exists as a profit-making center for the sponsoring company. As with the PCS, clubmakers who have passed the GCA's accreditation examination and achieved the distinction of Accredited, Professional, or Advanced clubmaker are definitely skilled in the craft. I know, because I not only helped create the first PCS Class A exam, I created the GCA's accreditation program. I can tell you that the examinations of both these organizations are thorough and are a true indication of the clubmaker's level of skill.

Another way to seek the name of a competent clubmaker is through two different clubmaker locator services offered on the Internet. The Professional Clubmakers' Society (www.proclubmakers.org) has a Clubmaker Locator link right on the home page of their Web site. Class A PCS members are identified clearly through this link. In addition, I have provided a Clubmaker Locator directory on the consumer Web site of my company at www.twgolftech.com. All the professional clubmakers listed on my company's consumer Web site are people whom I have either trained personally, or whom I have known for a long time in the craft. Both locator services can be reached by links on the Web site for this book: www.GolfClubLiteracy.com.

I do not want to leave you with the impression, however, that a clubmaker who does not have a PCS or GCA accreditation, or who is not listed through the PCS or my company's clubmaker locator is necessarily incompetent. Since the days of the original hickory shaft makers, club builders have been a notoriously independent lot and some are simply not "joiners." I know of a number of very skilled clubmakers who just plain don't feel a need to "pass a test to prove to anyone how good I am!"

Thus, if you find a clubmaker who does not hold either a PCS or GCA accreditation, or is not listed on either my company's or the PCS's Web sites, ask him or her to provide references. A good clubmaker will not at all mind your asking. Discovering if the clubmaker has attended any clubmaking schools is another way to get an idea of their level of skill and commitment to the craft. Again, just like a doctor, dentist, lawyer, or any professional from whom you seek service, you ask for references and make your own judgment based on what you find out.

One last point. Can you find a good clubfitter in a retail golf store or golf course pro shop? Yes, you can. But I am going be brutally honest about this—they're few and far between. Generally, they simply don't receive or seek the training necessary to become as skilled as the accredited and/or highly experienced professional clubmaker.

Among the off-course retail golf stores, many simply do not offer true custom fitting. By "true custom fitting," I mean being fitted from a selection of different clubhead, shaft, and grip designs and custom assembling them in-house to your individual specifications. Some retail stores do have accredited clubmakers on hand. (I think they ALL should have them.) If so, and if they offer fitting from a wide selection of different clubhead, shaft, and grip designs, then great. As Allstate says, "You're in good hands."

However, if the retail golf store offers to "custom fit" you from their existing clubs with no alterations, then forget it. That's NOT true custom fitting. If they offer to alter stock clubs to fit you, then (1) make sure you do NOT need a custom face angle on the woods to correct your slice, (2) be sure they will at the very least be altering the iron lies, length, swingweight, lofts, shaft weight, flex, grip, and grip size, and (3) be sure there is an experienced clubmaker on staff or out of store who they contract with for the alterations.

Then there are pro shops. In my career, I have had the opportunity to conduct quite a number of clubmaking and clubfitting seminars for PGA club professionals and assistants. Most definitely there ARE expert clubfitters among the PGA professionals who do a good job of teaching and administering the game. Most, however, simply do not receive adequate training. As a group they tend to impose far too much of their own likes and dislikes (i.e., the things that works best for their OWN golf clubs) in making equipment recommendations for their members and other golfers. Such pros tend to forget that YOUR game is likely quite different from theirs.

My friend Matz Evensson, the head professional at Nynashamms GC in Osmo, Sweden is what I consider to be the role model for all golf professionals. He is a skilled player, an expert teacher, and a true professional clubfitter and clubmaker. There are PGA club pros in every country who, like Matz, can conduct real fitting sessions and custom build your clubs to your individual needs. Unfortunately, there are not many. Because of my early career experiences as a PGA club professional, however, I do have a soft spot for club pros and the PGA of America. I hope to be able to work with them to help their members become better trained in the best principles of clubfitting.

The Acid Test

I want to be sure that I leave you with the ability to find a competent clubmaker/clubfitter, regardless if located in his or her own shop, a pro shop, a retail golf store, or their garage. While I've given you solid basics for this quest, I realize that some of you may want to be more sure before you trust your golf clubs (and your game) to a person you may not know from Adam.

The following Q&A section is offered for you to see whether a clubmaker is qualified to do a good job in your fitting session. No, don't go in with a pencil and paper. Just sort of casually bring up one or more of these questions when you're talking to him.

Q1. *How will you determine what is the best shaft flex for my game?*
Best Answer: I'll take a look at your existing shafts and ask you some questions about your experience and results with them, then I will measure your swing speed and look at your swing to determine what flex and what flex distribution (tip flexibility, butt flexibility, bend profile, etc.) is best matched to your swing and how you play.

Good Answer: I'll measure your swing speed and compare that to information I have about the swing speed requirement of various shafts I may have in mind for your game. Then I'll talk to you about the different options for different shot height and feel within these shafts that match your swing speed.

The "Walk Away" or "Hang Up the Phone" Answer: I'll watch you hit some shots and I'll know from my experience what flex you need. Or, I'll check your clubs and see what you play and decide from that.

Q2: What can you do to correct my accuracy problem with the driver?

Best Answer: I'll watch your ball-striking results on my swing computer/launch monitor to see your primary misdirection problem and how much the face is open/closed at impact. Then I'll ask you some questions about how you hit the driver off line and how much. I'll check your current driver to see whether its specifications are appropriate for what I see in my measurements and observations. I'll also check you carefully for the right driver length, shaft weight, flex, swingweight, and grip size and, from that, make a recommendation for the best driver face angle, offset hosel or not, length, total weight, swingweight, and grip size.

Good Answer: I'll ask you about the direction in which you miss the ball most often and talk to you about a different driver face angle. I'll also see what is the best length and swingweight for you to be able to hit the ball straighter.

The "Walk Away" or "Hang Up the Phone" Answer: Well, you probably need lessons to hit the ball more accurately, but stop by and I'll take a look and see.

Q3: What are some of the things you might be able to do to help me hit the driver farther?

Best Answer: I'll put you on our swing computer/launch monitor and measure things like your swing speed, launch angle, spin rate. Then I'll check your current driver for its specifications of loft, length, shaft weight, flex, and swingweight to see how well they fit you. In all likelihood you might be playing a driver that is too long, has too little loft, might be too stiff in the shaft, or the swingweight is off.

Good Answer: I will work with you on the proper loft, length, shaft, and swingweight because many golfers use clubs that are too long and have too little loft to achieve their maximum distance. Or, a little of the latter plus . . . I can fit you into the driver that you can hit the farthest for your swing speed and ability.

The "Walk Away" or "Hang Up the Phone" Answer: I can build you a longer driver and you might get a little more distance (or the person asks you what loft you are currently playing, you respond with a number lower than 10.5 and the person recommends a LOWER loft for more distance with the driver).

When No Clubmaker Is Available: Online Club Fitting

It's no secret that I believe any golfer, at any level, will benefit from custom built golf clubs. But, I am also a realist; I know that not everyone will have access to a qualified clubmaker. If you are in that position, the next best thing you can do is to take a look at purchasing from a qualified clubmaker *through the Internet*.

Let me be clear. Working with a clubmaker from afar is NOT as good as being able to work face-to-face with a skilled clubmaker in your area. That being said, let me also point out that it is FAR better than buying "off-the-rack." You can do it and get good results IF you do your homework.

Growing numbers of professional clubmakers have chosen to offer their services through Internet Web sites. Their methods are as varied as the clubmakers offering the service. Some ask enough of the right questions to do a good job; others don't. So if you are interested in this option, I urge you to take the same careful approach you would take in selecting any professional clubmaker.

Take a look at the online questions they use to make your fitting recommendations. At a *minimum*, they must include the following:

- *Some form of identification of your swing speed.* This can actually be in the form of asking whether you know your swing speed with the driver/3-wood and a middle iron, or inquiring about your carry distance with specific clubs.
- *Asking you for your height and arm length, or asking you to do a measurement of the distance from your wrist to the floor.* Some form of measurement must be taken in order for the clubmaker to approximate the proper length for your clubs. From this measurement, the clubmaker might also be able to approximate the best lie angle for your irons.
- *There should be questions about your swing and how you play, as well as what you wish to achieve in terms of shot changes with a new set of custom clubs.* The more extensive these questions, the better the depth of information the clubmaker will have in making the right decisions. Such inquiries should include questions about your swing tempo, swing path, strength, athletic ability, wrist-cock release position on the downswing, length of backswing, current common misdirection tendencies, the height/trajectory of your shots, what clubs you currently use, and any of the loft, length,

and shaft specifications for them that you may know. The questions should also ask you basic points such as whether you wish to reduce a slice or hook, hit the ball longer, hit the ball higher or lower than you currently do, or achieve a change in the feel of your new clubs such as a more solid impact feel or a different shaft bending feel. I understand you might not know the answer to all those questions, but the more of them that are asked, and the more you can answer, the better off you will be.

- There should be questions about what grip size you prefer, or a request for measurement of your hand size or finger lengths so as to try to ensure a comfortable grip size on your custom clubs.
- *There should be questions concerning your current set* including: set makeup, what is the longest club you hit with reasonable confidence in the woods and irons, as well as questions about what sizes or styles of clubheads you find acceptable.
- *You should at least try to satisfy yourself that the clubmaker is using top-quality components.* Sorry, but I am going to have to get in a gratuitous plug here. If they are using heads and shafts from my company, Tom Wishon Golf Technology, you are getting the highest possible quality (seriously). But I must be fair and point out that there are others who also do an excellent job. The thing is, you need to ask the clubmaker what brand of components he or she uses, and then do a little research to see how good that brand is.

Finally, you might want to call or e-mail to request references of other golfers they have fitted. Contact those customers and ask how well the clubs work for them, as well as their impressions of the clubmaker's service and follow-up.

As I said above, in all likelihood your clubs will not be quite as good as those done in a face-to-face custom fitting, but you will be astonished at how much better they will be than anything you can buy off-the-rack in standard form at any of the golf retail stores or golf course pro shops.

Golf for the Disabled

One of the areas of this book that I am most proud of is the section on "Golfers with Disabilities" in Chapter 10. It is something I've wanted to write about for a long time, and it's a topic that is long overdue for treatment.

If you would like more information about this topic, here are some places you might start.

NATIONAL ALLIANCE FOR ACCESSIBLE GOLF
501 North Morton Street
Suite 109
Bloomington, IN 47404

Phone: (812) 856-4422
TTY: (812) 856-4421
Fax: (812) 856-4480
e-mail: naag@indiana.edu
Web site: www.accessgolf.org

RESOURCE CENTER FOR INDIVIDUALS WITH DISABILITIES
United States Golf Association
1631 Mesa Avenue
Colorado Springs, CO 80906

Phone: 719-471-4810 x 15
e-mail: resourcecenter@usga.org
Web site: www.resourcecenter.usga.org

NATIONAL AMPUTEE GOLF ASSOCIATION
11 Walnut Hill Road
Amherst, NH 03031

Phone: 800-633-6242
e-mail: info@nagagolf.org
Web site: www.nagagolf.org

PHYSICALLY CHALLENGED GOLF ASSOCIATION, INC.
Avondale Medical Center
34 Dale Road, Suite 001
Avon, CT 06001

Phone: (860) 676-2035
Fax: (860) 676-2041
e-mail: pcga@townusa.com
Web site: www.townusa.com/pcga/
(They have an excellent state-by-state list of adaptive golf programs, by the way.)

EASTERN AMPUTEE GOLF ASSOCIATION
2015 Amherst Drive
Bethlehem, PA 18015-5606

Phone: (888) 868-0992
Fax: 610) 867-9295
e-mail: info@eaga.org
Web site: www.eaga.org/

THE ASSOCIATION OF DISABLED AMERICAN GOLFERS
P.O. Box 280649
Lakewood, CO 80228-0649

Phone: 303-922-5228
Fax: 303-969-0447
e-mail: adag@usga.org
Web site: www.golfcolorado.com/adag/

U.S. BLIND GOLF ASSOCIATION
3094 Shamrock Street North
Tallahassee, FL 32309

e-mail: usbga@bellsouth.net
Web site: www.blindgolf.com

Golf Club Components and the Barrel of Apples

As a 30+ year veteran of this industry, I am well aware of the ways big golf companies have negatively influenced many golfers' opinions concerning golf clubs built from components. And you know what? To a certain extent, they're right.

Most of the companies who sell component heads, shafts, and grips do not offer as high a level of design and manufacturing quality as the big standard made golf club companies. They represent, unfortunately, the bad apples that give those that DO offer "major brand" quality a "black eye."

So how do you know which companies are good and which are not? I would certainly tell you that my clubheads, shafts, and grips are within that group labeled: "Damn right they're good." Beyond that, I will not tempt the lawsuit gods other than to suggest you trust the judgment of your professional clubmaker.

If you have taken the time to seek out a skilled clubmaker, either from my advice in this Appendix or by probing on your own, then you'll be okay. You will be in the hands of someone who has pride in his or her work and cares for your needs. That person will not buy junk. He or she will choose quality heads, shafts, and grips from which to craft your custom made clubs.

Besides being technically skilled, the other thing that all good clubmakers have in common is that they CARE about each golfer they fit and serve. They know if your clubs don't perform, you'll be back. I can assure you, the only time they want to see you back will be: (a) if you add more custom clubs to your set; (b) if you bring a friend, spouse, kid to be fitted; (c) if you have taken lessons, gotten much better, and need to have adjustments made in your current custom set; or (d) if you want to drop off a bottle of wine in thanks for how much you like what they did to help you.

Most golfers are used to believing the best clubs are the ones they have seen on tour, in ads, and on TV. They have been carefully conditioned to NOT ask the question: "How could one size possibly fit all?" For them, going to a professional clubmaker will require a certain leap of faith. I understand that. The same thing happens to me when I need to take my car in for repair and there's no dealer in my little town of 15,000 here in the mountains.

I want to say this one last time because it's so important. *I truly believe that all golfers, at all skill levels, need to have aspects of their golf clubs customized. These very real needs will not be met by buying standard, off-the-rack, clubs.* I am not alone in this belief. The true professional clubmakers I have trained, helped, or just gotten to know, all have the same belief and passion for creating golf clubs that truly ARE better.

Take some time to find a good professional clubmaker in your area. If you do, and if you love the game as much as we all do, you will never regret it. May your clubs always bring you more enjoyment than sorrow!